GLOBALIZATION:

THE EXTERNAL

PRESSURES

GLOBALIZATION: THE EXTERNAL PRESSURES

Edited by

PAUL KIRKBRIDE

ASHRIDGE

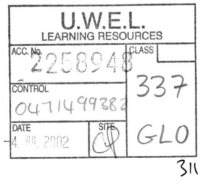
JOHN WILEY & SONS, LTD

Chichester · New York · Weinheim · Brisbane · Singapore · Toronto

National   01243 779777
International   (+44) 1243 779777
e-mail (for orders and customer service enquiries): cs-books@wiley.co.uk
Visit our Home Page on http://www.wiley.co.uk
or http://www.wiley.com

Other Wiley Editorial Offices

John Wiley & Sons, Inc., 605 Third Avenue,
New York, NY 10158-0012, USA

WILEY-VCH GmbH, Pappelallee 3,
D-69469 Weinheim, Germany

John Wiley & Sons Australia Ltd, 33 Park Road, Milton,
Queensland 4064, Australia

John Wiley & Sons (Asia) Pte Ltd, 2 Clementi Loop #02-01,
Jin Xing Distripark, Singapore 129809

John Wiley & Sons (Canada) Ltd, 22 Worcester Road,
Rexdale, Ontario M9W 1L1, Canada

British Library Cataloguing in Publication Data

A catalogue record for this book is available from the British Library

ISBN 0-471-49938-2

Typeset in 11/14pt Bembo by Dorwyn Ltd, Rowlands Castle, Hants.
Printed and bound in Great Britain by Biddles Ltd, Guildford and King's Lynn.
This book is printed on acid-free paper responsibly manufactured from sustainable forestry, in
which at least two trees are planted for each one used for paper production.

CONTENTS

9 THE GLOBAL PHARMACEUTICAL INDUSTRY

251

Malcolm Schofield

PREFACE

Since 1959 Ashridge has earned the reputation of being one of the world's leading business schools. Through all our activities, from executive education and post-graduate qualification programmes to research and consulting, we combine leading-edge thinking with a strong practical focus. We believe learning must be involving, challenging and above all real, so that it does make a significant difference when applied in the workplace. To this end we have reinforced and built upon the philosophy of our founders: that business needs to inform and reflect the environment in which it operates. Our work with clients and business school partners from all parts of the world endorses this still further.

We know globalization is not an isolated subject, as it integrates with all organizational activities and as such creates fascinating business and development opportunities. Our faculty's expertise in globalization has developed from research, observation, hands-on experience and passion for the subject. We are therefore delighted that our faculty members are able to share their learning and insights more widely by contributing chapters to two complementary books published by John Wiley & Sons.

I hope you find these two books, *Globalization: The Internal Dynamic* and *Globalization: The External Pressures* help you address your own particular issues and I would be pleased to hear your thoughts and comments on Ashridge's approach to globalization.

Leslie Hannah
Chief Executive

ACKNOWLEDGEMENTS

The original idea for this book and the companion volume (Kirkbride, P.S. and Ward, K. *Globalization: The Internal Dynamic*, John Wiley & Sons Ltd, 2001) came from Kate Charlton, then Director of Corporate Development and Paul Pinnington, Stream Director for Tailored Programmes at Ashridge. They had initiated discussions with publishers and my role as newly appointed Research Fellow was to bring the books to fruition. Kate and Paul were convinced that Ashridge had a wealth of talent that could be brought to bear on the topic of globalization and so the resulting works owe a debt to their vision.

Any editor of a collection such as this owes a debt of gratitude to the individuals who volunteered to provide chapters, often having to fit writing into a very busy teaching or consulting schedule. Thanks therefore to Paul Pinnington, Karen Ward, John Heptonstall, Jim Durcan, Mike Malmgren, Marcus Alexander, Roger Pudney, David Hennessey, Sarah Burns, Piero Dell'Anno, Samreen Khan, and Alex Poppleton for their sterling contributions.

Additional and special thanks must go to:

- My secretary, Tracy Bowdrey-Long, for her usual efficient work and for her calming influence;
- Rachel Oakley, from the Ashridge Graphics Department, for her excellent work on the Figures for the book;
- Leslie Hannah, Chief Executive, for his support and encouragement;
- Karen Ward, for her involvement in the development of the book and her constant encouragement and support;
- Claire Plimmer and her team at John Wiley & Sons for their expert advice and assistance;
- Staff at the Australian Graduate School of Management (AGSM) in Sydney, especially Dr. Robert Westwood, for providing me with a peaceful and relaxing venue to complete the final editing and writing while teaching a summer school in January and February 2000;
- My children, Daisy, Holly and William, for support and encouragement (as long as my writing did not intrude too far upon family activities!)

Paul Kirkbride
Reading, August 2001

EDITOR'S INTRODUCTION

Paul Kirkbride

EDITOR'S INTRODUCTION

*I*f the shelves of airport bookstalls are any indication, the 1990s were the decade of globalization. Whether in the fields of business, management, economics, information technology or e-commerce, the word appeared to be on everyone's lips. As a leading international business school Ashridge was not immune from such trends. The start of the decade saw Ashridge adopt a clear strategy of internationalization, if not globalization. It expanded its work in continental Europe as well as in Asia-Pacific and the United States.

In parallel with this move were several other trends within Ashridge. Obviously 'globalization' began to be taught more frequently on development programmes as a special topic, but also other parts of the 'curriculum' began to take on a more global dimension. Ashridge faculty were increasingly working with more 'global' clients and researching more into various aspects of globalization. For example, in 1993 we organized the Third Conference on International Personnel and Human Resources Management at Ashridge (Kirkbride, 1994). The theme for this conference was 'Human Resources Management in the New Europe of the 1990s' and it dealt with a number of globalization issues, including the role of national cultures, the developments in the European Union, the growth of Eastern Europe and the creation of pan-European managers. Ashridge also began a deliberate process of 'internationalizing' the faculty that led, by the end of the decade, to a faculty with very diverse cultural origins and working experiences.

However, part of the role of a high-quality business school is its ability to take an objective and critical look at topics and processes that might simply be passing managerial 'fads'. Our view is that innovations in terms of new concepts tend to go through two distinct phases. In the first phase, which we term recognition, the new concept attracts a great deal of attention. Many people jump on the conceptual bandwagon and dash into print with books and articles seeking to elucidate the concept. Managers rush to seminars and conferences to learn all about the new concept and the implications for their own organizations, often fearing that they may be missing out on something important. At the end of this phase the concept is high in the popular consciousness. Everyone has heard of it and has an opinion on it. However, while much heat has been generated in the discussions and debates around the topic, there is often not quite so much light. There are a number of examples of this process in recent years, ranging from 'lean manufacturing' to 'business process reengineering' to 'emotional intelligence'. Our argument is that globalization is yet another example of this trend. Indeed, we would argue that globalization is a particularly good example, as the globalization debate tended to get caught up within a more general '*fin de siècle*' or 'milleniumist' debate, which then saw globalization as the arrival of a new twenty-first-century epoch.

The second phase of dissemination, which we term understanding, is a more sober phase. Here the concept is held up to critical inspection and evaluation in an attempt to distil the real elements of the concept. The protagonists are not naïve supporters of the idea but objective observers. It is our contention that the concept of globalization is ripe for such a critical reappraisal. This notion, plus the fact that many from within the Ashridge faculty had been doing research, either pure or applied, into aspects of the topic, led to the suggestion that the faculty should pool their thoughts in a book on globalization. As this idea was debated two distinct books emerged and I was asked if I would take on the role of bringing together the collections and editing them. Both books are the products of authors who are full-time Ashridge faculty, recent Ashridge faculty and/or Ashridge associates.

This volume, *Globalization: The External Pressures*, seeks to examine the concept of globalization and the existence of global financial and labour markets. It looks at the pressures towards globalization and at how organizations are responding on a macro scale and in terms of their external interfaces with an increasingly global environment. The companion volume, *Globalization: The Internal Dynamic* (Kirkbride and Ward, 2001), focuses on the issue of global or transnational organizations. It essentially argues that, despite the rhetoric, few organizations are really global or transnational. This volume seeks to understand what such organizations would look like and the potential barriers to true global status. It offers practical advice in terms of what organizations would have to do to be really global in nature.

As mentioned above, the Ashridge faculty is now very international, both in terms of cultures of origin and working experience, and the contributors to this volume reflect this. Chapters have been written by American, British, Italian, Swedish and Venezuelan authors. But this simple listing of nationalities hides, as the authors of our final chapter note, further cultural complexities. Several authors have parents of different national origins and others are currently living and working in a country and culture very different to that of their birth. Even those, like myself, who are currently working in their 'own' culture have had extensive cross-cultural and international experience. I, for example, worked extensively in the 1980s in the Asia-Pacific region while based in Hong Kong.

PLAN OF THE BOOK

In Chapter 1, Paul Pinnington, Karen Ward and I try to evaluate critically the concept of globalization. We start with some definitions from various perspectives to try to get a broad view of the whole globalization arena. We then seek to delineate the various 'schools' of thought surrounding the globalization debate. We identify four distinct theses: the globalists; the sceptics; the transformationalists; and the anti-globalists. After extensively analysing each viewpoint, we come down on the side of the transformationalists, but with sceptical leanings. That is, we believe that the current epoch represents a historically unprecedented level of global integration, but that this will not necessarily continue as a simple linear trend, instead being subject to counter processes and potential fractures.

In Chapter 2, John Heptonstall evaluates the extent of the supposed 'global economy'. He considers world trade flows, terms of trade, capital flows and foreign direct investment, before concluding that in a strict sense the 'global economy' does not really exist. John offers a number of possible scenarios for the future. These range from the most optimistic, 'the best of all worlds', through the most probable, 'muddling through', to the worst, 'blood on the streets'. We have to hope that John is right and the most pessimistic scenario does not in fact materialize.

Jim Durcan, in Chapter 3, tackles the parallel concept of a 'global labour market' and again finds it wanting in reality. He considers a number of barriers to the creation of such a market, including demographics, patterns of migration, treatment of immigrants and agreements on transferable qualifications. Jim notes that national governments will continue to have labour market policies that seek to attract inward investment and that global corporations have great scope to influence global labour markets through their impact on both external and internal labour processes. However, he concludes by suggesting that the greatest force in the globalization of labour markets continues to be the millions of largely anonymous potential and actual migrants in search of work. Jim argues that the challenge for the twenty-first century will be whether globalization is as effective in meeting the needs of the suppliers of labour as it was in the twentieth century in providing opportunities for the suppliers of capital.

Chapter 4 sees a switch from the consideration of global financial and labour markets to the existence of what might be termed the 'global information market'; in other words, the Internet. Mike Malmgren considers the ways in which the Internet and e-business enable and even fuel the globalization process. He begins by examining the global business drivers that affect the extent to which an industry will be affected by the Internet revolution. In this analysis he considers issues of information value, network reach, cultures and languages, and economies of scope. Mike then provides us with a framework for assessing the Internet's effect on products and services. This framework measures the degree of digitization, the efficiency of transactions and the global potential of the products and services. During the course of his analysis he provides a number of illustrative examples of how global companies are using the Internet to change their business models.

In Chapter 5, Marcus Alexander examines the role of the corporate parent in the multinational business. He considers how corporate parents either add value to the subsidiary businesses or risk destroying value through their actions. Marcus then focuses his attention on the embryonic transnational organization and examines both the challenges and the opportunities facing corporate parents trying to globalize. He concludes by suggesting that globalization is an extremely important issue for the corporate parent and providing a number of questions that should be posed, and answered, by multibusiness companies attempting to globalize.

Chapter 6 continues this organizational theme by focusing on the issues involved in designing and managing global partnerships and alliances. Drawing heavily on his on-going Global Partnership Study, Roger Pudney introduces his SCOPE model, which describes the key factors and decisions involved in establishing and maintaining successful international partnerships. Liberally sprinkling his arguments with practical cases from his research work, Roger goes on to describe a step-by-step approach to the partnership development process that is so important to global businesses in industries often characterized by extensive networks of such partnerships and alliances. He concludes by suggesting that strategic partnerships and alliances will continue to increase in importance as a major weapon of globalization. However, he notes that the success rate will continue to be low unless senior managers realize that the key success criteria are the 'soft' cultural and relational factors rather than the 'hard' technical ones.

In the next two chapters, David Hennessey focuses on the 'pull' towards globalization that comes from the market and from customers. In Chapter 7, he examines the complex opportunities that companies face when they market products or services globally. He covers the methods companies use to screen such global opportunities as well as how they respond in terms of multidomestic, regional and global marketing strategies. Drawing on a number of real examples, David considers product, pricing, distribution, branding and advertising strategies on a global scale. He concludes by suggesting that while there are a number of questions that companies seeking to globalize have to answer, the real issue is how well they can learn during the process.

In Chapter 8, David focuses on the key aspects involved in the process of developing and managing global customers. He examines a number of important issues, including the factors driving customers to be global; how to determine which customers to serve globally; and what customers actually want from global suppliers. Using examples from leading companies worldwide, David describes how to develop a global account programme and the barriers to success. However, he counsels that establishing a global account programme requires radical change for most organizations; thus it may be better for a firm to continue to serve customers locally or regionally until sufficient leadership and/or competence has been developed to support the necessary changes.

In Chapter 9, Malcolm Schofield uses pharmaceuticals as an example of an industry experiencing globalization. Drawing on his extensive experience in this industry, he traces its history from humble origins to near global status. He then discusses a number of issues that have been raised with globalization, including the role of the corporate parent, the global/local tension, processes of consolidation and convergence, and the use of international partnerships and alliances.

In Chapter 10, Alex Poppleton, Sarah Burns, Samreen Kahn and Piero Dell'Anno join cross-cultural forces to present a personal critique of globalization. They note that globalization seems in some way to be 'glamorous' and that this can be part of the reason for its success as a concept. They then review globalization as a force and consider its economic, political and social dimensions. They conclude by noting our personal roles in the globalization process. Thus, globalization is not an irresistible force that we must either support or resist, but instead a process that will continue to be influenced and shaped by human action.

References

Kirkbride, P.S. (1994) *Human Resource Management in Europe: Perspectives for the 1990s*, Routledge, London.

Kirkbride, P.S. and Ward, K. (2001) *Globalization: The Internal Dynamic*, John Wiley, Chichester.

THE STATE OF GLOBALIZATION TODAY

Paul Kirkbride, Paul Pinnington
and Karen Ward

CHAPTER 1

THE STATE OF
GLOBALIZATION TODAY

Globalization may not be a particularly attractive or elegant word. But absolutely no one who wants to understand our prospects at the century's end can ignore it . . . In France the word is *mondialisation*. In Spain and Latin American, it is *globalizacion*. The Germans say *Globalisierung*. (Giddens, 1999: 7)

*T*here is little doubt that globalization has been a 'buzz' word in the business literature and managerial community for the last 10–15 years. Everywhere one turns there is more and more discussion of the subject. Debates have ranged around the essence of globalization itself, around the extent of global business networks and around the existence and power of supposedly 'global' corporations. Indeed, some have argued that the concept is *passé*, having either been done to death or only been a passing 'fad'.

Our view is that globalization is more important than these dismissive responses would imply. We may disagree as to what it really is, but something is happening and it cannot be ignored. In this volume we will examine the concept of globalization in some detail and consider how organizations react to it and to some of the external realities. In a companion volume (Kirkbride and Ward, 2001), we will focus on the concept of the 'global organization' and what organizations have to do to go, and be, global.

WHAT IS GLOBALIZATION AND WHAT IS IT NOT?

Globalization has been defined in many ways. Some definitions are relatively concise, while others are more vague and evocative. In the latter category we could locate Govindarajan and Gupta:

> What do we mean when we say that we live in an increasingly global world? If you are a Hollywood producer, it means that you care not only about whether your movies will be a box office success in the home market, but also and perhaps even more so about whether it will be a successful export and earn several times as much outside the North American shores. If you are a CEO of Black & Decker, it means that, in reviewing your strategy for the North American power tools market, you look at the strategies of competitors such as Makita and Bosch not only in North America but also worldwide. If you are the chairman of British Steel, it means that you wake up every morning acutely aware of the fact that over 60 per cent of your company's shares are owned by Americans rather than by perhaps more patient local investors. If you are the CEO of Ford Motor Company, it means that, as you enter and expand into emerging markets such as China or India, you do not need to design new cars from scratch and that you can enter these markets more quickly, more economically, and at lower risk by creating modified versions of global platforms such as Escort or Ka. If you are the Finance Minister of India, it means that you regard the integration of the country's economy with the rest of the world as fundamental to the realization of your homeland's potential as an economic superpower. And, last but not least, if you are a recent MBA and a junior manager at Proctor & Gamble, you vow never to forget that you do not have a prayer of ever making it into the top ranks of the company unless you combine superb on-the-job performance with extensive international experience. (Govindarajan and Gupta, 2000: 274)

From a slightly more academic perspective, we have the following definitions from authors who are generally proponents of globalization.

> Globalization is the integration of business activities across geographical and organizational boundaries. It is the freedom to conceive, design, buy, produce, distribute and sell products and services in a manner which offers maximum benefit to the firm without regard to the consequences for individual geographic locations or organizational units. There is no presumption that certain activities must be located in certain places or that existing organizational boundaries are inviolable. Instead, the global firm stands ready to respond to changing market conditions and opportunities by reconsidering its options from a broad economic perspective and choosing the alternatives which are thought to be best in the long run. Globalization incorporates a willingness to consider world-wide sourcing for parts which were previously manufactured in our own at-home

plant, the development of relationships for distribution and selling through otherwise unrelated firms located in other countries, and the use of joint ventures with international partners to develop and exploit a new technology. The global firm is not constrained by national boundaries as it searches for ideas, talent, capital and other resources required for its success. In short, the global firm operates with few, if any, self-imposed geographical or organizational constraints on where or how it conducts its business operations. (Ray Reilly, University of Michigan, and Brian Campbell, TriMas Corporation, quoted in Barnett, 1992: 322)

The capacity to treat the world as one market while paradoxically dealing with it as many culturally diverse merchants. It requires a totally new human engine for corporations, one that can deal with the paradoxes of:

1 Global economies of scale and local customization
2 Transnational and domestic mind-sets
3 Speed and quality. (Noel Tichy, University of Michigan, quoted in Barnett, 1992: 322)

The collective capability to differentiate and integrate five components of competitive advantage – resources, information, processes, products and markets – between two or more countries, through structures that are managerially enacted rather than geographically imposed. (Karl Weick, University of Michigan, quoted in Barnett, 1992: 323)

Globalization is the conscious and disciplined management process of stepping out of the intellectual and operational confines of a domestic enterprise to fully recognize and address global opportunities and threats in a strategically and operationally integrated manner. Globalization is much more than setting up plants and offices in foreign countries: it is a total approach to managing business around the world that seeks the whole to be greater than the sum of the parts. In a successful global company, each geographic entity enriches the other in more ways than providing an outlet for product or services. (Deb Chatterji, The BOC Group, quoted in Barnett, 1992: 329)

Others, from a critical perspective, have suggested that often globalization has been only vaguely defined, if defined at all. Such authors tend to suggest that globalization has been asserted rather than defined. As Hirst and Thompson note, 'We can only begin to assess the issue of globalization if we have some relatively clear and rigorous model of what a global economy would be like and how it represents both a new phase in the international economy and an entirely changed environment for national economic actors' (1999: 7). Hirst and Thompson seek to define a globalized world and economy by contrasting it with an open international economy. Such an open international economy would be one characterized by open 'exchange between relatively distinct national economies and in which many outcomes, such as the competitive performance of firms and sectors, are substantially determined by processes occurring at the national level' (1999: 7). They see this international economy as one characterizing the period of the mid-nineteenth century up to the First World War and again the more recent post Second World War period in the major advanced economies.

In contrast, a globalized economy would be one where national economies are subsumed into wider international processes and transactions. The 'global economy raises these nationally based interactions to a new power. The international economic system becomes autonomized and socially disembedded, as markets and production become truly global . . . As systemic interdependence grows, the national level is permeated by and transformed by the international' (Hirst and Thompson, 1999: 10). Such an economic system would have some fundamental consequences:

- One consequence would be the problem of governance. How would it be possible to create integrated patterns of national and international public policy formulation and implementation that could cope effectively with autonomous market forces?
- The second consequence of such a global system would be that multinational companies (MNCs) would be transformed into transnational companies (TNCs). TNCs would represent genuinely 'stateless' capital without any national identification or loyalty, which would be willing to locate anywhere in the world to secure the most advantageous terms or returns. Such organizations would source, produce and market at the global level as strategy and opportunities dictated.
- The third consequence would be the continuing decline in the international political influence and national and local economic bargaining power of trade unions and other forms of organized labour.
- The final and ultimate consequence of such a system would be a 'withering away' of the hegemonic nation state as an actor and the

corresponding rise of alternative agencies that could obtain legitimacy from consumers and citizens across national boundaries.

Without attaching themselves to any one school of thought regarding globalization (see section below), Held *et al.* (1999) offer a precise definition of globalization as:

> A process (or set of processes) which embodies a transformation in the spatial organization of social relations and transactions . . . generating transcontinental or interregional flows and networks of activity, interaction, and the exercise of power. (1999: 16)

They argue that this formulation enables one to differentiate globalization from other spatial forms of social relations such as localization, nationalization, regionalization and internationalization, as in Figure 1.1. They also suggest that the globalization form can be assessed on a number of key dimensions:

- How extensive are global networks of relations and connections?
- How intensive are the flows and levels of activity within these networks?
- How fast are the global flows of trade, exchange and information?
- How great is the impact of these processes on particular communities?
- To what extent is there an infrastructure (physical, legal, technological or symbolic) to support processes of globalization?
- To what extent have such global networks and relationships become regularized and institutionalized in a number of different social domains?

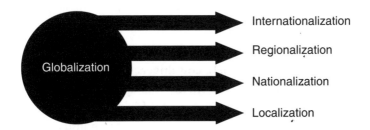

Figure 1.1 Levels of spatial organization.

- To what extent has globalization transformed the organization, distribution and exercise of power to create specific patterns of stratification?

THE GLOBALIST THESIS (GLOBALIZATION IS HERE TO STAY)

One clear school of thought in the literature is that of the 'globalists,' who are perhaps best represented by Ohmae (1990, 1995, 2000) and Yip (1995). For these and other writers in this vein, globalization represents many different things. However, what is not questioned is the fact that globalization exists and will be a major factor for large organizations in the decades to come. To these theorists, globalization represents:

- A convergence of tastes and an increasing homogeneity that allows for the use of standard products and services worldwide.
- The process of integrating purchasing and manufacturing processes on a global scale to achieve cost efficiencies.
- Industries dominated by a few major players worldwide.
- Large organizations with global cultures and mindsets.

Yip sees globalization as a process driven by a series of global industry drivers (see Figure 1.2).

> What aspects of strategy should be globalized? Managers can answer this question by systematically analyzing industry conditions or 'industry globalization drivers', by evaluating the benefits and costs of globalization, and by understanding the different ways in which a globalization strategy can be used through 'global strategic levers'. (Yip, 1995: 6)

These drivers are market drivers such as common customer needs and the existence of global channels; cost drivers such as global scale economies and global sourcing efficiencies; economic drivers such as trade policy and deregulation; and competitive drivers such as the existence of global competitors. Readers can rate their own industry against this list of drivers by considering Figure 1.3.

Figure 1.2 Yip's model of globalization.
Source: Yip (1995).

	Very weak			Very strong	
	1	2	3	4	5
Market drivers – Common customer needs – Preference for latest products – Potential for parallel imports – Global customers – Global channels – Transferable promotional mix					
Cost drivers – Global scale economies – Global sourcing efficiencies – Low logistics costs – Fast-changing technology					
Government and economic drivers – Policies that promote world trade – Integration of world capital markets – Compatible technical/environmental standards – Deregulation					
Competitive drivers – Globalized competitors – Transferability of competitive advantage					
Overall score					

Figure 1.3 Industry globalization drivers.

Yip suggests that faced with a number of global industry drivers, firms have to respond by setting their global strategic levers appropriately. Such levers would include global products, global location, and global marketing and positioning. These forces and levers are then balanced by a number of global organizational factors, which make it easy or difficult for a firm to 'globalize'. These factors are considered in more detail in our companion book on the internal dynamics of globalization (Kirkbride and Ward, 2001).

Of course, industry sectors are not simply either global or local. As the industry drivers increase, industry sectors move gradually from more domestic to more global in their dynamics. Thus we can delineate a series of different stages that industries move through as they globalize (Pinnington, 2000). In Stage 1 early globalizers appear who are seeking competitive advantage through first-mover status. In Stage 2 the industry evolves to favour global or regional players. Other companies begin to globalize to match the advantage gained by the early movers. In Stage 3 the industry consolidates into global, regional and niche groups and the global responses ('levers'), such as global account strategies, become more important. Finally, in Stage 4 the industry becomes dominated by between four and ten global players and the playing field moves from products and prices to intangibles such as branding and learning (see Figure 1.4).

If one looks at globalization from a managerial perspective, two of the most influential writers and consultants in this field are Christopher Bartlett and Sumantra Ghoshal. So what are the key threads of their thesis on globalization? Probably the most notable idea is their claim that 'the dominant vehicle of globalization is the Multi National Corporation (MNC)', thus placing managers of these organizations squarely at the centre of the globalization debate. (MNC is defined as an organization with substantial direct investment outside its domestic market, which undertakes active management of these offshore assets both operationally and strategically.) This is in contrast to some of the other globalists who take a broader technological, economic or social perspective on globalization. Bartlett and Ghoshal note that in the post-war period, MNCs have accounted for 40 per cent of the world's manufacturing and almost 25 per cent of world trade and GNP.

	Stage 1	Stage 2	Stage 3	Stage 4
Industry examples	Legal services, real estate agents, food, wine	Financial services, retailing, utilities, beer	Pharmaceuticals, automotive, white goods, airlines	Soft drinks, sporting goods, consultancy firms, PCs
Industry evolution	Early globalizers emerge who believe their industry is beginning to globalize and that there are first-mover advantages	Industry evolves to favour global or regional players; lead players continue to build their global businesses; other players consider their options	Industry consolidates into global, regional or niche players; acquisitions continue, especially in emerging markets; global account strategies become more important	Industry dominated by 4–10 global players; global players compete on intangibles (brand, learning); non-market forces become more important
Actions	Visionaries lead	Companies are acquired; global alliances form	Acquired companies are integrated to form a global organization	A learning organization is developed
Key issues to be addressed	Regulatory and political hurdles; competitive reaction; building global skills and resources; timing the global strategy launch	Identification of similarities across markets and the definition of the industry globalization logic; development of a long-term brand and positioning strategy; development of processes to acquire and integrate companies and build global alliances	Need to squeeze global efficiencies; need to develop strategies for emerging markets; development of a global organization (global processes, global human resources, global corporate culture, global learning, global structure)	Attracting, developing and retaining global talent; developing processes to manage non-market factors

Figure 1.4 Globalization stages.

Their study of MNCs has taken a historic perspective and analysed how this organizational form has emerged in the last 50 years, exploring the rationale behind its rise in power and influence. Interestingly, one of the key findings of their work is that MNCs do not usually start out with clearly defined global objectives or a well-crafted global strategy, but rather emerge piecemeal, driven incrementally from a home-market strategy. This should offer encouragement to smaller, less experienced organizations that are dipping their toes into the global pond for the first time.

Bartlett and Ghoshal argue that initially organizations venture outside their home markets in search of access to low-cost factors of production or to secure key supplies, often to give themselves a competitive advantage back in their home market. They note that this might be an initial step on the journey to globalization, without the organization acknowledging this. However, increasing competitive pressure in home markets with reducing product life cycles and increasing research and development costs then leads these organizations to engage in market-seeking behaviour outside their home market. Often the initial choice of overseas markets is opportunistic, based on existing internal preferences and networks, as opposed to carefully crafted strategic choices.

More recently, Bartlett and Ghoshal have noted a third reason for MNCs pursuing a globalization strategy, which is the need for global scanning of the external environment and learning from ideas globally to enhance competitive positioning. Figure 1.5 illustrates these three core strategic drivers for MNCs pushing globalization.

Bartlett and Ghoshal have therefore argued that these strategic drivers have led to globalization following an evolutionary pattern, with organizations moving through phases or stages. These phases have been defined as international, multinational, global and ultimately transnational, with each phase having distinct characteristics. (see pp. 11–14 of Transnational Management (2nd Edition) for a detailed definition of each stage) Figure 1.6 illustrates how these stages map on to the key strategic drivers discussed earlier.

Despite the widespread coverage of Bartlett and Ghoshal's basic thesis in management texts on globalization, more recent research in

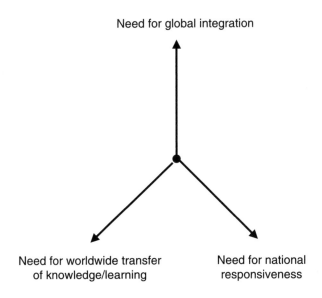

Figure 1.5 Global strategic capabilities.

Figure taken from *Managing Across Borders (2nd Edition)* by Bartlett & Ghoshal, published by Random House Business Books (1998). Used by permission of The Random House Group Limited.

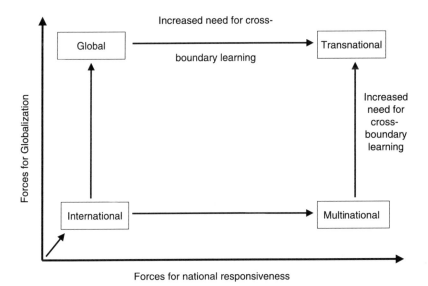

Figure 1.6 Forms of global organization.

Data compiled from *Managing Across Borders (2nd Edition)* by Bartlett & Ghoshal, published by Random House Business Books (1998).

this field (Barham and Heimer, 1998) has offered a critique of this evolutionary perspective, while retaining the MNC at centre stage. Looking at the emergence of 'new' forms of global players, which have challenged the dominance of old-economy MNCs, this recent work has attempted to combine the perspective of business strategists and business psychologists to understand the seemingly unstoppable trend towards 'global connectedness' (Barham and Heimer, 1998: 165).

Barham and Heimer argue that this focus on stages or phases of globalization is both misleading and unhelpful for individual organizations and managers. First, the focus on phases carries with it the implication that the final phase – that of transnational – is the ideal organizational form for operating globally and that organizations are unavoidably on an incremental path towards this goal. Yet there are many examples of organizations operating successfully outside their domestic markets without being transnational, and most commentators admit that in reality there are few examples of organizations that are operating with the characteristics of a transnational, even the much (over?) hyped ABB.

Second, Barham and Heimer argue that the 'phase' approach tends to focus manager's thinking on the question 'Where are we?' instead of the more helpful questions of 'What is changing in our marketplace? And where do we need to go?' The evolutionary model provides a descriptive framework without underpinning it with a diagnostic tool, which would assist managers in assessing whether they have what it takes to be a successful MNC. After all, even Bartlett and Ghoshal acknowledge that there are some preconditions for organizations aspiring to operate globally as MNCs. They argue that organizations need to have:

- the motivation to invest directly outside their home market;
- the strategic competencies to compete effectively;
- the organizational capability to implement their strategic choices;

yet provide no criteria for organizations to assess whether they have these prerequisites.

The final and central critique of the evolutionary phase model is that it does not acknowledge that globalization is a process of culture change with profound impacts on many, if not most, of the staff within

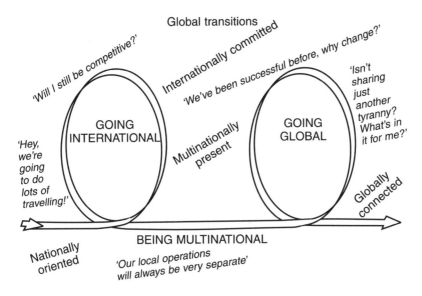

Figure 1.7 An alternative model of global organization.
Barham and Heimer (1998). Reproduced by permission of Pearson.

an organization (Barham and Heimer, 1998: 166). Barham and Heimer argue that the change processes and emotional reactions to globalization are masked by this focus on an evolutionary process, despite evidence that globalization is often achieved at great personal cost to the individuals involved.

Barham and Heimer therefore offer an alternative model of globalization that is based on the notion of transition: that any organization in any industry needs to make choices about how it wants to operate globally and then it needs to be thoughtful about how it implements these choices. The choices they offer (see Figure 1.7) are:

- *Going international* – being internationally committed. Operating outside the home market is no longer peripheral but a strategic imperative.
- *Being multinational* – having a multinational presence. The key issue is the extent of centralization vs decentralization within the organization. There is little incentive to think of the organization as a globally integrated entity.

- *Going global* – being globally connected. The key issue is accelerated learning and encouraging independent action, yet a feeling of being connected to a bigger whole that adds value to the parts.

Barham and Heimer hypothesize that the choice to transition to a different organizational form should be based on:

- opportunity
- intent
- readiness
- capability.

They provide a diagnostic framework to help managers assess what choices would be appropriate for their organization (see Table 1.1).

Table 1.1 Engaging the organization

How to engage your organization in 'going international'

- Organize mind openers. Take people to different places and let them experience a different country with its smells, tastes and people.
- Go out there. Take as many people from different hierarchical levels with you as you can. Meet local expatriates.
- Hire people with international experience, but think about how you will integrate them.
- Protect your international pioneers. If there is no critical mass, people are likely to reject what they have to say about the organization.
- Go on benchmarking visits to other countries.
- Systematically debrief people. Share their experiences when they go abroad, to avoid superstitious learning.
- Find a way for people to see the benefits and discover what is involved for themselves. Telling doesn't work.
- Send people on international projects.
- Give key people responsibility for important international accounts.
- Take trade union representatives with you on a trip abroad.

How to engage your organization in 'being multinational'

- Hold your meetings in different countries.
- Let local people run the local companies.
- Bring large numbers of international people into the head office.
- Make international experience a requirement for promotion.
- Consciously develop a breed of international managers.

- Make international assignments attractive.
- Make sure the country managers have something to gain from co-operating with other countries.
- Create greater co-operation and coherence by starting up regional head offices.
- Bring people across the globe together to think about the strategy of the organization.
- Create functional best practice forums to engage people around the world in thinking about how to improve what they do. Appreciate the way different cultures work. Then they will understand what benefits co-operation can bring.
- Set up international teams – they provide learning that helps stretch the organization into becoming global.

How to engage your organization in 'going global'

- Develop a vision of what the organization could be. Communicate it, even by using the media.
- Provide clear measures of performance globally. Make people's performance transparent.
- Break down country fiefdoms. Create operational and knowledge-sharing networks across the globe.
- Run global management development programmes. These will ensure a rich pool of international talent.
- Create a 'cultural whirlpool' for key people who need to be international. Create geographically dispersed international teams that meet in different locations every time – this avoids their falling back into their national complacency.
- Provide a global IT infrastructure for communication.
- Allow as much freedom to experiment as possible. Global co-operation requires spontaneous opportunities for people to come together and ignite around ideas.
- Make people responsible and accountable for global co-operation.
- Change the roles of the country managers. Alternatively, link them up with people who look at the whole globe.

Source: Barham and Heimer, 1998: 170–73.

Thus, after this long excursion through the main globalist thinkers, we can capture the central features of the globalist position as follows:

- Globalization represents a new global age.
- The power of national governments is eroded in the face of global capitalism.
- The central driving forces are modern capitalism and new technology.

- Industries are becoming more global as the globalization drivers increase.
- Organizations are having to respond and are becoming more international, multinational, global and transnational.
- The outcome will be the creation of a new 'borderless world' and the end of the nation state.

THE SCEPTICAL THESIS (OH NO IT'S NOT – IT DOESN'T EXIST)

That the concept or notion of globalization has captured the managerial and popular imagination is beyond doubt. But does globalization really exist? Is there in fact a global economy and global organizations? Or is globalization an over-hyped and misleading myth? There are a number of authors (Gordon, 1988; Hirst and Thompson, 1999; Thompson and Allen, 1997; Weiss, 1998) who have challenged the globalization orthodoxy. Hirst and Thompson (1999: 2) point to three disturbing problems with the globalist thesis:

- The general absence of a clearly defined model of the supposed new global economy and a clear articulation of how this differs from previous economic systems.
- The tendency to cite convenient and illustrative examples of globalization processes and the internationalization of sectors as if this proves the existence of a new global economy. An excellent example of this genre is Pico Iyer and his notion of the global 'soul': 'For more and more people, then, the world is coming to resemble a diaspora, filled with new kind of beings – *Gastarbeiters* and boat people and *marielitos* – as well as new kinds of realities: Rwandans in Auckland and Moroccans in Iceland. One reason why Melbourne looks more like Houston is that both of them are filling up with Vietnamese *pho* cafés; and computer technology further encourages us to believe that the remotest point is just a click away. Everywhere is made up of somewhere else – a polycentric anagram – that I hardly notice I'm sitting in a Parisian café

just outside Chinatown (in San Francisco) talking to a Mexican-American friend about biculturalism while a Haitian woman stops off to congratulate him on a piece he's just delivered on TV on St. Patrick's Day' (Iyer, 2000, 10–11).
■ The lack of any historical depth to the analysis, which allows current trends to be seen as unique and without precedence. Such an ahistorical analysis also allows commentators to propose that the globalization trend will persist long into the future without change.

The sceptics generally adopt an economic analysis and seek to show that the current global economic system is either far from the picture presented by the globalists or little different from previous economic systems or epochs. Typical of this genre is the seminal work of Hirst and Thompson and we can sum up the essence of the sceptic's approach in their words with the following summary of their position (1999: 2–3):

1 The present highly internationalized economy is not unprecedented: it is one of a number of distinct conjectures or states of the international economy that have existed since an economy based on modern industrial technology began to be generalized from the 1860s. In some respects, the current international economy is *less* open and integrated than the regime that prevailed from 1870 to 1914.

2 Genuinely transnational companies appear to be relatively rare. Most companies are based nationally and trade multinationally on the strength of a major national location of assets, production and sales, and there seems to be no major tendency towards the growth of truly international companies.

3 Capital mobility is not producing a massive shift of investment and employment from the advanced to the developing countries. Rather foreign direct investment (FDI) is highly concentrated among the advanced industrial economies and the Third World remains marginal in both investment and trade, a small minority of newly industrializing countries apart.

4 As some of the extreme advocates of globalization recognize, the world economy is far from being genuinely 'global'. Rather trade,

investment and financial flows are concentrated in the Triad of Europe, Japan, and North America and this dominance seems set to continue.

5   These major economic powers, the G3, thus have the capacity, especially if they coordinate policy, to exert powerful governance pressures over financial markets and other economic tendencies. Global markets are thus by no means beyond regulation and control, even though the current scope and objectives of economic governance are limited by the divergent interests of the great powers and the economic doctrines prevalent among their elites.

Thus, the essence of the sceptical position on globalization can be summed up as follows (adapted from Held *et al.*, 1999: 10):

- Globalization, global markets and global organizations do not exist.
- The current world economic system is less global and interdependent than in some earlier periods.
- Driving forces are still states and markets.
- The power of national governments is reinforced or enhanced.
- Globalization is really regionalization or internationalization.
- The future could be the clash of regional blocs.

THE TRANSFORMATIONAL THESIS (IT DOES EXIST BUT IT IS MORE COMPLEX)

Held *et al.* (1999) distinguish a third potential approach to globalization that they term the 'transformational thesis'. This approach is particularly associated with the work of Giddens (1996, 1999) and Rosenau (1990). Unlike the sceptics, the transformationalists are characterized by the 'conviction that contemporary patterns of global economic, military, technological, ecological, migratory, political and cultural flows are historically unprecedented' (Held *et al.*, 1999: 7). Globalization is seen as the central driving force behind a number of the rapid changes (social, political and economic) that are reshaping the world order. As a result, globalization is conceived as a powerful transformative force responsible for a 'massive shake-out' of nations, economies, international institutions and the whole world order. As Giddens notes:

> I would have no hesitation, therefore in saying that globalization, as we are experiencing it, is in many respects not only new, but also revolutionary. Yet I don't believe that either the sceptics or radicals have properly understood either what it is or its implications for us. Both groups see the phenomenon almost solely in economic terms. This is a mistake. Globalization is political, technological and cultural, as well as economic. It has been influenced above all by developments in systems of communication, dating back only to the late 1960s. (1999: 10)

Unlike the globalists or sceptics, the transformationalists are very unclear about the direction or outcome of this 'shake-out' of the world order. This is because they tend to see globalization as a long-term historical process (rather than as a recent 'event') that is contradictory in nature (rather than certain in direction). As Giddens pithily puts it, 'Globalization thus is a complex set of processes, not a single one. And these operate in a contradictory or oppositional fashion' (1999: 12–13). For example, globalization can be seen as the 'pulling away' of power from local communities or the nation state while, at the same time, it can also be seen as 'pushing downwards', creating new pressures for local autonomy. Thus, as Daniel Bell (1973) has noted, the nation state becomes not only too small to solve the big problems, but also too big to solve the small problems.

For the transformationalists, the possible existence of a global system is not taken as confirmation of the arrival of a global economy, global convergence or a new world order. Instead, the consequence of globalization is seen as a 'sea change' in the existing social order and the creation of new patterns of global stratification. Thus, for transformationalists, globalization is a story of winners and losers in the global power balance. Some communities and nations become increasingly entwined in the new global system while others become marginalized. Simple dualities such as North/South and First/Third World are replaced by a more complex pattern of stratification involving elites, the contented and the marginalized (Hoogvelt, 1997).

Thus the central features of the transformationalist position can be captured as follows (adapted from Held et al., 1999: 10):

- Globalization represents a historically unprecedented level of global interconnectedness.
- The power of national governments is both reconstituted and restructured by globalization processes.
- The central driving forces are the combined processes of modernity.
- The process will lead to the transformation of political communities and a new architecture for the world order.
- The outcome will be contradictory processes of global integration and fragmentation.

THE ANTI-GLOBALIST THESIS (IT'S HERE AND WE DON'T LIKE IT)

Unlike the sceptics, the anti-globalists do not question the existence of a new global economic system. They are certain that such a system exists but, unlike the globalists, they are not enamoured with its effects on employees, communities, nation states and the environment. For them the global economic system, its institutions and its transnational corporations are as real as they are for the globalists. Indeed, the only point of real departure is over the nature of the effects.

The anti-globalists challenge the view that globalization is an inevitable, naturally occurring phenomenon, by arguing instead that it is a hegemonic strategy pursued ideologically by a few small but powerful international bodies without transparency or democratic oversight. The institutions usually singled out for attention include the World Trade Organization (WTO), the World Bank (WB), the International Monetary Fund (IMF) and international trade agreements such as the General Agreement on Tariffs and Trade (GATT) or the North American Free Trade Agreement (NAFTA). These institutions are viewed as covertly pursuing an ideological agenda under the pretence of neutrally promoting economic growth and trade. That agenda is seen as the liberalization of capital markets and trade flows and the creation of free-market economies to the benefit of the largest transnational corporations and the world superpowers such as the G7 group of nations. Global Exchange, an anti-globalist website, cites as evidence the words of Joseph Stiglitz, former chief economist at the World Bank:

> There never was economic evidence in favor of capital market liberalization. There still isn't. It increases risk and doesn't increase growth. You'd think [defenders of liberalization] would say to me by now, 'You haven't read these 10 studies', but they haven't, because there's not even one. There isn't the intellectual basis that you would have thought required for a major change in international rules. It was all based on ideology. (globalexchange.org, 6 September 2000)

Why do the anti-globalists reject globalization? We can summarize some of the key arguments in point form (from globalexchange.org):

- *Globalization creates greater inequality.* Until comparatively recently (150 years ago), there was relative equality between the major parts of the world. Since then, processes such as slavery, colonialism and globalization have slowly transferred wealth from the South to the North. Today the richest 20 per cent of the world's population receives 83 per cent of the world's income, uses 70 per cent of the world's energy, 75 per cent of the world's metals, 85 per cent of the world's wool and 60 per cent of the world's food, while producing 75 per cent of the world's environmental pollution. In contrast, the poorest 60 per cent of the world's population receives just 5.6 per cent of the world's income.
- *Economic growth is not a panacea.* Globalists argue that if economic growth rates across the world could be increased, everyone would benefit. But for those without the opportunity to participate, such growth can simply serve to amplify inequalities. 'The data shows that during a period of significant growth in world trade (1960 to 1989) global inequality got significantly worse: the ratio between the richest 20 per cent and the poorest 20 per cent of the world population went from 30 to 1 to 59 to 1.'
- *The key institutions (WB, IMF, WTO) and the transnational corporations do not promote 'development' as they claim,* but instead seek to incorporate the ruling elites of Third World economies into the global system of rewards and punishments. The WB, IMF and WTO represent a 'new colonialism' in an era when old-style colonialism is no longer tolerated or fashionable. Through processes of

loans to the Third World and debt creation, these institutions produce a 'debt treadmill'. The institutions can then promise new cash flow if Third World countries will implement policies that are advantageous to the First World elites and the transnational corporations. This process represents a collusion between First World and Third World elites. Entrepreneurs and transnational corporations are allowed to extract natural resources and wealth and in return the local elites get a cut of the profits, which they spend on control apparatus to perpetuate their rule.

■ *The free-market policies promoted by the WB and IMF have been disastrous.* The 'structural adjustment policies' (SAPs) of the WB and the IMF ensure that Third World countries pay off their debt, but at the expense of increasing poverty, exploiting local workforces, reducing social services and reducing the ability to develop a strong domestic economy. Thus, the WB and IMF 'sap the poor to fatten the rich'.

■ *The 'free-market' economic model promoted by the WB and IMF to the Third World is not the one the First World advanced economies actually used to develop themselves.* The major economies such as the US, Japan, UK, Germany and France, as well as some of the new Asian 'tigers' (Korea, Singapore and Taiwan), used a heavily state-interventionist model to build and develop their economies and only at that point came to free-trade and free-market economics.

■ *The policies of the WB and IMF, especially on expanding exports, have been disastrous for the environment.* The WB/IMF policy of expanding Third World exports leads countries to overexploit their natural resources. 'They are cutting down their forests . . . pumping chemicals into their land to produce export crops . . . ripping minerals out of the ground at a frantic pace . . . [and] overfishing coastal and international waters.'

Thus the central features of the anti-globalist position can be captured as follows:

■ Globalization represents a new form of colonial exploitation.
■ National governments have been replaced as colonial aggressors by the global institutions and the transnational corporations.

- The central driving forces are free-market capitalism, liberalization and Third World debt.
- The outcome will be the creation of a 'global economic elite' whose interests transcend national boundaries and a marginalized and subjugated 'world proletariat'.

IS THIS THE GLOBAL AGE?

We have already seen that the various schools of thought on globalization take different positions on the question of whether we are in a global age. The globalists and the anti-globalists tend to assume that in the post-war period we have entered a distinctive and clearly delineated globalization epoch. However, both are rather ahistorical in their approach and tend to cite fairly recent trends or examples as decisive evidence of a new 'global age'. The sceptics take a much more historical perspective and see several 'eras' of globalization, with the current simply being the most recent. The transformationalists tend also to see globalization in a long-term historical perspective, but view the current era as representing a 'revolutionary' or 'disjunctive' turning point in world history.

Held *et al.* (1999), in their seminal study, take a more agnostic view and neutral position: 'Globalization as a historic process cannot be characterized by an evolutionary logic or an emergent telos. Historical patterns of globalization have been punctuated by great shifts and reversals, while the temporal rhythms of globalization differ between domains' (1999: 414). From their research they delineate a fourfold periodization of globalization:

- *Premodern globalization.* This covers the period from the start of history until around the Renaissance. It was an era when globalization is best characterized by interregional or intercivilization encounters within Europe and Asia. The drivers for globalization in this period include the establishment of political and military empires (Indic, Han Chinese and Roman), the spread of world religions (Christianity, Islam, Judaism), and large-scale migratory movements (Roman, Germanic, Mongol).

■ *Early modern globalization (1500–1850).* Globalization in this period is a function of a number of factors. Key among these were the demographic flows between Europe, the Americas and Oceania. In addition, this period saw the rise of the 'nation state', the expansion of great trading companies, more long-lasting political and military relationships and the formation of European global empires (British, Portuguese and Spanish).

■ *Modern globalization (1850–1945).* This period saw the rise of industrialized capitalist economies with advanced defence capability and powerful state institutions. European power began to stretch around the whole globe and this led to the (often forced) 'opening up' of Africa, China and Japan. This period also saw the beginning of economic globalization as global trade and FDI (foreign direct investment) soared. New communication technologies (railways and telegraph) opened up one culture to others on an unprecedented scale.

■ *Contemporary globalization (1945–present).* 'In the period since 1945 there has been a renewed wave of global flows and interconnections . . . Of course, in terms of the extensity of global linkages, the appearance is one of catching up; a return to the *status quo ante* of the classical Gold Standard era. But we argue that in nearly all domains contemporary patterns of globalization have not only quantitatively surpassed those of earlier epochs, but have also displayed unparalleled qualitative differences – that is in terms of how globalization is organized and reproduced. In addition, we argue that the contemporary era represents a historically unique confluence or clustering of patterns of globalization in the domains of politics, law and governance, military affairs, cultural linkages and human migrations, in all dimensions of economic activity and in shared global environmental threats. Moreover, this era has experienced extraordinary innovations in the infrastructures of transport and communication, and an unparalleled density of institutions of global governance and regulation. Paradoxically, this explosion of global flows and networks has occurred at a time when the sovereign territorial state, with fixed and demarcated borders, has become the near universal form of human political organization and political rule' (Held *et al.*, 1999: 424–5).

So what do we believe? Is this the global age or not? Our position is probably closest to the transformationalist position, although with sceptical overtones. We believe that many of the claims of the globalists have been correctly exposed as excessive hyperbole and lacking in both intellectual rigour and historical context. We do not believe in the existence of either a global economic system or a global market. We also believe that the incidence and truly 'global' nature of transnational corporations have been greatly exaggerated. However, we do accept that the contemporary age is increasingly global in many respects, while noting that this is not the first global epoch. Current trajectories and trends may be reversed or changed and this current global age is unlikely to be the last.

Nevertheless, globalization does exist and firms and companies have to deal with an increasingly borderless world. Globalization presents many challenges and opportunities for organizations, but for us it is not the *sine qua non* of modern management. As the above analysis demonstrates, globalization has been around for a very long time. For us, what is distinctive about the current age is the degree of extensity and intensity of the phenomenon leading to a classification of the current period as 'thick' globalization. Thus in some senses there is little that is 'new' in this global age, except the fact that globalization is affecting more and more individuals, communities, organizations and states than ever before.

IS GLOBALIZATION A GOOD OR A BAD THING?

Is this a question that should even be asked? As Giddens notes, 'Is globalization a force promoting the general good? The question can't be answered in a simple way, given the complexity of the phenomenon' (1999: 17). It is a question, however, that sharply divides the schools that we have delineated in this chapter. The globalists would generally line up on the 'good' side of the proposition, while the anti-globalists would unequivocally be on the 'bad' side. The sceptics can be found on both sides of the debate, although probably with more on the 'bad' side. Finally, the transformationalists would tend to sit on the fence, as they see globalization not as a linear phenomenon but as a process that contains internal contradictions and countervailing pressures. Even if the question can be asked, we are not sure it can be definitively answered; and certainly not within the short confines of this volume. However, we would hope to add to the debate through these chapters.

References

Barham, K. and Heimer, C. (1998) *ABB – The Dancing Giant: Creating the Globally Connected Corporation*, Prentice Hall, London.

Barnett, C.K. (1992) 'The global agenda for research and teaching in the 1990s' in Pucik, V., Tichy, N.M. and Barnett, C.K., *Globalizing Management: Creating and Leading the Competitive Organization*, John Wiley, New York.

Bartlett, C.A. and Ghoshal, S. (1998) *Managing Across Borders: The Transnational Solution*, Random House, London.

Bartlett, C.A. and Ghoshal, S. (2000) *Transnational Management: Text, Cases, and Readings in Cross-Border Management*, McGraw-Hill, New York.

Bell, D. (1973) *The Coming of the Post-Industrial Society*, Basic Books, New York.

Giddens, A. (1996) 'Globalization: a keynote address', *UNRISD News*, 15.

Giddens, A. (1999) *Runaway World: How Globalization is Reshaping our Lives*, Profile Books, London.

Gordon, D. (1988) 'The global economy: new edifice or crumbling foundations', *New Left Review*, 168, 24–64.

Govindarajan, V. and Gupta, A. (2000) 'Analysis of the emerging global arena', *European Management Journal*, 18, 3, 274–84.

Held, D., McGrew, A., Goldblatt, D. and Perraton, J. (1999) Global *Transformations: Politics, Economics, and Culture*, Polity Press, Cambridge.

Hirst, P. and Thompson, G. (1999) *Globalization in Question*, 2nd edn, Polity Press, Cambridge.

Hoogvelt, A. (1997) *Globalisation and the Postcolonial World: The New Political Economy of Development*, Macmillan, London.

Iyer, P. (2000) *The Global Soul: Jet Lag, Shopping Malls and the Search for Home*, Bloomsbury, London.

Kirkbride, P.S. and Ward, K. (eds) (2001) *Globalization: The Internal Dynamic*, John Wiley, Chichester.

Ohmae, K. (1990) *The Borderless World*, HarperCollins, New York.

Ohmae, K. (1995) *The End of the Nation State*, Free Press, New York.

Ohmae, K. (2000) *The Invisible Continent: Four Strategic Imperatives of the New Economy*, Nicholas Brealey, London.

Pinnington, P. (2000) 'The local route to global success', *Directions: The Ashridge Journal*, July, 22–7.

Rosenau, J. (1990) *Turbulence in World Politics*, Harvester Wheatsheaf, Brighton.

Thompson, G. and Allen, J. (1997) 'Think global, then think again: economic globalization in context', *Area*, 29, 3.

Weiss, L. (1998) *The Myth of the Powerless State: Governing the Economy in a Global Era*, Polity Press, Cambridge.

www.globalexchange.org/economy/rulemakers, 6.9.2000.

Yip, G. (1995) *Total Global Strategy: Managing for Worldwide Competitive Advantage*, Prentice-Hall, Englewood Cliffs, NJ.

THE
GLOBALIZATION
PROCESS IN THE
WORLD ECONOMY

John Heptonstall

CHAPTER 2

THE GLOBALIZATION PROCESS
IN THE WORLD ECONOMY

*T*he term 'globalization' is widely used, increasingly controversial, rarely defined and not very well understood. This lack of precision has led, among other things, to the use of such terms as 'the global economy'. This chapter will not be about the 'global economy', however – because no such thing exists. In a truly global economy there would be free circulation of people, goods and services, technology and knowhow, capital and information. In such an economy, companies would be indifferent as to where their plants – or their legal residences – were located. There would be no differences between countries or regions in the cost of capital or in return on investment. Differences in economic performance would be negligible and transitory.

Reality is very different. At the time of writing, the European Union subsidizes the export of agricultural products and the United States imposes a quota on sugar imports. Whole sectors of the Indian economy are closed to foreign investors. Japan imposes a 'voluntary' limit on some car exports and protects its own highly inefficient rice producers. Sony is arguing with the European Union about the treatment of its Playstation 2, which the Union considers to be a games machine (high tariff) and the company claims is a computer (lower tariff). Disagreements between the European Union and the USA about the duties to be charged on bananas from Central America vs those from the Caribbean have almost led to a trade war. Meanwhile, the USA and Canada have been enjoying five years of quite extraordinary economic growth and may or may not be now approaching a 'soft landing'. The Eurozone countries have been underperforming, and even the massive undervaluation of the euro itself has done little to stimulate the economy. The third member of the 'Triad', Japan, has been stuck in near stagnation for seven years. Even within the eurozone, Ireland's economic growth rate is three times that of Germany and Italy. There are still massive differences between the economic performances of countries, the stability of their currencies, their openness to trade and investment flows and the wealth and well-being of their residents. There probably always will be.

Even though a 'global economy' does not exist, however, globalization as a *process* very definitely does. One of the most striking developments of the period since the Second World War has been the steady erosion of tariffs and other protective barriers, and the consequent growth in world trade. This was followed, during the 1970s and 1980s, by the development of the first truly international capital markets and a spectacular growth in global flows of funds. In recent years the growth in foreign direct investment and in portfolio investment flows has been even more rapid than the growth in trade, while the era of major cross-border mergers is just beginning to take off.

Interestingly, the process is not a wholly new one. In some ways the international economy had made significant progress towards globalization in the late nineteenth century, and the process continued well into the twentieth. Much of what had been achieved was lost during the late 1920s and the 1930s, however, so some of the progress made recently has been no more than recovering lost ground. The fact remains, nevertheless, that although the process of globalization is not yet complete, the world is a lot closer to being a global economy than it used to be.

Sadly, hopes that the globalization process would produce unequivocal gains for the developing world and bring about an end to world poverty have not been realized. Some countries and regions have made spectacular advances. Others have been largely by-passed and some have become poorer. The gap between rich and poor has increased – both within countries and between countries. The resultant disenchantment surfaced at the WTO conference in Seattle in 1999 and is becoming ever more vocal. It is increasingly argued that 'globalization' is just another term for the ways that multinational companies use to exploit the less developed parts of the world.

The purpose of this chapter is to review the progress that has taken place in the trend towards a global economy and the benefits and the problems that have resulted, to try to put the criticisms into perspective, and to present some differing possible scenarios for future development.

WORLD TRADE – DEVELOPING A GLOBAL MARKET

It is in the nature of economies to grow and in the period since economic data started to be systematically collected and reported there have been very few years in which world output (measured as gross domestic product, or GDP) has failed to increase. This growth in output has been accompanied by a growth in world trade. In the early 1980s, world exports were growing at around 4 per cent per year. By the mid-1990s, that rate had more than doubled to 9.2 per cent and in 2000 reached a massive 12%. It would be very surprising, however, if there had been no such increase in world trade. It would seem reasonable to assert that true globalization is taking place *only if trade is growing significantly faster than world output*: that is, that *world exports as a percentage of world GDP* show a systematic increase.

This is one of the areas in which early progress was subsequently reversed. In 1900 world exports were already about 8 per cent of world GDP, and by 1929 that figure had increased to almost 10 per cent. During the traumas of the subsequent stock market crash and the horrendous recession of the early 1930s, this trend was sharply reversed. Many industrial countries resorted to protectionism and even currency convertibility was severely restricted. The outbreak of war led to further obvious distortions, and as late as 1950 the export ratio was still no higher than its 1900 level. The figure of 10 per cent of GDP was not reattained until 1965. Since then, however, growth has been rapid. A ratio of 12 per cent was reached by 1980 and 15 per cent by the mid-1990s. World trade – and probably the exports-to-GDP ratio – fell sharply during 1998/99 in the wake of the 1997 Asian crisis, but is now rapidly reviving as the region consolidates its recovery.

The progressive improvement in the exports-to-GDP ratio has coincided with an equally progressive elimination of tariff barriers and similar protectionist measures. The General Agreement on Tariffs and Trade (GATT), introduced as a stop-gap measure in 1946 after the failure of the Bretton Woods conference to reach agreement about the role and powers of a proposed World Trade Organization, has facilitated a remarkable degree of trade liberalization – at least in manufactured products. In the immediate post-war period the average tariff level was close to 30 per cent. By the beginning of the final GATT 'Uruguay round' negotiations, the level had fallen to 15 per cent in developing economies and to 5.4 per cent in countries that are members of the Organisation for Economic Co-operation and Development (OECD). By the end of those negotiations the figures were 11 per cent and 3 per cent respectively. Much remains to be done in removing protection in some specific areas – agricultural products, man-made fibres and intellectual property in particular – but there is little doubt that trade liberalization – the movement towards a world free market – has been a major factor behind trade growth.

Understandably, the pattern of world trade still largely reflects economic development. Almost three-quarters of all trade remains intra-OECD, although this will eventually change. By the mid-1990s, intra-OECD trade was growing at a fraction less than 8 per cent. Trade between the OECD countries and the rest of the world was growing at more than 10 per cent, however, and that among the non-OECD countries by no less than 15 per cent. This in itself would appear to suggest that it is the less developed parts of the world that have been the main beneficiaries of the growth in world trade.

Closer examination of the trade flows unfortunately reveals that the growth pattern has been far from uniform. Of the total non-

OECD world trade during 1995, the developing countries of Asia accounted for 25 per cent, up from 16 per cent in 1990. The countries of Latin America also enjoyed an increased share. The share of Middle Eastern countries, on the other hand, declined. Africa was the source of only 2 per cent of total non-OECD trade in 1995, and this figure was actually lower than that for 1990.

This picture of regional inequality becomes even more striking once world trade is broken down into its component parts. The fastest-growing segment is trade in services: during the 1990s trade in commercial services grew twice as rapidly as trade in manufactured goods or materials. Within the services sector, the fastest-growing element is of course telecommunications. More than 40 per cent of exports of services come from the European Union countries, with the balance fairly equally divided between Asia (including Japan) and North America. This will continue to be the fastest-growing sector in world trade – and this is growth in which the rest of the world plays virtually no part at all, except as customers.

The conclusion here is inescapable. Looked at from the viewpoint of trade, the world has indeed become more open, more interdependent and more 'global', and it is to be hoped that the process will continue. The development continues to be highly uneven, however. Some countries have scarcely shared in the globalization process at all.

There is one further current development that is likely to have a significant impact on the future growth and distribution of world trade: the proliferation of trading 'blocs'. The European Union has been around for so long in some form that it is largely accepted, despite its manifold restrictions on trade. More recently, however, the world has seen the development of the North American Free Trade Agreement (NAFTA) and Mercosur (a Latin American common market), the probable expansion of the Association of Southeast Asian Nations (ASEAN), a projected Asia-Pacific Conference and most recently the establishment of an East African free trade area. Those which are true 'free trade areas' without a common external tariff (which NAFTA is, so far) are relatively benign. Any which follow the lead of the EU and form 'customs unions' with common external protective mechanisms are far less benign on a world scale, despite the advantages that they may develop for their members. But above all, if such groupings continue to be established, the burden will fall most heavily on those few countries – probably the poorest – that are not members of any club at all.

TERMS OF TRADE – A GLOBAL RIP-OFF?

The previous section has indicated that the benefits of global trade growth have not been evenly distributed. Much of the protest at Seattle and elsewhere, however, has put forward a considerably more serious criticism – that *international trade has actually damaged some of the poorer countries*. To justify this viewpoint it would be necessary to show that these countries have experienced a consistent deterioration in their terms of trade – and that countries and companies in the developed world have somehow manipulated these terms.

Such a viewpoint would have been much easier to support during the earlier high-water mark of globalization a century and more ago. There can be little doubt that the former colonial powers did dictate the terms of trade between themselves and their colonies. British trade with India certainly benefited the Lancashire cotton textile industry more than it did the people of India. But those days are long past. The colonial heritage is now more typically represented by the efforts of France and Britain to preserve some privileged access for the exports of their former colonies into the highly protected European Union markets. Recent efforts to manipulate the terms of trade have come rather more from the producers of primary products – particularly oil – than from the mature industrial economies.

The real problem arises not from any cynical 'rigging' of the terms of trade, but from their volatility. The market prices of primary commodities are, by their very nature, more volatile than those of manufactured products and services. Swings in world economic output directly determine demand for such primary products – and therefore affect the economies of the commodity-producing countries much more than those of either the OECD countries or the newly industrialized nations of Asia. To the extent that many developing countries are excessively dependent on one or two commodities, their vulnerability is correspondingly greater.

The aftermath of the 1997 Asian crisis makes a good example. The immediate impact was a sharp fall in output in the Asian countries themselves, together with a collapse in their currencies and equity markets. But by 1998, according to figures published by UNCTAD (1999), the terms of trade of all the Asian economies except Indonesia and Taiwan in fact improved by amounts ranging from 0.2 per cent (Korea) to 5 per cent (Thailand). In Africa, on the other hand, the general slowdown in world output and trade immediately after the crisis was by this time showing in falling commodity prices. Ghana and Cote d'Ivoire were hit by lower cocoa prices, Malawi by tea and tobacco prices, Kenya by coffee prices and Mauritius by sugar prices. For Africa as a whole, the terms of trade deteriorated by 9.9 per cent, leading to a fall in real incomes of 2.4 per cent. Nevertheless, tragic though this is, it is not manipulation but a fact of economic life.

CAPITAL MARKETS – GLOBAL BORROWERS AND LENDERS

In no area has the globalization process been more obvious or more dramatic than in the capital markets. Prior to the 1950s no truly international capital markets existed. The only financial transactions that could be considered international were borrowings in the major national capital markets by non-resident borrowers, primarily through the issuing of 'foreign' bonds in these markets. The beginning of global financing came with the development of 'parallel' or 'offshore' markets, in which a currency is borrowed and reloaned by financial institutions domiciled outside the country issuing that currency – and consequently not subject to regulation by its central bank. Such markets quickly came to be called the 'Euro-currency' markets. The freedom from regulation, and the purely 'wholesale' nature of the transaction, gave the banks operating in these markets a clear cost advantage, so that they were able to lend at rates below those in domestic banking. Inevitably, therefore, the market grew rapidly.

Although the 'Eurobanks' were willing to make fairly long-term loans, their prime source of funds was short-term deposits. It would have been disastrous, therefore, for the banks to lend at fixed rates of interest. The transactions were made at floating rates, typically reviewed every six months. The rates were set at a 'spread' or margin above the wholesale cost of funds in London, known as LIBOR (the London Interbank Offered Rate), which was now usually said to be 'the most important interest rate in the world'; truly a major step towards globalization.

By the 1960s the Euro-currency market was well established and a parallel offshore 'Eurobond' market had emerged. A decade later, syndicated lending in the Euro-currency market had become one of the world's biggest financial sectors – and certainly the most controversial.

A primary concern here must be the contribution of these markets to the globalization process. That contribution rapidly became significant – if not always benign – as funds raised in these markets replaced more traditional forms as the major source of funds for the developing world.

The main problem for less-developed countries is that development requires capital. Such countries have such low incomes and savings rates, however, that they have little chance of generating the necessary capital themselves. The whole development process, therefore, is dependent on access to external funding. It was this fact that led to the creation of the various World Bank institutions and to the regional development banks. During the 1950s and 1960s, these were the chief sources of loans for the developing world, together with bilateral loans and grants from developed-country governments. However, in the 1970s there was a dramatic change. During the period 1975–82, such official sources made up just 32 per cent of net capital flows to the developing world. Direct investment by western companies accounted for only 9 per cent. The balance, well over 50 per cent of total capital flows, took the form of borrowings from the western banking system. Most of these loans were very large syndicated 'sovereign' credits, usually of a billion dollars or more in a single transaction, made to third-world governments or to agencies with a government guarantee. Virtually all of them were made in dollars, but at floating interest rates and at a spread of 1 to 3 per cent above LIBOR. This would eventually trigger a crash.

The surge in lending to the developing countries certainly allowed them purchase far more, of both manufactured goods and energy, than they could otherwise have done, and therefore contributed to the further growth of world trade. In the wake of the 1973 oil price rise, when the newly inflated surpluses of the Organization of Petroleum Exporting Countries (OPEC) poured into the international banks, the developing countries were for a while the only available borrowers – and their willingness to borrow kept the wheels of finance turning. Without their purchases the impact of the recession on the industrial world would have been much worse. But by 1982 just three Latin American countries – Mexico, Argentina and Brazil – owed well over $200 billion to the western banking system. The magnitude of the loans, together with the exposure to any rise in interest rates, left the borrowers horribly vulnerable.

The day of reckoning came in 1982 with the Mexican loan default and the onset of the 'debt crisis'. Prior to this time, the US Federal Reserve had carefully regulated American interest rates. The new Chairman of the Fed, Paul Volker, switched to a completely different approach based on 'monetarist' economics. He concentrated on controlling the monetary aggregates, but allowed interest rates to find their own level. It now became all too clear just how global the financial markets had become. US interest rates shot up and LIBOR followed. At a peak LIBOR rate of 22 per cent, many of the least developed countries (LDCs) were obliged to pay interest at 25 per cent. It was the final straw. Default in Mexico was followed by defaults in Brazil, Argentina and many smaller countries. The boom in bank lending to the developing countries quickly came to an end.

During 1983–89 only 16 per cent of capital flows to the region took the form of bank loans. Nevertheless, the damage had been done. Many developing countries had borrowed more than they could ever repay. Much of the debt remains outstanding – and the pleas for debt forgiveness are currently a significant part of the anti-globalization 'protest' platform.

The international capital markets did of course recover from the LDC debt crisis. The syndicated credit market, in which the crisis had arisen, was out of favour for a while. Private-sector borrowing recovered strongly as the industrial economies emerged from the recession, but now increasingly used the Eurobond markets rather than syndicated borrowing. The development of interest rate swaps gave an even greater impetus to the bond markets, as highly rated companies found that issuing fixed-rate Eurobonds and then swapping the proceeds was the cheapest way of obtaining floating-rate funds. By the end of the 1980s the Eurobond market was by far the biggest component of the international capital markets.

New forms of financing also developed, primarily a Euro commercial paper market in which borrowers increasingly side-stepped the banks and raised money by issuing their own paper. This in turn led to the emergence of the medium-term note (MTN) technique for financing, now the most flexible and fastest-growing of all financial markets. The syndicated credit market also revived and continues to be the favoured method of financing in high-risk situations such as 'project financing' and leveraged buyouts. By the mid-1990s the international financial market was bigger, and offered a more varied range of activities, than ever. Some particular transactions, often involving simultaneous issues in both the Eurobond and foreign bond markets and sometimes as large as $5 billion, came to be known as 'global' issues. The total size of the international financial markets is virtually impossible to measure, but is usually estimated to be somewhere between $5 trillion and $10 trillion.

Only in the area of equity financing has there been relatively little progress towards globalization. Certainly, some transnational companies do list their stocks on multiple exchanges: a German company, for example, may choose to list on London, Amsterdam and New York as well as on the Frankfurt exchange. The reason may be to tap a deeper pool of potential investors, or simply for publicity and prestige. But this in fact indicates that it is still the individual exchanges that matter, and that there is as yet no truly international exchange. Equally, the 'depository receipt' technique by which some companies seek to gain access to foreign exchanges without incurring all of the legal and accounting costs of a full listing simply endorses the importance of the individual exchanges. But even in this area we are seeing the beginnings of a move towards an international market, in that some major international banks have been willing to enter into syndicates to under-write equity issues in just the same way that most Eurobond issues are launched, and to make a market for the shares thereafter. The past track record of the financial world suggests that once such a process is established, it may be expected to develop very rapidly.

However, problems emerged again in the 1990s. Developing countries still needed development capital – far more than the World Bank or the regional development banks were able to provide. The international banking system was again more than willing to step into the breach. Bankers seem to have short memories and an unwillingness to learn from the mistakes of their predecessors; or perhaps it is fairer to say that they simply learnt the wrong lessons. They had become somewhat more reluctant to lend to the governments of developing countries, but happily loaned to private-sector banks and companies in those countries. The lending was again indiscriminate. No single bank seemed to know just how much borrowers in, say, Thailand, Malaysia or South Korea had already borrowed. The result was the Asian crisis of 1997, followed closely by the Russian default of 1998.

Here at least the anti-globalization protesters have some justifica-tion. The international – and in this case one can truly say global – financial markets are a very impressive development. They allow capi-tal to be raised cheaply and efficiently and to be moved around on an unprecedented scale. But they are also completely unsupervised and unregulated – in effect, a jungle into which borrowers venture at their own risk. The governments of some of the developing countries are certainly open to criticism. They chose to borrow the funds and must have realized the dangers involved. It is true, also, that in many cases the proceeds were used unwisely, on grandiose projects that were never completed – and that in some cases they found their way into private bank accounts.

Nevertheless the western banks are also very open to criticism. Their lending was unco-ordinated and frequently appears to have been based on very shallow credit analysis. Smaller banks apparently thought that everything must be under control if Citibank/Chase/Deutsche/UBS/HSBC or similar 'names' were the co-lead managers in the syndicate. Perhaps the larger bankers assumed that if the worst came to the worst the International Monetary Fund (IMF) would step in and sort things out. One of the most unfortunate results has been that the IMF has indeed become involved in many resultant rescue and refinancing operations, and in its desire to inject some fiscal discipline is now widely seen as one of the 'bad guys'. This is, in short, one of the more questionable aspects of the globalization story.

FOREIGN DIRECT INVESTMENT – TOWARDS THE GLOBAL COMPANY

The flow of capital from the developed to the developing countries has again changed dramatically in recent years. Official funds – government aid grants and development agency lending – had by the 1990s fallen to 20 per cent of total funding. Lending by the western banking system had recovered from its post-crisis lows to reach 24 per cent. But the most important item, providing 34 per cent of the total, was now foreign direct investment – the process by which corporate entities invest in branches, subsidiaries, acquisitions and joint ventures in countries other than their own domicile. This has become the most important mechanism through which the globalization process operates.

One might again argue, as with foreign trade, that in the light of continued (if erratic) world economic growth, some increase in direct investment is predictable and expected. Again, therefore, it seems reasonable to claim that the investment process is contributing to globalization *only if it is increasing significantly faster than world GDP*. The claim is, once more, easily justified. The FDI-to-GDP ratio has in fact been increasing much faster than the exports-to-GDP ratio examined above. In 1980 the figure was just 5 per cent. By 1997 it had increased to almost 12 per cent.

Not only has the rate of foreign investment been accelerating, but also the sums involved are consequently very large indeed. In 1998, total foreign direct investment stocks had grown to almost $4.1 trillion. The total sales of foreign affiliates were $11.4 trillion and their gross profits $2.3 trillion. These affiliates in turn generated a further $2.3 trillion of exports, a significant contribution to world trade and to the globalization process.

Predictably, most foreign direct investment flows from the developed areas of the world (see Table 2.1). The most striking feature here is the emergence of East and South Asia as a source of outward investment rather than just a recipient. Investment by the 'offshore Chinese' into China has played a key role here. Nevertheless, the major mature industrial countries continue to play the leading role. During 1998 the biggest outward investor was the US, with outflows of $133 billion. In second place came the UK, with $114 billion, then Germany with $87 billion. The other leading countries, in order of magnitude, were France, the Netherlands, Canada and Japan.

Table 2.1 Total outward FDI expressed as a percentage of GDP

	1980 (%)	1997 (%)
European Union	6.2	18.6
North America	8.2	11.5
South America	0.2	1.9
Central and Eastern Europe	neg.	1.2
Africa	0.2	3.7
Western Asia	0.4	1.6
Central Asia	neg.	neg.
East and South Asia	1.4	9.3

Source: United Nations Conference on Trade and Development (1999).

Once again, it is important to keep matters in perspective. The main foreign direct investment flows, as with the main foreign trade flows, are *intra-OECD*: investments made by companies in developed countries into other developed countries. In 1998 some $460 billion – about 71 per cent of all foreign direct investments – flowed into developed countries. Investments into the developing world have been growing rapidly, however. A total of $700 billion flowed into developing countries during 1990–97 and a further $166 billion during 1998 alone.

As with trade growth, the growth in direct investment has been very unevenly distributed. During the 1970s Latin America was the favoured area. After the 1980s debt crisis South and East Asia became the main recipients for a while. During the early 1990s it appeared that the 'transitional' countries of Central Europe would become the principal recipients of investment flows from western Europe as their economies were deregulated and privatized, but the region has failed to live up to its expectations so far, and since the mid-1990s China has become the favourite destination. During the second half of the 1990s, in fact, one-third of all FDI flows to developing countries were to China.

Here again, as with foreign trade, it is the least developed countries that have gained least investment, and the share going to sub-Saharan Africa in particular goes down and down. During 1998, for example, Asia enjoyed a total of $84.9 billion of new inflows, with China receiving $45.5 billion, Singapore $7.2 billion, Thailand $7.0 billion and South Korea $5.1 billion. Total flows to central and eastern Europe were only $19 billion. Lending to the *whole* of Africa during the year was just $7.9 billion, with only Nigeria and Egypt receiving more than $1 billion. It is scarcely surprising that the development process is uneven and that the gulf between the richer and poorer countries continues to grow. More significantly, China is rapidly being integrated into the world of global companies, while the countries of Africa are marginalized.

The pattern of investment flows into specific industries is also very uneven – and again there have been significant shifts in the pattern over time (see Table 2.2). Clearly, some industries are also becoming more global than others, with the finance industry and trade leading the way.

Recent changes in the regional pattern of investment flows have coincided with a further significant development: an alteration in the nature of the investment transactions themselves. In the past a high proportion of inflows have been 'greenfield' developments. The dominant form of transaction in the past couple of years, however, has been cross-border merger and acquisition activity. As recently as 1991, greenfield developments in developing countries were about $16 billion, compared with mergers and acquisitions of just $9 billion. By 1997 greenfield investments were still only $20 billion and acquisitions increased to more than $90 billion. This development accompanies – and perhaps reflects – a further important shift: from investment in the primary (natural resource) and secondary (manufacturing) sectors and towards the tertiary (services) sectors. This trend has been established in investment patterns into developed countries for some time, but is now

Table 2.2   Investment flows into specific industries

	FDI inflows: millions of dollars (percentages)	
	1988	**1997**
Agriculture, forestry and fishing	8577 (9.2)	8591 (4.3)
Manufacturing – total	34 974 (37.5)	70 281 (35.4)
of which:		
chemicals and chemical products	5721 (6.1)	9368 (9.8)
publishing, printing and recorded media	5510 (5.9)	889 (0.4)
machinery and equipment	4255 (4.6)	8078 (4.1)
Services – total	39 999 (42.9)	105 241 (53.0)
of which:		
finance	12 639 (13.6)	38 908 (19.6)
trade	7376 (7.9)	24 119 (12.2)
business services	7262 (7.8)	14 181 (7.1)

Source: United Nations Conference on Trade and Development (1999).

clearly spreading to developing countries as well. During the 1990s investment flows into the services sector exceeded those in the other sectors in a number of developing countries, including Argentina, Brazil and Mexico, Indonesia and Thailand.

To what extent are the criticisms of globalization valid in this area of activity? Leaving aside the obvious inequalities in the distribution of investment flows, is the process itself on balance good or bad? Here there will always be some disagreement. The benefits of FDI – particularly investment into developing countries – have frequently been listed. In particular:

■ Inward investment generates employment and enhances the skills base. The investor almost always transfers capital into the host country, and for the past three decades FDI has been consistently increasing as a percentage of total capital formation.

■ The investor also transfers technology, frequently advanced technology, as FDI becomes increasingly important as a way of spreading development costs over a broader market. Additional transfers are production and managerial knowhow, brands, and training and personnel management techniques. Even though the original motivation may have been import substitution, the recipient industries and firms frequently become more competitive in export markets. Statistical surveys carried out by UNCTAD show a strong correlation between per capita inward FDI and export performance in manufactured goods. In most cases (although not invariably) this has also led to an improvement in the developing country's trade balance.

- The transnational company often makes a contribution to the host country environment by introducing cleaner technologies and environmental management systems.

- Finally, FDI often produces a 'multiplier effect' in the host country by stimulating both upstream and downstream investments, so that according to one study (Borzenstein *et al.*, 1995) 'the total increase in investment is estimated at between 1.5 times and 2.3 times the increase in the flow of FDI'.

So what criticisms can be levelled at FDI? One has been that the foreign investor, once established, then raises further funding in the local capital market, which in typically thin markets tends to 'crowd out' local borrowers. Hard evidence of this is difficult to find, however. It has also been suggested that the easy access to technology and know-how that FDI provides inhibits the development of indigenous research and development capability. The most frequent objection is the obvious one: that control of assets passes out of the hands of residents and into those of foreign companies – and that in the process the major multinationals become even bigger, more powerful and less controllable. The swing from greenfield development to the acquisition of local companies can only intensify this criticism.

It is estimated that there are between 50 000 and 60 000 transnational companies (TNCs) involved in some degree of foreign investment. However, a handful of large companies dominate FDI flows. The World Investment Report states, 'Although there are many TNCs in the world, FDI is actually concentrated in relatively few of them. In many countries, only a small number of firms account for the bulk of outward FDI.' This is certainly true. And here at least the pattern has been fairly consistent. Most of the companies that were listed in the 'top 100' list of outward investors five years ago remain in that list today. Predictably they are companies whose domiciles are in the major mature industrial economies. Of the current top 100, the country league table is as in Table 2.3.

Table 2.3 Top outward investor countries

Country	No. of companies
United States	27
Japan	17
France	13
United Kingdom	11
Germany	11
Netherlands	5
Canada	3
Sweden	3
Italy	3
Others	7

Source: United Nations Conference on Trade and Development (1999).

In terms of the degree of involvement in international operations of these 100 companies, the following figures are pertinent:

- Total assets $4200 billion, of which $1808 billion (43 per cent) are foreign.
- Total sales $4128 billion, of which $2149 billion (52 per cent) are foreign.
- Total employment 11.8 million, of which 5.9 million are foreign, i.e. not citizens of the country in which the company is domiciled.

Interestingly, the overseas assets of these companies appear to generate more sales per dollar of investment than the domestic ones.

It is clear, then, that a high proportion of FDI is undertaken by a handful of very powerful companies. In fact, *the UN estimates that these 100 companies produce somewhere between 4 and 7 per cent of total world GDP.* Given their size and power, and the fact that they are increasingly using acquisitions as their preferred method of investment, it is not surprising that their activities cause concern. The main areas of concern are as follows:

- The ownership and control of those local companies with most development potential is passing into foreign hands.
- The host government has little or no control over the activities of such investors.
- Most or all of the profits of the acquired companies are owned by foreigners and are likely to be repatriated.
- The new owners may undertake consolidation and rationalization activities that will reduce employment.
- Acquisitions and rationalization may reduce competition in the host country.
- Investment through acquisition, unlike greenfield investment, does not initially produce any inflow of capital in the early stages.
- TNC investors may pressure host governments to reduce their tax rates – and threaten to move their investments elsewhere if they do not.
- Above all, the fact that *the overall objective of the TNC is not the same as that of the host government*. The government wishes to stimulate economic development. The immediate objective of the TNC's investments is to make itself more competitive in world markets. Its ultimate objective is increasingly argued to be the maximization of the wealth of its shareholders.

In these circumstances, it is clear that the activities of TNC investors will be increasingly closely scrutinized – particularly their growing investments in the developing world. The ways in which they respond to this scrutiny will largely determine the future development of globalization.

FUTURE GLOBAL DEVELOPMENT – THREE SCENARIOS

The preceding discussion has suggested that, while the rapid movement towards a more global economy has on the whole been beneficial, some criticism is justified. Some of the poorer countries have been left behind. The international banks behaved with massive irresponsibility in the past and the debt overhang that resulted is with us still. Some of the TNCs have not taken as much care as they might have done to understand and to try to accommodate the needs and objectives of their host countries and their governments. The World Bank and the IMF have sometimes seemed 'high handed' and have not always done their homework as well as they might. And the WTO is not noted for its communication skills so far!

Scenario one – which might be called, after Voltaire, 'all for the best in the best of all possible worlds' – is one in which there is an honest, systematic and co-ordinated attempt to put things right. This would clearly involve debt forgiveness on a scale beyond anything that has been seen so far. It is, of course, relatively easy for governments to forgive debts. Private-sector banks with shareholders find it more difficult, but if most of the debts are unlikely ever to be repaid and if any write-off can be set against taxes, the write-offs should not be too painful. (One of the bitterest criticisms of the banks, indeed, has been that they have taken tax losses through provisions but still kept the debts on their books.)

This scenario would also require some measures by which the poorest countries could be given access to investment funds, and thus enabled to improve their productivity and play a larger role in world trade. The readiest solution might seem to be to enhance the role of the IDA (the International Development Agency, that part of the World Bank Group that makes 'soft loans' available to the poorest countries), by guaranteeing to it adequate funding instead of the present situation in which it has to go 'cap in hand' to its richer members periodically and beg for donations. This would be only a partial solution, however. Development requires not just capital but all of those other things that FDI so efficiently provides, so the real challenge would be somehow to motivate the TNCs to direct some of their investment activities to the poorest parts of the world.

The third main requirement under this scenario would be a 'code of conduct' in good corporate citizenship, to which all TNC investors agreed and adhered. In the absence of any appropriate regulatory authority, the application of such a code would be a matter for self-regulation by the international corporate community; a very pious hope perhaps. Yet the current behaviour of the international banks in terms of their acceptance of Bank for International Settlements (BIS) directives regarding minimum capital to loan ratios and their self-imposition of sophisticated internal risk-management schemes contrasts dramatically with their behaviour in the 'cowboy' days of the 1970s and 1980s, and suggests that a degree of self-policing might also be feasible among the non-bank TNCs.

Finally, the scenario assumes that progress towards trade liberalization continues. All of the loose ends left behind by the Uruguay round are tied up. The European Union actually does honour the agreement to end agricultural subsidies. The Multi-Fibres Agreement is revoked, and free trade in services and the protection of intellectual property are finally achieved. Any regional groupings that develop are of the 'free-trade area' type, and do not impede world trade.

This scenario would effectively defuse the various protests and criticisms that are currently placed in the path of further progress towards globalization. Sadly, it is not likely to happen – although one might hope that parts of it at least could eventually become reality.

The second scenario, which might be called 'muddling through', is a much more likely development. Under this scenario there is no general co-ordinated reform programme, but the main problems are addressed and partial solutions found. The international agencies improve their procedures and train their staff to be more sensitive to local needs and concerns. The funding of the IDA is put on a more regular footing. The World Trade Organization does achieve a degree of credibility and a new trade round is inaugurated.

One of the major improvements under this scenario is in relations between TNCs and host governments. No general code of practice is developed. But the governments of the developed countries increasingly urge behaviour standards on their 'local' TNCs (as the US has already done through its 'Model Business Principles'). Most of the TNCs become increasingly sensitive to differences in national concerns and cultures, and handle their foreign investments with increasing skill.

World trade, however, remains far from completely free – especially in agricultural products. The European Union continues to be protectionist, although the 'eastward extension' and the incorporation of Poland, Hungary and the Czech Republic in the near future necessitate some reductions in level of subsidies.

In this scenario, however, the debts of the developing world continue to be rescheduled rather than written off. Trade flows and investment patterns continue to be uneven. The gap between rich and poor does not close, but perhaps does not increase at quite its recent rate.

The result of this scenario is probably that some criticisms are blunted, while others become even more vociferous. Protest against globalization does not disappear. The globalization process continues, but the road is at times a very rocky one.

The third scenario could be called 'blood in the streets'. Under this scenario there is no change at all in the current patterns. International banks and TNCs continue to think of little else but the interests of their shareholders. The European Union and Japan continue their current levels of protectionism and both are frequently involved in bitter trade wars with the United States. There is little progress in debt forgiveness. Most foreign investment continues to pour into a handful of already emergent nations in South-East Asia and Latin America, and very little flows to the poorest countries. The World Bank and IMF are increasingly seen, in the Third World, as being the tools of the rich countries. The IDA continues to be chronically underfunded. Protest, under these assumptions, becomes so bitter and so aggressive that the WTO never does manage to hold a further round of trade talks.

It is to be hoped that this third scenario is unlikely. It is not impossible, however. If it were to occur, it would severely limit any further progress towards globalization.

References

Borzenstein, Eduardo, de Gregorio, José and Lee, Jong-Wha (1995) 'How does foreign direct investment affect economic growth?', working paper no. 5057, National Bureau of Economic Records, Cambridge, MA.

United Nations Conference on Trade and Development (1999) *World Investment Report: Foreign Direct Investment and the Challenge of Development*, United Nations, New York and Geneva.

GLOBAL LABOUR
MARKETS

Jim Durcan

CHAPTER 3

GLOBAL LABOUR MARKETS

'Keep, ancient lands, your storied pomp!' cries she
With silent lips. 'Give me your tired, your poor,
Your huddled masses yearning to breathe free,
The wretched refuse of your teeming shore,
Send these, the homeless, tempest-tost, to me,
I lift my lamp beside the golden door!'

Emma Lazarus, 'The New Colossus', 1883

*I*n the years that have passed since Emma Lazarus wrote the verse
that was inscribed on the Statue of Liberty, the international migration
of labour has continued on a massive scale. Whether it is the 'yearning
to breathe free' or 'the golden door' that fuels the aspirations of migrant
workers is an issue with contemporary relevance. Either way, millions
of migrants and would-be migrants have continued to add to the
cultural diversity and economic resources of many nations. Such mass
migration involves a complex mixture of hopes and fears, generosity
and self-interest from all involved. Continuing rapid population
growth and urbanization have added to the 'huddled masses'. Poverty
continues to characterize the 'wretched refuse'.

After 120 years, it is surely worth asking whether migration is
still the surest hope of a better life. It is also worth reviewing whether
the keepers of the 'golden door' still offer a welcome to the tired and
poor.

In this review there are several areas of questioning. One concerns
the process of globalization itself. Does the globalization of the world
economy render mass migration unnecessary or does it give even

greater urgency to the struggles of millions of individuals who seek a better life by seeking work in more prosperous areas? Does the free movement of capital mean that capital naturally flows to those areas where capital is scarce, bringing employment and prosperity in its wake? Do global corporations with their capacity to move productive capacity and jobs regardless of national boundaries mean that the 'huddled masses' no longer need to abandon their homes and risk the tempests?

The second is concerned with the available evidence on the continuing pattern of migration from poorer to richer countries. How do we explain the continuing flows of migrant workers risking even death to secure work in developed countries? How do we explain the evident willingness of migrants and their families to invest heavily through cash, time and energy to secure opportunities to work, perhaps illegally, in richer countries? How do we explain the characteristics of those migrant workers?

The third area of questioning concerns government policy. Does commitment to the free movement of capital and of goods and services mean that the free movement of labour is unnecessary? Or should a commitment to free markets and to human dignity and development require that governments demonstrate as great an enthusiasm for free movement of labour as they have for the free movement of capital? How can we explain government policies that embrace tougher measures to deter would-be migrants with simultaneous efforts to recruit skilled labour from poorer countries?

This chapter seeks to set out some of the key economic issues that arise in the way the process of globalization affects labour markets in a context of rapid technological change and major demographic shifts. It explores some of the forces at work in labour markets across the world and the role of labour mobility in adjusting to those forces. It considers the impact of demographic changes on the demand for and supply of labour. It looks at the costs and benefits of international labour mobility for the individuals and countries concerned. It also discusses the role played by global corporations and their scope to support or reduce labour mobility.

GLOBALIZATION AND LABOUR

Globalization may be seen as a process whereby local, regional and national markets are merged into worldwide or global markets. These markets may deal in particular commodities such as oil and grain, or goods such as cars and computers, or services such as insurance and finance. Globalization has proceeded much more quickly in some markets than others. In some markets many barriers remain around local, regional and national markets. These barriers may reflect government-endorsed standards or requirements, tariffs and taxes, customers' cultural preferences, physical accessibility, languages, or conditions in related markets. Some of these factors may consciously be co-ordinated to protect local interests, for example the difficulties of accessing local distribution systems may prevent foreign companies from accessing key national markets. In other cases government policy and business interests may diverge, for example tax policy aimed at attracting inward investment may reduce the profitability and market share of local businesses.

Agreements between governments to reduce exchange controls have done much to promote a global market in financial capital. The work of a wide range of public and private-sector financial intermediaries has reinforced these trends. Successive rounds of international negotiations have reduced the levels of tariffs on a wide range of goods and services. Other negotiations have lessened non-tariff barriers to trade.

This progressive opening of markets has increased the numbers of potential competitors and customers. The reduction in all kinds of barriers lessens the insularity of markets and leaves them more exposed to the fluctuations and changes taking place elsewhere. While such openness heightens the vulnerability of domestic markets to external pressures, it also provides domestic markets with access to a much wider range of customers and suppliers to alleviate domestic market pressures. For example, buying food from elsewhere when harvests are poor reduces the risks of famine. Exporting food to markets where prices are higher raises domestic prices as well. The collapse in Asian financial markets in 1998 was a tribute to the volatility of short-term finance. The subsequent rebound and rapid growth in those Asian economies reflects, in part, the role of wider markets in reducing and accommodating greater turbulence.

Of course, international trade has existed for thousands of years and has served to link markets in the ways described above. In part, what characterized the late twentieth century was the willingness of so many governments to increase the scope of international trade by reducing market barriers. International trade, by definition, focused on those goods and services that are exportable. One consequence was that goods and services that were not traded internationally were not subject to international competition. Economists talked in terms of 'tradeable' and 'non-tradeable' sectors in domestic economies. Tradeable sectors were subject to international pressures on price and quality. Commercial organizations needed to be internationally competitive if they were to survive. In contrast, in 'non-tradeable sectors' commercial organizations only needed to be domestically competitive to survive.

Globalization has dramatically altered that situation. The growth of global corporations has spread the impact of globalization far beyond that of internationally traded products and services. Global corporations, with their access to mobile financial capital, their technology and their marketing prowess, have brought global pressures to the most domestic of markets. Service organizations that do not trade internationally, such as restaurants, are subject to the attentions of global corporations and have, in consequence, become part of the global markets. Of course, global corporations are not always wholly committed to the elimination of barriers between markets. The existence of markets in 'grey goods' – those that are bought from a global corporation in one national market and resold at a profit elsewhere – indicates that global corporations are prepared to utilize and even create market barriers when it enhances their profitability. The continued growth of trade in grey goods despite the restrictive efforts of global corporations reflects the market pressures that exist to undermine strategies elevating the interests of shareholders over those of consumers.

Two key forces can be seen as having accelerated the process of globalization: the willingness of governments to reduce the barriers between markets; and the growth of global corporations, which has brought new competitors to localized markets. The strength of the former may be seen in the creation of such institutions as the European Union, which has transformed not just the economic but also the political landscape of Europe. Belief in the success of such institutions in enabling poorer areas to share in the prosperity of the rich is reflected in the number of countries applying to join the European Union. Widening markets is not cost or risk free, but many governments obviously believe that the costs and risks are dwarfed by the advantages. At the same time, global corporations have anticipated the widening of market areas by switching production to eastern Europe and by opening new outlets to compete with domestic distributors.

GLOBAL LABOUR MARKETS?

This broad canvas of global markets for goods and services is widely recognized and studied. This chapter focuses on particular types of markets – those for labour. It is concerned with the trends and forces at work within the global markets for labour and with the activities of global corporations within those labour markets.

External Labour Markets

Labour markets can be defined as areas where buyers and sellers of labour interact to set levels of pay and employment. The term 'external labour markets' is used to define those areas where there is relatively free movement of labour and employers seek to meet their labour needs through external recruitment. Employers seeking workers advertise their vacancies in the wider world. Workers seeking employment respond to job opportunities. Labour market adjustments come about through labour mobility between organizations, wage movements in response to shortages and surpluses, and changes in the numbers and types of jobs on offer.

Within the broad framework of external labour markets, specific labour markets may be defined in terms of particular jobs or employees within defined geographical areas, e.g. the market for teachers in London. If teachers within London are reluctant to leave the capital and if employers can recruit enough teachers from the geographical area of London, then to talk of a London labour market for teachers reflects reality. If London teachers are prepared to move to other parts of the country and London employers are prepared to recruit nationally, then the effective labour market may be described as national rather than local. If London schools, despite advertising nationally, are unable to fill their vacancies, respond to this shortage by advertising their vacancies in other English-speaking countries and begin to recruit in significant numbers from other countries, then the market has become multinational rather than national.

Volumes of jobs and workers are important in this context. In the 1960s a handful of British soccer players were recruited to play for clubs in other parts of Europe. Such a trickle of players did not mean that the British labour market for soccer players – which clearly embraced England, Northern Ireland, Scotland and Wales – had become a European labour market. By the late 1990s the flows of players to and from clubs outside Britain, at the highest level, had created a European labour market for top-quality soccer players, even though those clubs in lower divisions continued to depend heavily on British sources.

Obviously, one can trace some degree of linkage between all labour markets. These linkages may be strong or weak, but they exist. Factors that influence the degree of linkage include individuals' range of skills and the interconnectedness of geographical areas. Individuals may have skills that are saleable through a number of different job markets, e.g. a qualified doctor who is also a talented actor and a successful playwright could seek work in a number of very different labour markets. Such individuals, by choosing to move from one job market to another, serve to link markets that might be seen as different, e.g. military pilots who transfer to civilian airlines link markets that are otherwise dominated by very different institutions and practices. Individuals who are prepared to travel 100 miles to work link many more labour markets than those who are only prepared to travel 10 miles. Workers who are prepared to move their residence provide a link between their originating and destination markets, even if these are thousands of miles apart.

In theory, all labour markets could be global. Given the falling cost of travel and the growing accessibility of job information from electronic networks, all labour markets might encompass the globe. The willingness of major corporations to advertise their job vacancies through their websites suggests that they believe they operate in wide labour markets. There is little systematic evidence of the extent to which such advertisements attract responses from outside national boundaries. The falling costs of travel and the ease of communication have lessened some of the costs to would-be migrants of seeking work outside their home countries.

Boundaries of external labour markets

Although labour markets could be global, they are typically characterized by barriers and restrictions that serve to fragment and diminish their scope. The geographical limits of labour markets are set by the willingness and ability of workers to move. The ability of workers to move is more restricted than their willingness. Government restrictions on workers' freedom of movement are widespread. Many governments impose strict controls on inward and, in some cases, outward migration. Although the costs of movement and the uncertainty about employment prospects may serve to reduce the willingness of would-be migrants to travel, the efforts of governments to control and restrict their flow suggest that government restrictions are a far bigger hurdle than workers' preference to stay at home.

The scope of labour markets is further restricted by employers' specifications of the type(s) of workers they wish to hire. These specifications are designed to delineate particular jobs and the kinds of workers who could fill them. These specifications weaken or eliminate the linkages between labour markets that might otherwise exist. By specifying qualifications, experience and ability, and by including social, legal and cultural norms and prejudices concerning gender, age, race, religion, disability or other personal qualities that are not directly related to the individual's ability to do the job effectively, organizations discriminate against and disadvantage individuals and groups. Such employer-created barriers may be supported by some or all of the existing workforce, but their impact is to narrow the scope of labour markets and limit the opportunities for labour mobility. Individual workers who are able to meet such specifications benefit by having fewer competitors for such jobs. Conversely, those excluded from these 'favoured' labour markets face more competition, lower wages and greater insecurity of employment in the unrestricted labour markets. Such restrictions have traditionally weighed heavily against women and against members of particular ethnic minority groups. The overall impact of such barriers is to fragment and isolate labour markets, to the detriment of all those who do not come within their scope.

In theory, labour markets could be as narrow as a village or as wide as the world. Also in theory, labour markets could be as confined as a single job, e.g. President of the United States of America, or as wide as a universal activity, e.g. cleaning. In practice, it seems that real labour markets are far more narrow and constrained than wide and universal. In assessing whether this matters, one might consider not only the economic consequences of labour market barriers, but also the social and personal costs to those individuals and groups who are denied the opportunity to compete for jobs that offer higher standards of living and a better quality of working life.

Internal Labour Markets

In addition to external labour markets there are many 'internal labour markets'. The term is used to describe those situations in which at least of some of the jobs in an organization are not advertised externally. Many organizations operate internal labour markets where available jobs are allocated to existing employees and where pay levels reflect internal criteria rather than market rates. Such labour markets offer potential benefits in terms of cost savings and reduced risks to employees and employers in terms of exchange of reliable information about jobs and individuals' capacities to fill particular jobs. They also offer greater security of supply for employers and of work for employees.

Employers in internal labour markets are more willing to provide training and development because they believe employees are less likely to leave. Lower rates of labour turnover imply greater duration of employment, which means that the costs of training and development can be recouped over a longer period. Employees are more willing to engage in training and development for tasks and behaviours that are specific to that organization, e.g. internalizing corporate culture or operating organization-specific procedures, as these will enhance their value to the organization and increase their job security. Internal labour markets may play a vital role in developing those competences that provide the organization with its competitive edge in the marketplace.

In its most extreme form, an internal labour market only recruits at one level – one entry point to the internal market. Internal movement fills all other vacancies. Police forces in the UK continue to insist that all police officers must begin their service as constables, regardless of their qualifications or experience. Other organizations operate partial internal markets, with some jobs being filled internally or where existing staff are given prior consideration for vacancies.

Internal labour markets and equality of opportunity

Internal labour markets reflect implicit or explicit contracts between the employer and the existing employees, replacing the competitive pressures of external labour markets by internal procedures and criteria that allocate employees to jobs and set pay rates that encourage labour retention and development and reflect shared perceptions of equity and consistency. In seeking to insulate themselves from external pressures, employers and employees also exclude those not currently represented in their workforces. The impact of such exclusion on women and members of ethnic minority groups and the consequent continuation of patterns of discrimination and exploitation have been widely recognized. The impact of exclusion from internal labour markets on migrants has been less widely studied, but there seems little reason to suppose that its effects are any less severe. It has also been recognized that the impact of internal labour markets on issues of discrimination and exploitation depends on the specific criteria and procedures adopted. By choosing appropriate criteria and procedures – particularly in relation to the point of entry to the internal labour market – organizations may play a major role in promoting equal opportunities for all. In some instances, as global corporations have come under pressure to promote equal opportunities among their workforces in western countries there have been beneficial spin-offs in other countries.

Causes and consequences of internal labour markets

Many internal labour markets developed in large organizations in response to the twin pressures of tight external labour markets and highly unionized workforces. Labour shortages encouraged employers to consider more effective means of retaining labour while controlling wage costs. Total reliance on external markets would mean that organizations would give up any pretence of control over wage rates – they would simply follow the market rate. Any increase in their wage rates would have to be paid to all their existing workers in order to prevent them from quitting. Wage adjustments in response to labour shortages have significant effects on overall costs. Unions, committed to equity and conscious of the need to contain the potential tensions between different groups in the workforce in order to maximize their bargaining strength, are usually supportive of the development of internal labour markets. Replacing uncontrolled market forces by negotiated criteria and procedures enables unions to meet their objectives and to extend their influence and appeal to members.

Protecting internal labour markets from market pressures has a clear rationale and obvious benefits to those involved. It also carries some risks, particularly at a time when globalization is generating new and stronger market pressures. Insulating organizations from market pressures may foster a mindset that sees internal pressures as being more important than external ones. Organizations that become internally focused may fail to react in time to external market developments that affect the demand for or supply of their products. Changes in competitor activity or consumer tastes may be ignored in the short term. For example, the inability of management and unions in the UK car industry to establish constructive working relationships in a highly protected market in the 1960s distracted their attention from the competitive pressures that emerged in the 1970s as trade barriers were reduced.

Organizations that fail to respond to market pressures risk losing their competitive advantage and with it market share and profitability. Declining market share and falling profitability typically trigger cost–cutting activity. At the organizational level, such dynamics may include job losses and pay cuts that break the implicit contract of the internal labour markets. Such pressures were very evident in the 1980s, when the growth of new competitors from Asia and the increasing pressures from globalization resulted in widespread recession and industrial restructuring. Conventional wisdom (and business school prescriptions) changed rapidly. The merits of large, highly integrated corporations occupying multiple stages in the value chain were dismissed in favour of 'focus, focus, focus'.

This new conventional wisdom decreed that organizations should concentrate on those activities in which they have significant competitive advantage. Any 'non-core' activities should be outsourced. Organizations were to be pared down to those activities in which they had a clear competitive advantage. In reality, the cold logic required to determine which were 'core' and which 'non-core' activities was frequently clouded by executives' personal value sets and the impact of organizational cultures that valued some activities more highly than others. The logic was beguiling and the opportunity to walk away from difficult management issues very attractive. Much was written about the advent of the 'virtual corporation' that would only exist as a brand. Labour market problems were to be vanquished in the electronic lightning of new technology.

Global internal labour markets

However, while organizations were slimming down to their core activities, globalization pressures were encouraging them to expand their geographical reach, so that the new organizations became more global and more focused. Running these new global corporations required new global managers. These appeared to be in short supply. One response was to reinvent internal labour markets, with corporations seeking to attract and retain managers around the world who could be developed to provide the global management they required. Management development programmes aimed at identifying and developing young, high-potential managers became a major new source of activity for corporate human resources departments.

In addition to the response of employers to the globalization of competitive pressures, governments also intervened. Much of that intervention was designed to enhance the flexibility of national labour markets to enable the nation state to survive in a globalized economy. Such government interventions included the gradual adoption of privatization programmes to introduce competitive pressures into the public sector and, by implication, to weaken or destroy the internal labour markets that had developed in those sectors. Government interventions also included legislative changes to reduce the collective power of individual unions and to reduce entitlements to social security benefits, which were seen as inhibiting labour market flexibility. These efforts really serve to underscore the extent to which labour markets can be characterized as fragmented and insulated.

LABOUR MOBILITY ACROSS BORDERS

In the context of globalization, the continued existence of so many barriers and restrictions to the free operation of labour markets contrasts sharply with developments in other markets. It is of course true that within some of the new trading blocs, e.g. the European Union, there is a commitment to the free movement of labour. In reality, the scope to move depends on language skills, on the wider acceptance of qualifications and credentials and on the absence of discrimination. Other trading blocs, e.g. NAFTA, have not sought to encompass freedom of movement. Many, if not all, of the more developed countries are united in their resistance to uncontrolled immigration. Desperate migrants struggle against such restrictions by seeking to enter 'Fortress

Europe' or to cross the Rio Grande. Their desperation is reflected in the numbers who die in the attempt. The tragedy in the summer of 2000 when 58 Chinese would-be immigrants suffocated while crossing to Britain is only one example of the risks taken and the costs incurred.

This resistance to immigration, although explicable in terms of political and social pressures within the developed countries, ignores the massive contribution made by mobile labour to the process of economic and social development. The exploitation of natural resources and the process of industrialization have resulted in massive population shifts within and between countries. The population movement within Britain from agriculture to manufacturing during the Industrial Revolution is widely recognized as having been crucial to that process of transformation. The later development of heavy industries and coal mining resulted in significant population shifts within Britain and from Ireland to Britain. The rapid growth of the USA as an industrial power also required continued immigration throughout the nineteenth century. The recovery of the West German economy through the 1950s was supported by the continuing flow of refugees from the East. Without this mobility of labour, these phases of economic development would have been severely stunted and may have simply withered.

Government policies towards labour mobility reflect an interesting but confusing (and confused?) mixture of approaches. Many governments have taken steps to reduce perceived rigidities in their national labour markets by embracing privatization and limiting collective rights. At the same time, governments have responded to immigration pressures by tighter controls and only accepting 'genuine' refugees. When that approach seemed inadequate, refugees were reclassified to separate out 'genuine refugees' and 'economic migrants'. A desire to escape poverty at home and build a better economic future elsewhere was not sufficient to justify refugee status.

Who Migrates?

Conventional economic analysis suggests that labour mobility will be positively related to the perceived difference in earnings between origin state and destination state. The definition of earnings needs to be stretched to include pay rates for particular jobs at particular points in time and the likelihood of finding and retaining employment. If future prospects only stretch to a lifetime of unemployment, the incentive to move is high although not necessarily overwhelming. Labour mobility is negatively related to the perceived costs of moving. Such costs include not only travel and subsistence but also the loss of family, friends and familiar surroundings. The more highly valued are these latter factors, the less likely the would-be migrant is to leave. Consequently, standard economic analyses of labour mobility focus attention on the demographic profile of migrants compared with the host population. Migrants are more likely to be young, both because the expected returns to migration will be available for a longer period and because the loss of family and friends is perceived as partially compensated by the experience of travel and new surroundings. In addition, one might suppose that migrants and non-migrants from the same communities have different values. Migrants may value the possible future returns more highly and attach more weight to the possibility of change and difference. Non-migrants may value their current circumstances more highly and discount the benefits of travel and new experience.

In so far as new technology has resulted in a greater spread of information about other countries – in particular about more affluent countries – it has contributed to raising expectations about the benefits of mobility. Differences in material standards of living and, by implication, differences in expected earnings have become highly visible through satellite TV. As technology has reduced the cost of travel and lessened the difficulties of maintaining contact with family and friends, it has lowered the perceived costs of movement.

These effects cannot be dismissed as perceptions distorted through the lens of mass-media broadcasting. Some 10 per cent of the world's population receives 70 per cent of its total income. Average incomes in the world's 20 richest countries are 40 times that of the world's poorest. Forty years ago that ratio was estimated to be 20, a hundred years ago it was close to 5 and in 1820 it was about 2. (This data was compiled by the economic historian, Angus Maddison (Wolf, 2001)). The gap between the richest and poorest has widened very substantially over a long period. In part this is because the countries that were growing in the nineteenth century have continued growing while the poorest countries have stood still. The poorest countries have not become poorer in absolute terms, but the gap between them and the richest countries has widened and widened.

Newspaper and television reports of African migrants seeking to enter the Spanish enclaves of Ceuta and Melilla to infiltrate 'Fortress Europe' are simply explicable by the fact that globalization has done little to improve the plight of the poorest countries. It is entirely understandable then that, if employment and prosperity are not available in their own countries, migrant workers will strive to secure the potential gains of mobility. The technological trends that have contributed to a shrinking globe have intensified the pressures for freer labour markets by broadcasting images of what life could be for those able to live and work in another country.

Different Rules for the Highly Skilled?

Despite the political pressures to maintain labour market barriers and restrictions, some labour markets are more global than others. In some highly regulated professions such as medicine, there is a long history of labour movements as doctors have moved from poorer to richer countries in search of higher living standards. Such movements become possible when the national professional bodies recognize qualifications from elsewhere. Ironically, it could be argued that it is the very success of the national professional bodies in restricting the supply of labour in their domestic labour markets – through demanding entrance standards and extended qualifying periods – that created shortages that could only be resolved through migration.

Most developed countries that permit immigration operate systems that favour the highly qualified – particularly those highly qualified in occupations where there are high levels of domestic vacancies. A number of European governments recently announced their willingness to relax restrictions on the migration of IT professionals as the expansion of that sector outstripped available domestic capacity. At

the other end of the scale, a number of governments have been prepared to relax controls on workers arriving to fill vacancies disdained
by the domestic population, e.g. the hundreds of thousands of Asian
workers in the Gulf states. In the latter cases it is commonplace for
governments to insist on fixed-term contracts to ensure that such migrants are not encouraged to settle.

All these groups are subject to significant restrictions and controls.
Would-be migrants may be required to demonstrate the possession of
particular qualifications or competences. They may need sponsorship
from employers. The duration of their stay may be subject to strict
controls. They need information about the existence of vacancies and
about employers' requirements.

All these requirements are also attached to the other significant
group of migrant workers – employees of global corporations. The key
difference between poor would-be migrants and their corporate
cousins is that for the latter the obligation of satisfying governments'
restrictions and constraints is met by the corporation, not the individual. These global internal labour markets provide opportunities for
managers and a wide range of professionals and technical staff. Of
course, the more global corporations can rely on the expertise of their
expatriate staff, the less labour force development they need in poor
countries to run their operations.

GLOBAL CORPORATIONS AND
LABOUR MOBILITY

It seems a curious paradox that, at a time when the governments of
developed countries are reinforcing their restrictions on would-be immigrants, the governments of poorer countries are persuaded, through the
power of global corporations, to facilitate reverse migration flows. It is,
of course, argued that, by siting production facilities in poor countries,
global corporations create employment and opportunities for development. It is also argued that these facilities may require expatriate staff
initially to get them set up and operational. Despite these potential
benefits, it would seem a curious feature of globalization if the traditional

national barriers to labour mobility were replaced by one-way valves controlled by global corporations based in the developed countries.

The shift in responsibility from individual migrants to organizationally sponsored key workers is accompanied by an equally dramatic shift in risks and costs. The power of the global corporations can and do reduce the risks and costs of mobility to the individuals concerned. Mobile workers are usually more highly rewarded for international assignments. The corporation deals with the issues of work permits, travel arrangements, housing etc. Workers are provided with opportunities to return to their home countries on a regular basis. While working in poorer countries their lifestyle, in comparison with their hosts, is well to do. The contrast between this protected existence and the difficulties endured by would-be individual migrants is shockingly apparent. Internationally mobile key workers, employed by global corporations, experience the difficulties of living and operating in different national cultures, but their experience is softened by the support of the global corporations. Many large corporations in the USA have been forced to amend their internal labour markets through pressures for equal opportunities. Global corporations that brought the same degree of commitment to all of their employees in their global operations could act as a powerful and progressive force for the development of global labour markets.

In part the route taken by global corporations in the future will depend on the values espoused by their managements as well as any pressure brought to bear by national governments or international agencies. Global corporations might decide to extend the benefits of global internal labour markets to residents of poorer countries as part of a policy of corporate good citizenship. Such good intentions will have limited impact, however, unless global corporations simultaneously redefine their own activities. The corporate pursuit of 'focus' has led to wide-scale divestments, outsourcing, reorganization and job losses. By definition, such 'focused' corporations can only offer limited, narrow internal labour market opportunities.

The range of opportunities available could be widened if global corporations redefined themselves. A significant assumption underpinning the 'focused' approach is that other enterprises are available, ready and willing and better able to supply those goods and services that the focused corporation no longer wishes to produce for itself. Moving work from conglomerates to these new enterprises may shatter the old internal labour markets, but it does not necessarily reduce the overall level of employment. If the assumption that other enterprises are available, ready, willing and better able is not met, then the rationale for the 'focused' approach is significantly diminished. Some countries and regions lack the industrial infrastructure of a wide range of highly focused enterprises available to supplement the activities of global corporations. In such circumstances, global corporations face the decision of whether to take on directly a much wider range of activities and employees or to seek to import these complementary activities.

Khanna and Palepu (1999) have argued cogently that restructuring conglomerates in emerging markets needs to reflect the absence of infrastructure taken for granted in the developed markets. Consequently, they argue that corporations in emerging markets need to internalize many functions that would be outsourced in developed economies. In this analysis, emerging corporations within the poorer countries may decide to develop as 'broad corporations' with a wider range of activities that permit them to develop effective internal labour markets to retain and enhance scarce labour resources. By definition, the reach of such emerging corporations remains limited, although it is expanding. Global corporations originating in developed countries could choose to emulate this practice to enhance the scope and scale of their own global internal labour markets. Each of these markets would create opportunities of employment and development for would-be migrants. Such migrants might eventually choose to move with sponsorship from the corporation. Alternatively, the effective lessening of the gap between rich and poor implicit in such arrangements might obviate the need for migration.

LABOUR MOBILITY AND PUBLIC POLICY

Technological change has not only altered the expectations and perceptions of mobile workers. It continues to alter the nature of labour markets themselves. The combination of technological change and market changes resulting from growth and from differential patterns of growth has significant impacts on labour markets. The location, scale and nature of employment opportunities all change rapidly. Employers and governments face the dilemma of encouraging employment opportunities to move or encouraging workers to move (see Table 3.1).

Table 3.1 The impact of labour market changes

Pace of skills change	High	Greater education and development	More skilled, more mobile
		Familiar skills, familiar surroundings	Foot-loose and focused
	Low		
		Low	High

Pace of location change

Responding to rapid changes in either the nature or the location of employment opportunities is likely to cause significant social dislocation. Responding to both simultaneously is likely to generate pressures that pass far beyond the boundaries of single labour markets. If countries differ in their capacity to respond to such challenges – and we will show later that they do – such pressures are bound to have international repercussions.

Economists have repeatedly drawn attention to the economic benefits derived by labour-importing countries. Migrants tend to be younger, more highly skilled and more willing to embrace change than non-migrants. As the costs of migrants' initial upbringing and education are met by their countries of origin, labour-importing countries benefit from migrants' tax and national insurance contributions, from their production, and from their contribution to reducing labour market pressures that would otherwise add to inflation. If the migrants stay in the host country in their old age, then the host will bear costs in terms of health and social care provision but, taken over their lifetime, migrants' ratio of contribution to costs will be greater than for those who spend their whole lifetime in one country.

These benefits need to be balanced against the pressure exerted by migrants on social capital, e.g. housing, schools, hospitals, although investment in these areas may contribute to a higher overall level of prosperity. There are also non-economic factors. Migrants are frequently met by hostility and fear from host populations concerned about their effects on jobs and troubled by obvious differences in culture. Such hostility and fear may result in social and political conflict, even when migrants have been resident for several generations, if they are not assimilated into the host population. The recent opening of Holocaust memorials is, in part, a reaction to the continued occurrence of ethnic conflict, brutality and genocide. Recent events in countries as far apart as Fiji and Kosovo reflect continuing reactions against older waves of migration and the tensions that exist between political and economic forces. Some countries, such as the Gulf states, seek to avoid such difficulties by refusing to grant political rights to migrant workers. These policies clearly strengthen the control of the host population at the expense of their migrant workforces.

If labour-importing countries benefit economically from migration, does it follow that labour-exporting countries lose? The answer is not clear cut because it depends crucially on the alternatives to migration. When unemployed workers seek employment in other countries, the immediate impact is a reduction in the social security burden and some flow of remittances from those able to find work elsewhere. The scale of remittances is affected by a range of economic and cultural factors and by the policy of the labour-importing country in permitting entry to migrants' families. There are thus some short-term benefits to labour-exporting countries and regions.

There are also substantial costs. Labour-exporting countries lose the talent and capacity of their migrants. The society receives little return on its provision of education and healthcare in the migrants' early years. If migrants are more willing to embrace change than nonmigrants, the society overall may have lost some of its capacity for development. If a significant proportion of those migrating are drawn from the highly skilled or highly educated, then the potential for economic loss is multiplied.

Exporting unemployed workers may be a 'safety valve' for the domestic political system as it masks the failure of the domestic economy to generate sufficient jobs. Large numbers of unemployed workers may pose a threat to political stability and to the political interests that are entrenched by that stability. For instance, over generations Ireland has been a net exporter of its people. Irish migrants and their descendants have spread far and wide. Mass migration continued to be a feature of Irish life even after the country had become politically independent of Britain in 1922. Economic policies aimed at self-sufficiency and protectionism did nothing to reverse the outflow of labour. The impact of migration to Britain on whole towns in Ireland is vividly chronicled in Frank McCourt's novel *Angela's Ashes* (1996). The change of political power that accompanied the ousting of Eamon de Valera as Taioseach in 1959 reflected a change in political priorities. The new government, headed by Sean Lemass, was less inclined to accept continued migration to fill low-paid jobs in other countries as the inalienable birthright of the Irish people. The government also displayed a greater awareness of the personal and social costs associated with the Irish diaspora. The success of the Irish economy in the following 40 years is a tribute to the foresight and determination of those who laid down the initial outlines of a new economic policy. Recent developments that have seen Irish governments seeking to attract returning migrants and others reflect the capacity for economic growth to create employment opportunities and are a hopeful reminder that migration can be a two-way process.

By exporting its younger, more highly skilled, more change-oriented workers, a country may become less attractive to employers – national and global – and less likely to attract domestic or inward investment. If the impact of migration on the country's demographic profile is severe, it may result in an ageing population, with the social and economic costs that implies. High levels of migration, for instance those from rural to urban France, may contribute to a progressive depopulation and underutilization of social capital. Houses are abandoned or only occupied for parts of the year and schools close for lack of children.

GLOBAL LABOUR MARKETS AND DEMOGRAPHIC CHANGE

As the above analysis indicates, labour mobility may contribute significantly to demographic changes. Labour mobility itself is also being heavily influenced by demographic changes. Among the major social changes of our time has been the conscious individual reordering of demographic patterns as women have reduced the number of children they bear. Demographic changes on a huge scale are already in train. Within the European Union only two countries, Greece and the Irish Republic, still have young and growing populations.

A number of developed countries, including most of western Europe and Japan, have experienced a substantial fall in their birth rates to levels below those consistent with a stable population in the long term. These changes appear to have been influenced by their rising standards of living, by the availability of effective birth control technology and by changing social norms about the importance of children compared with careers and higher living standards. In many of these countries the full extent of these changes has been masked. The large numbers of people of working age who are still active in the labour markets is a product of baby booms in the late 1940s and again in the late 1960s and early 1970s. In addition, labour force participation by women has risen substantially. A growing population of working age and an increasing rate of labour market participation has therefore disguised labour shortages. As that growing population of working age inevitably becomes a growing population of pensioners, the demographic effects will be revealed.

There is widespread recognition that the numbers of people of pensionable age will rise substantially due to both longer life expectancy and the post-war baby booms. There is also recognition that these demographic shifts will lead to a much higher ratio of workers to non-workers and to pension funding problems. There is less recognition that falling birth rates and increasing education levels have reduced the numbers of young people entering labour markets. These demographic factors are already adding to labour market pressures as employers seek to attract young people to occupations experiencing shortages. Labour market pressures place substantial pressure on social barriers to the free movement of labour. Such pressures may be of great benefit to particular groups within society. In Japan, a mixture of labour market pressure, legislative reform and social change that is leading to later marriages is slowly transforming the role of women in the labour market, for example.

Some employers have sought to respond to these labour market pressures by transferring production and employment to other countries, for example the growing volumes of car production in eastern Europe and Latin America. Switching production in this way serves to amplify the process whereby developed economies engage less in manufacturing and expand their service sectors. While switching production may dampen some of the labour market pressures, other factors serve to intensify them, including the growing demand for services. As societies become more prosperous, there is more rapid growth of spending on services than on goods. Some services can be imported. Holidaymakers who travel to other countries are effectively importing the services of those countries by going abroad to consume them. Other services (such as call centres) can be located in different countries to those in which the telephone calls originate. Still more services, such as health and social care, require local delivery. In simple terms, higher levels of prosperity and ageing populations will increase the demand for locally provided services at a time when demographic change and competing employment opportunities will reduce the numbers of workers available. Increasing the numbers of migrant workers may be necessary to make good the shortfall. Press reports of UK hospitals recruiting nurses from all over the world suggest that some of these pressures are already acute.

Outside the most developed countries the demographic pressures are quite different. It is widely reported that life expectancy in Russia is falling and that the birth rate there has also fallen. China's efforts to reduce its population growth have slowed the rate of childbirth, but the working population continues to expand through rising life expectancy and major shifts of population from rural to urban areas. In many other countries high birth rates accompanied by rising life expectancy result in rapid population growth. Growing numbers entering labour markets in economies where growth is insufficient to generate enough jobs results in rising unemployment – particularly among the young.

In these circumstances, the imbalances in the global demand for and supply of labour that have fuelled mass migration in recent years seem unlikely to diminish. Differences in living standards and employment prospects will continue to encourage migration from poorer to richer countries. The growing demand for services that accompanies rising living standards makes it unlikely that sufficient employment opportunities can be transferred to poorer countries to generate full employment. Demographic changes indicate continuing opportunities for migrants in the developed countries.

CONCLUSION

Governments' policies towards labour market mobility reflect the confusions of a range of interacting and conflicting pressures. The struggle of nation states to protect domestic jobs and prosperity against the pressures of mobile financial capital has encouraged them to take steps to enhance labour market flexibility and internal mobility. In some cases, for example in the European Union, governments have co-operated to support mobility between countries, although inter-state mobility in Europe is reported to be only one-fifth that in the USA. Government policies aimed at restricting immigration to the highly qualified seem inequitable and are probably damaging to labour-exporting countries. Heightened barriers to labour mobility in the face of labour market pressures and demographic changes seem likely to encourage the growth of illegal enterprises that profit from smuggling would-be migrants.

Global labour markets already exist, although often in restricted and attenuated forms. Global corporations have significant scope to influence global labour market pressures through their impact on external and internal labour markets. By shifting their operations and changing their sources of supply, global corporations can either heighten or diminish the prosperity of individual nation states. Ireland's continued economic expansion owes much to its success in attracting inward investment from global corporations. The most discernible and persistent strand in UK industrial policy in the last twenty years has been its efforts to attract inward investment. But these examples, while acknowledging the employment and prosperity that flow from international capital movements, reflect the tendency of global corporations to invest more heavily in developed economies. Global corporations also have scope, through their internal labour markets, to foster greater equality of opportunity and to facilitate the employment and development of at least some of the would-be migrants.

However, the greatest force in the globalization of labour markets continues to be the millions of largely anonymous migrants and would-be migrants. These people, who believe in the prospects of a better life, who are prepared to invest their savings and risk their lives in pursuit of their dreams, provide a continuing silent testimony to the inequalities that persist in the global economy. Their struggles and their successes will provide inspiration for millions more. One challenge for the twenty-first century is whether globalization will be as effective in providing opportunities for suppliers of labour as it was in the twentieth century in providing opportunities for suppliers of capital.

References

Khanna, T. and Palepu, K. (1999) 'The right way to restructure conglomerates in emerging markets', *Harvard Business Review*, July–August.

McCourt, F. (1996) *Angela's Ashes*, HarperCollins, London.

Wolf, Martin (2001) 'Growth makes the poor richer', *Financial Times*, 24 January.

ON THE INTERNET ALL BUSINESS IS GLOBAL (LIKE IT OR NOT)

Mike Malmgren

CHAPTER 4

ON THE INTERNET ALL BUSINESS IS GLOBAL (LIKE IT OR NOT)

*T*he Internet's global nature and universal connectivity immediately force businesses, large and small, to consider the implications for customer relationships on a global scale. This universal connectivity requires a new set of dimensions with which to evaluate the globalization drivers in different market sectors and industries. In this chapter we develop a framework to separate out the Internet-related forces that drive companies to establish global organizations and business processes.

The Internet also challenges the traditional view of which parts of business processes should operate on a global basis. To understand which specific products and services are affected by the Internet, two further frameworks are introduced. With this as a basis, we can evaluate if the products and services will stay local or have global potential.

We will give examples of traditional businesses that make use of the Internet and new technologies to achieve cost-effective geographical expansion as well as developing new business models and move up in the value chain. The chapter will conclude with a future scenario of the speed with which the Internet globalization drivers are affecting large parts of the economy.

A FUNDAMENTAL SHIFT FROM THE PHYSICAL TO THE DIGITAL DOMAIN

The most fundamental implication of the Internet for globalization and business in general is the shift in value of products and services from the physical to the digital domain. Much has been said about the new knowledge economy, but it is only when this knowledge can be defined as products and services that value can be attributed to it. Within existing organizations there is a need to separate what is in the digital domain and what is in the physical world to evaluate the real effects of the Internet.

With the strong growth in computing devices used throughout the business process, the balance between the physical and digital domain has changed dramatically. As late as 30 years ago banks and finance departments were full of accounts clerks filling in ledgers of transactions by hand and adding them up for transfer to other ledgers. Today even a self-employed craftsman enters his accounts information in a simple accounts package such as Quicken, connects to his bank to get his current account balances, checks his share portfolio and renews his car insurance directly over the Internet.

This example may sound self-evident, but let us consider its full implications. The bank's original role was to provide a safe store of money in times when leaving your money in the house was risky and law and order not always at hand. In return for this the bank could lend money to others, taking a margin to compensate for the risk and make a profit. What is our general view of the value of a bank today? How many see the bank as a physical store of money or as an institution providing accurate information in real time offering valuable services to a very different set of customers?

Customers today carry out more and more sophisticated business processes from home, in the car or on the move. This development can only take place because the information is in a digital format and standardized ways of transmitting it have been developed. The question for the financial services sector is how this digitization is driving them to consider organizing themselves for a global customer base rather than a local community centred on a high-street branch.

This digitization of products and services is even more interesting when we are considering its effect on physical products and services. What the Internet provokes is a challenge to what the customer values in the product and service. The example of pay-per-wash, see page 111, demonstrates that the Internet has the potential to create new business models and change the position in the value chain of very traditional business such as the manufacture of washing machines. Or consider the example of Volvo Truck Corporation, see page 112, that through the use of Internet technology must consider if it is a manufacturer only or a transport solutions company providing transport on a global scale. The Internet opens up the question of the scope and purpose of organizations in many markets.

The Internet evolved from American origins and has a bias towards English and an Anglo-Saxon view of what the user wants. However, language and cultural considerations continue to be very important when evaluating the globalization forces of the Internet. At a very simple level, it is not much good offering telephone support for a global site using an 0800 free-phone number in the US and only support in the English language. The technology is there to deal with some of the language barriers and cultural differences for global Internet sites, but the solutions are often costly and not as functional as desired. This makes decisions on the balance between central control and local adaptation of websites and IT infrastructure key factors for success in global markets.

At the macro level, the development of the Internet is not uniform in different geographical regions. This is due to differences in economic development, but also to cultural differences resulting in varying adoption rates of new technologies and methods of communicating. The type of devices, such as PCs, mobile phones and interactive televisions, that are used to connect to the Internet vary considerably in different countries, hence the globalization effect will be patchy and sometimes relatively slow.

GLOBAL DRIVERS: THE GLOBALIZING ROLE OF THE INTERNET

The traditional view has considered economies of scale in manufacturing (e.g. automotive and oil extraction) and deregulation of markets (the telecommunications industry and banking) as strong drivers of globalization. This is still the case and will not be covered in this chapter. What the

Internet has introduced is a new and different effect on business and customer interactions that requires consideration of additional forces.

Four groups of industry globalization drivers – information, network reach, language/culture and economies of scope – represent the effect that the Internet has on an industry sector.

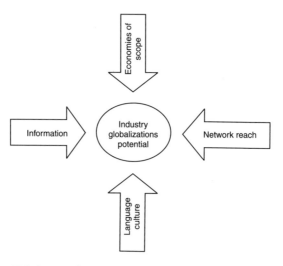

Figure 4.1 Globalization framework.

By considering how business processes are becoming increasingly digitized, hence offering the potential to expand business scope and economic models, we can understand the capability of the Internet to reach a global market quickly. Differences in language and cultural preferences will determine the speed of up-take among customers and the design and content of the website will be important when competing with local Internet sites. The bullets below will give definitions of the forces of globalization.

- *Information:* If the product or services have high information value or are in (or can be transferred to) a digital format, the globalization driver is strong.
- *Network reach:* The penetration and growth of Internet access via landline or wireless devices will determine the timing and scale of globalization.

- *Language/culture:* The extent to which the population is willing to adopt and then communicate, negotiate and transact with a low-touch medium such as the Internet will affect the strength of the globalization driver.
- *Economies of scope:* If the opportunity to alter the traditional value chain is strong, it will drive the globalization of the participants in the industry. This is difficult to assess but a potentially ground-breaking aspect of the Internet.

All the forces above have a time dimension to their development. This is partly linked to rates of investment in connecting devices by customers or in IT infrastructure by governments and organizations, but also to the rate of innovation in technologies to improve the user interface and cost-effective delivery of enhanced products and services. An example of infrastructural constraints is the deployment of broadband access. This has been available as a technology for several years, but the economic return of old analogue technology has been very attractive and is a disincentive for telecom operators to invest in digital equipment and high-bandwidth networks.

The next sections will discuss each of the four forces in detail and offer a set of evaluating questions to use for diagnostic purposes.

INFORMATION

In traditional globalization strategy the location of production on a global scale has often been an important definition of a global business. This is still true in many industry sectors, but the Internet has brought a new angle to the question. The importance of information, both as a product and as a means of evaluating a product, is now one of the main globalization drivers. Why information? Because it is easily converted or is originated in digital form and hence can be accessed from anywhere in the world 24 hours a day at low cost.

Many large businesses today are in essence databases of information stored in large computers that can be located anywhere in the world. Obvious examples of this are AOL, Yahoo!, Microsoft, Reuters and the Financial Times, but also Cisco as a technology hardware manufacturer, retailers such as Tesco.com in the UK and Quelle, a large German catalogue business. These all create value through information technology. The financial services market sector has the potential of being transformed at a global level largely due to the high information content and digital storage of financial information.

Traditional industrial markets such as heavy engineering, manufacturing and transport are also being transformed. Over the next few years companies in this category will become knowledge-based corporations. Companies such as ABB, with 160 000 employees and operations in 140 countries, have a wealth of knowledge and technological expertise deeply buried within their organization. In January 2001 the recently appointed CEO, Jorgen Centerman, commented 'We are responding to a silent revolution in the market that is completely changing the business landscape. Faced with the increasing complexity and speed – much of it driven by the Internet – our customers want clarity and simplicity' (Milner, 2001). ABB aims to harness its knowledge and make it commercially available to its customers and partners. This knowledge is global, as ABB's products are made and sold all over the world using the same technology and knowledge base. The connectivity of the Internet makes knowledge a valuable resource available anywhere at a marginal cost close to zero. It may be merely a coincidence that Jorgen Centerman has spent his career in ABB's high-tech automation division rather than the heavy engineering side of the business.

A recent development is Internet-based on-line marketplaces in vertical markets, such as chemicals and energy, and in horizontal markets, such as office supplies. These new intermediaries connect buyers and sellers and offer the potential for significantly reduced transaction costs. Importantly, they also create the possibility of price transparency in products and services that was previously not readily available. Information on prices, supply and demand, together with connections between buyers and sellers all over the world, allow the possibility of fast globalization of a range of products and services that used to be considered slow to move to global supply.

A further benefit is more efficient matching of supply and demand. A large part of the costs in the value chain is spent on finding, negotiating and comparing prices from suppliers and partners. Suppliers find themselves with excess inventory, while buyers may have production problems because of a shortage of key production supplies. It has been estimated that the Internet could reduce input costs by up to 10 per cent in the next 10 years by improving price transparency and matching supply and demand more efficiently.

Box 4.1   Diagnostic questions relating to information-based globalization forces

- Is the product in a digital format (music)?
- Is the product information rich (software)?
- Is the product in a digital format before final production (books, government advice)?
- Is product support in a digital format before final production (technical support, drawings, instructions, software upgrades)?
- Can product development be shared between parties in digital format (design, CAD drawings, software, project management)?

NETWORK REACH

A very important aspect of market development is the Internet's network effect. The idea behind network effects in packet-switched communication is attributed to Bob Metcalf. He is one of Silicon Valley's legends from his time as researcher at Xerox Palo Alto Research Park and as founder and CEO of 3Com. In the 1970s he postulated the magic of interconnections: 'connect any number, "n" of machines – whether computers, phones or even cars – and you get "n" squared potential value' (Gilder, 1993).

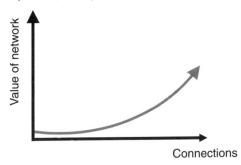

Figure 4.2   Networks effect on value of connections.

With 196 million users in 1999 and a prediction of 502 million users in 2003 (IDC, 2000), the value of the Internet has the potential of increasing exponentially, both in terms of accessible information and commercial transactions completed or strongly influenced by information on the Internet.

Even three years ago, the common wisdom in the car retailing industry was that such an emotive, high-value purchase would not be suitable for the Internet. I think we can now safely say that this is incorrect. All manufacturers today see the Internet as a very important sales channel and they offer some of the most innovative and interactive websites. For example, at www.edmunds.com an amazing amount of information is available to purchasers, down to the actual dealer margin on the car. If you want to locate a second-hand car, go no other place than your PC. There are numerous sites such as Autobytel (www.autobytel.com and various international sites) and CarPoint (http://carpoint.msn.com) where you can search for a car, see pictures of it, obtain performance information and find out which dealer has it in the showroom. Many dealers will bring the car to your house, take you for a test drive and sell you the car in your living room.

PC and Mobile Penetration

In the case of network reach, the globalization driver in a geographical market can differ between consumers and organizations. There are also different adoption rates for landline-based and wireless communication. Taking Italy as an example, the business community is as well connected as the neighbouring countries in Europe, but the adoption rate of home PCs and on-line access (16 per cent in Italy) is lower than, say Germany (23 per cent). On the other hand, Italy has a very high penetration of mobile phones (44 per cent compared with 27 per cent in Germany). It has been suggested that the Italians have a strong preference for personal contact and relationships when they communicate, hence the preference for mobile phones rather than on-line access

Table 4.1 Mobile telephone usage statistics

	Australia	France	Germany	Netherlands	Italy	Poland	South Africa	Spain	Sweden	UK	USA
Population (m)	19	55	84	15	58	38	43	39	9	56	264
Mobile penetration (%)	35	36	27	32	44	12	19	36	52	45	38
Mobile market size (%)	6.6	21	23.4	6	29	4.6	8.2	14	6	25	101
Market value (US$ bn)	n/a	7	n/a	n/a	n/a	n/a	1.8	n/a	n/a	n/a	40
Internet device penetration (%)	10	n/a	n/a	n/a	n/a	n/a	n/a	n/a	n/a	<1	40
On-line access (m)	6.5	4	19.5	4.2	8.2	2.6	1.5	<3	4	18	119
On-line access (%)	43	11	23	28	16	7	3.5	<7	44	33	45
Secure servers/million	130	15	40	<10	<10	<10	<10	15	75	55	190
(% of adults) shopped on-line	14	4	14	12	3	<3	<3	2	21	12	33

n/a = not available.

Source: Compilation by Chris Turner, Ashridge, from CIT publications, Australian Communications Authority, US cellular Telco Association, African Cellular Communications unit, *Warsaw Voice*, *Financial Times*.

via the PC. It is likely, however, that other aspects such as costs and reliability are also at play when adoption rates differ in different markets. Furthermore, the economic structure and prosperity in Italy are different in the industrialized north and the rural south of the country. Any assessment of network reach must take a more fine-grained view than country statistics and generalized views would offer.

An important consideration is the governmental attitude to large infrastructure investments. For example, the Swedish government has pledged to wire up the majority of the country's 5 million homes with broadband access by 2004. Sweden currently has one of the highest usages of PCs per capita, which in part can be explained by the Swedish trade unions' decision in the late 1990s to offer all their members attractively priced PCs payable by interest-free monthly payments drawn directly from their salaries. The country's very high penetration of mobile phones (52 per cent) has less to do with government investment and more with openness to technological innovations.

Box 4.2 Diagnostic questions relating to the network reach-based globalization forces

- How many of the users in the value chain are connected to the Internet?
- Are landline or wireless connections used?
- How fast is the user base growing?
- Are different geographical areas growing at the same speed (e.g. north/south Italy)?
- Is standardization taking place (e.g. XML)?
- Is a dominant global vendor emerging?
- Are there other digital communications standards in use (e.g. EDI)?

LANGUAGE AND CULTURE

When analysing globalization drivers, it is important to realize that the Internet does not eliminate local market drivers. Language and culture continue to be important differentiating factors in national markets. Put a group of reasonably Internet-experienced people from different countries in front of a PC and the French will soon dial up Wanadoo.fr, the Swedes are likely to log in to Spray.se or Yahoo.se and the Japanese would log on to Biglobe.ne.jp and Yahoo.co.jp. This is natural, as they are based on local languages, offer local services and address specific interests, with the cultural differences showing through both in terms of content and site design. In the case of Yahoo! the design of the website and structure are the same in all countries with only the language changed, Spray uses a different layout for the Swedish user compared with a Finnish user. The underlying balance to strike in site design is cost efficiency versus local preferences.

To understand cultural differences, geographical markets must be analysed off-line in a traditional way rather than extrapolating from Internet usage between countries. For example, the density of the Japanese population means that there are large shopping centres in close proximity to the consumer. Local convenience shops open 24 hours a day, 7 days a week are focal points in the daily lives of a Japanese household, to the extent that they are used as delivery points for goods purchased over the Internet. Although DHL operates in Japan, it is not the preferred method for delivering direct to the doorstep of a private household.

Payment preferences in Japan are quite different compared with, for instance, the USA. In the annual consumer survey by Bank of Japan, the preferred payment methods are cash (50 per cent), bank transfer (39 per cent) and credit card (11 per cent) (Ishiguro, 2000).

This is in contrast with Sweden, which has one of the lowest population densities in Europe and long distances between services and shops, hence the Internet offers convenience and cost benefits to the user. The local village post office, or post bus in remote areas, is an important link for deliveries of products that are only available in larger towns and cities. The preferred payment method is cash on delivery at the local post office.

With the Internet's bias towards English, the globalization driver is partly connected to people's ability to read and write in English. Table 4.2 shows the language used as a percentage of Internet users.

However, English is only the third most common first language, spoken by 322 million, behind Mandarin Chinese, spoken by 885 million people, and Spanish, by 332 million. An important question is

Table 4.2 Main languages of Internet usage

Language	% of Internet users
English	61
Japanese	7
German	5
Spanish	5
French	4
Chinese	3
Italian	3

Source: eMarketeer, 2000 and McKinsey

what usage percentages are likely to be in 10 years' time. With high birth rates in India, China and South America and low birth rates in the US and other English-speaking countries, languages other than English are likely to be of increasing importance.

Table 4.3 The world's most commonly used first languages

Language	No. of speakers (millions)
Mandarin Chinese	885
Spanish	332
English	322
Bengali	189
Hindi	182
Portuguese	170
Russian	170
Japanese	125
German	98
Wu Chinese	77
Javanese	76
Korean	75
French	72

Source: SIL.org (1999), Top 100 Languages by Population. Reproduced by permission of SIL International.

Other differences to look out for occur in the translation of words used in different parts of the world. Rubber in the UK means the same as eraser in the US, whereas rubber in the US means a condom. This problem is particularly challenging, as many sites are using database publishing techniques that store phrases and words in the database and convert them between different languages automatically. Search engines such as Altavista.com offer translation software on their sites and by applying the software a foreign site can be translated on the fly. In Box 4.3 a news bulletin from German portal T-Online has been translated via the Altavista translation engine at http://world.altavista.com. The results can be quite amusing at times.

Box 4.3 Translation of T-Online news bulletin

> **Violent Storm Gusts**
> Meteorologists announced storm gusts with rates up to 100 km per hour. With Ludlow in central England two humans died, when with heavy storm a umstuerzender tree fell on their auto. A third person came with lethal heading and back injuries into the hospital.

Text can either be pasted into a window on the Altavista site or directions can be followed to another website that is then translated by the Altavista translation software. The translation is fast, but the grammar and choice of words are not perfect. Although the software is quite crude, it will improve over time and will be an acceptable way of accessing information in foreign languages. This is another example of how technology is globalizing local information and making it available to anyone with Internet access.

It should be noted that national boundaries are not necessarily the relevant criteria when dealing with the Internet. Many countries have several language regions, such as Belgium (Dutch, Flemish and French) and Switzerland (German, French and Italian), hence there is a need to treat these as different markets when designing websites.

Traditionally, international trade has had to deal with different currencies when expanding beyond home markets. The constant changes in exchange rates between currencies have often been used to maximize profits by maintaining different price levels in different markets. It was difficult for customers to compare prices and to shop around, until the Internet shifted the balance of power from the seller to the customer. The introduction of the euro has been quoted as a strong force for equalizing prices through the price transparency it offers between European countries. The issue of price comparisons is, however, becoming irrelevant on the Internet, as sites can easily include a real-time currency converter and calculate any price in any currency in which the customer wishes to trade. The overall effect is thus high price transparency and a levelling out of price differentials between national markets.

Payment methods and behaviour in establishing prices are important factors when considering the globalization drivers of the Internet. In the US credit card payments are widely used, but that is not the case all over the world. In Japan credit card sales amount to only 0.5 per cent of consumer purchases; 50 per cent is settled in cash. Japanese on-line shoppers used credit cards in 9.4 per cent of purchases in 2000 (down from 15 per cent in 1996), while payment on receipt increased from 38 per cent in 1996 to 53 per cent in 2000 (Ishiguro, 2000). In places such as the bazaars in the Middle East or the food markets in Asia, where the daily buying process includes good-humoured haggling over price, the list prices shown on a website may not have the same function even if the price is attractive. Alternatively, an on-line auction could begin to replicate the traditional behaviour in these places, but may not be the preferred process for Swedes who have never haggled over the price of a consumer item in their lives.

Making an assessment of the propensity for a country or language region to communicate and transact business over the Internet is not easy. By its nature it has to be made based on assumptions on cultural biases with limited facts at hand. This is, however, not a new challenge and traditional methods for evaluating market entry are still applicable.

Box 4.4   Diagnostic questions relating to language/culture-based globalization forces

- Is English used in the target market?
- Is more than one language used (India, China, Netherlands)?
- Is it costly to translate into the local language?
- Is the meaning of your company name in the local language appropriate?
- Can you secure the local URL?
- Are the current colours and website design acceptable in the country/area?
- Is the society cash based?
- Is the penetration rate of credit card use high?
- Is it the norm to accept the product list price rather than to haggle over price?

ECONOMIES OF SCOPE

The potentially most powerful effect of the Internet on globalization comes from changes in the economies of scope for a wide range of organizations. Business value is increasingly linked to information and connectivity between parties in the value chain. This has the potential to break down the traditional definitions of industries and market sectors and completely change a business's economies of scope. Examples of this include rapid convergence in the telecom, media and technology sector (TMT) where information businesses are buying media businesses (for example AOL and Time/Warner). In the bids for third-generation (3G) communication licences in Sweden, several of the consortia are innovative groupings of skills in order to best match the requirements. One group is based around Orange (telecom), Skanska (one of the world's largest construction companies), Schibsted (a media concern that includes the second largest broadsheet newspaper in Sweden) and Bredbandsbolaget B2 (a Swedish technology company specializing in broadband networks).

However, forming alliances between organizations with very different business models has never been an easy route to take. Skanska's skills include working on large hydroelectric dam projects in the Third World lasting over 20 years, whereas Bredbandsbolaget is a new-economy creation full of young techies who live their lives at Internet speed. Add to this a telecom business with roots in the UK and a Norwegian-owned media concern full of journalists and creative media

Box 4.5 Diagnostic questions relating to economies of scope-based globalization forces

> - ■ Vigorously challenge the accepted view of the value chain.
> - ■ Separate all value creation that can be produced in a digital format and ask:
>   - − Who else can provide this information?
>   - − What skills are required?
>   - − Are costs fixed or variable?
>   - − Is it a people- or technology-based resource?
> - ■ Based on the above, how could a new value chain be constructed?
> - ■ Who has the best skills and resources for this new value chain?
> - ■ Who in this new value chain has the bargaining power and why?

people and cultural differences are in abundance. Although the scope of this chapter is not how to make alliances and partnerships work, it is clearly one of the main challenges and therefore the potential scope of competitive advantage the emergence of the Internet is offering.

Two examples of firms thinking about how universal connectivity offers potential to create economies of scope are Electrolux and Volvo Truck Corporation.

Electrolux is the leading manufacturer of household appliances such as refrigerators, washing machines and dishwashers. By broadening the definition of the value delivered from these appliances and the role they play in the life of a household, new business models are beginning to emerge. As a result, Electrolux and Ericsson, the telecommunications company, formed a joint venture called e2 in 1999.

Occupying the central place in the household; the kitchen, provides the opportunity to maintain unprecedented relationships and knowledge of the users' behaviour. It also offers the scope for new and extended services far beyond the traditional role as appliance and telecoms equipment manufacturers.

At the time of writing, the Volvo Truck Corporation is seeking EU and US approval for its recent acquisition of Renault/Mack, which will make it the second largest truck manufacturer in the world. Like companies in the car industry, Volvo Truck is facing increased price pressures and a need to amortize increasingly costly R&D and product development costs over a larger number of vehicles. When asking the Volvo Truck employees what business they are in, they are most likely to say that the company makes and sell trucks of high quality and reliability. In the future, however, this may prove to be a narrow definition of the value the customer receives from Volvo (see box on page 112).

Over the next two to three years, the scope to build new and enhance existing business models in traditional industries such as white goods and truck manufacture is one of the strongest drivers of operating in a co-ordinated way on a global basis. Using the Internet's connectivity to capture value from information and services as a means of climbing up the food chain and get closer to the user is increasingly essential to compete in a global marketplace.

CASE STUDY – The pay-per-wash model

The price of household appliances has been decreasing for many years, hence Electrolux's share of household expenditure has gradually diminished. Reliability has also improved, so Electrolux is only getting a relatively small income from the initial sale, compared to the lifetime value of providing clean clothes for the 10 years the machine is expected to last.

With the ability to connect appliances such as a washing machine to the Internet and in partnership with an existing billing infrastructure, a new business model has been considered. In partnership with Vattenfall, a large electricity utility in Sweden, Electrolux is currently testing a concept called pay-per-wash in a small town in Sweden. Electrolux is providing the washing machine free of charge with all maintenance included at an attractive cost per wash. The connection via the Internet and the billing facility are provided by Vattenfall, which already have a relationship with the user.

This new business model offers the opportunity to charge a low cost per wash to the user while extracting an attractive net present value of the future cash flow over the lifetime of the appliance. But is this really a different model when renting of appliances has been available for many years?

It is the addition of the connection to the Internet that is the difference. In the scenario of making your Screenfridge (see www.electrolux.se), the information hub of the family, there are many products and services that can be bundled together and sold via this channel. Many companies, from Microsoft to infrastructure providers such as Cisco, from utility companies to appliance manufacturers such as Whirlpool and Electrolux, are drawing up plans to capture this central space in our lives.

The other aspect is gaining detailed knowledge of how different appliances are used. Both manufacturers of appliances and auxiliary products such as detergents have in reality very limited data and information on how their products are used by different categories of users. By monitoring actual usage the information may be just as valuable for new product development as the additional revenue a new business model could offer.

The drive for economies of scale used to be in manufacturing. However, the cost and complexity of operating on the Internet drive a need for global scale just as much as manufacturing did.

The four forces discussed above have different strengths for different market sectors and will change at different speeds. The research

CASE STUDY – The Volvo total solution model

From the customers' perspective, both individual owner-drivers and large fleet operators, what Volvo offers is highly reliable and cost-efficient transport of goods in the form of a truck. A marginal improvement in operational availability is highly valuable and the purchase decision is often measured as the cost/mile to operate the truck. To meet this requirement Volvo is offering a pan-European call service centre in Brussels, which can direct service operators to a broken-down truck and get it back on the road as quickly as possible. However, although this is a valuable service, it addresses a problem only after the event.

Today's trucks are highly computerized with sophisticated software monitoring the performance of all vital functions during operation. With the development of computerized vehicle management systems, connections to global positioning systems (GPS) and the Internet, it is technically possible to monitor remotely the detailed operation of a truck and its position. This opens up the strategic question of who could take most value from the information now available.

For the individual owner-driver, Volvo has the ability to set up an infrastructure with mobile service vehicles and delivery of the required parts on a pan-European if not global basis. This creates a potentially profitable opportunity to take stronger control of the lucrative after-market and to maintain a close relationship with the truck drivers. The large fleet operators are themselves big enough to manage this type of operation, but may see benefits in the possibility of pan-European coverage. The new devices with large colour screens that are being planned in future trucks and cars also offer significant opportunities to bundle services and information benefiting the driver. One of the world's largest oil companies is currently investing in mobile technology with a view to being the central point in the driver's cab in a similar way as Electrolux is planning in the kitchen. The race is on to capture a dominant position in this new space.

From Volvo's point of view, the fleet operators are consolidating at some considerable pace and are increasingly putting pressure on prices. This in the long term is an unattractive development, placing more bargaining power in the hands of the customer. Volvo's strategists are asking themselves which business they should be in the future and what skills and resources it will take to get there. Could the Internet connectivity create a new source of revenue and a stronger position in the value chain?

data needs to be continuously updated to establish development trends over time. The speed of development of the Internet and technology in general is very fast and this should be weighted against the softer factors, including adoption rates and change in cultural acceptance, which are far slower in development than the technology would sometimes suggest.

The next step is to analyse products' and services' propensity to be affected by globalization forces available from the Internet.

A FRAMEWORK FOR ANALYSING THE INTERNET'S EFFECT ON MARKETS AND PRODUCTS

The following framework illustrates a two-step approach to assessing how the Internet is affecting the globalization drivers of products and services. The framework measures three aspects, the degree to which the product or service is or can be digitized; how efficient the transaction is between supplier/provider and customer; and how global the products and services could be using the Internet. Box 4.6 defines these two aspects.

Box 4.6 Definitions of digitization framework

Definition of degree of digitization	Definition of transaction efficiency
Measures the degree (high, medium or low) to which a product or service is in the digital domain. The digital domain means that the product or service can be stored on a computer (e.g. Reuters news or the weather) or that it has been in digital format at a late state of the production process (e.g. a book or government advice).	A measure (high, medium or low) of how fast, easy and inexpensive it is to obtain or deliver the product or service. The measure can either be seen from the seller's point of view (e.g. cost and complexity of distribution, ease or difficulty in reaching a defined customer segment) or from the buyer's point of view (e.g. ease of locating a seller of a product and ease of purchase transaction).

Figure 4.3 shows how these two aspects can be represented diagramatically. The Y-axis, representing the degree of digitization, should reflect the situation today. Few products other than information products such as news are currently in the digital domain at the point of delivery. Others that are currently in a physical format, such as music CDs, books and software, are in digital formats at a very late stage in the production process, but are then printed on paper or on CDs and thus have a medium degree of digitization. The same applies to products such as advice (e.g. legal, business and governmental information), which are often stored in a digital format and then printed, resulting in a medium degree of digitization. Petrol and out-of-print (secondhand) books are not in a digital format, hence they are low on the degree of digitization scale.

The next step is to evaluate how technological developments are changing the degree of digitization of the products or services. Some products, such as software and music CDs, will move straight up and then to the right. The developments of compression techniques and delivery direct to the listener via the Internet, either for storage or immediate consumption through an Internet-connected device, are

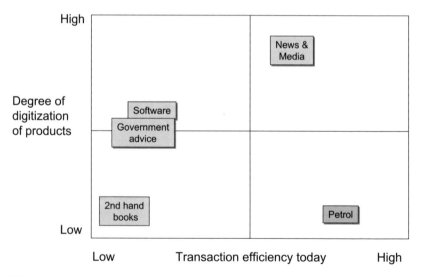

Figure 4.3 Transition towards higher transaction efficiency (without the Internet).

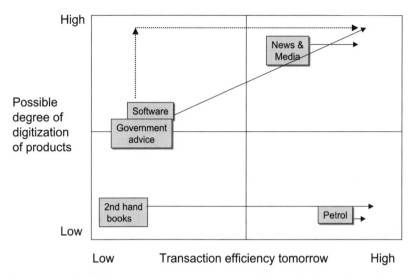

Figure 4.4 Transition towards higher transaction efficiency (with the Internet).

transforming the music industry. Others, however, will not become more digital, such as petrol or secondhand books.

What should then be considered is how Internet connectivity can improve the transaction efficiency for the business and/or for the customer. Even petrol sold through forecourts will have some potential to improve transaction efficiency, as in the future the majority of new cars and trucks will have Internet-connected information systems offering directions to the nearest station, the current price level and possible waiting time. A major oil company is currently developing a comprehensive WAP (wireless application protocol) website offering valuable travel information including (of course) directions to the company's petrol stations across Europe.

To make full use of the framework, it is important to break down the business process in some detail. In a major building company in the UK, the concrete and building materials are not likely to move into the digital domain, but job planning, computer-aided design (CAD) drawings and communications with customers and suppliers are held on computers before being printed out and sent by paper mail or fax.

Several on-line services are being launched that will hold job planning and project management information on a web server, including sms (short messaging services) to direct the teams who are spread out over many sites and continuously on the move. On the basis of this type of analysis, the company is considering moving much of its operations, products and services on to the Internet. The importance of challenging the way a business is run is one of the most fundamental aspects of the Internet. Companies will be born and die based on their ability to understand and harness the new connectivity in a wired-up world.

It is important to challenge established assumptions and redefine current business models. An interesting example of this is the second-hand book business. It has traditionally been a manual, inefficient and quite local trade of rare and out-of-print books and printed material. The books are located in thousands of secondhand book shops and out of this a broking-style activity developed, which connects potential buyers and sellers through advertising in specialist magazines. The search process often takes two to six months and sometimes fails to find a rare book that is in fact on a dusty shelf somewhere. Interestingly, it turns out that the Internet is an ideal vehicle for the secondhand book business. This market is being transformed from an inventory-based business to an information-based business, information about where a specific book can be found. The Internet's connectivity has demolished geographical barriers and the only remaining issue is to offer search facilities in all languages, making it all of a sudden a truly global business. A tip for the reader is to visit Bibliofind.com, where there are over 20 million books that can no longer be purchased in normal bookshops.

We are now ready to map the globalization effect against products and services. The example of secondhand books is a good introduction when evaluating the potential for global reach for a product or service. By mapping the possible degree of digitization against geographical reach, the globalization potential can be evaluated, as is shown in Figures 4.5 and 4.6.

Through the Internet's connectivity it is possible to reach a global audience in search of rare and out-of-print books in a highly cost-efficient manner. Of course, the physical distribution of the book still

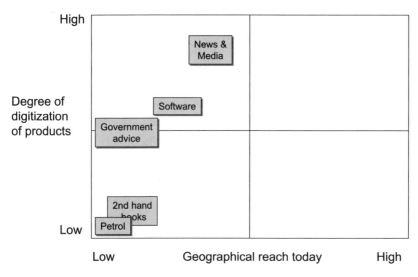

Figure 4.5   Transition towards greater globalization (without the Internet).

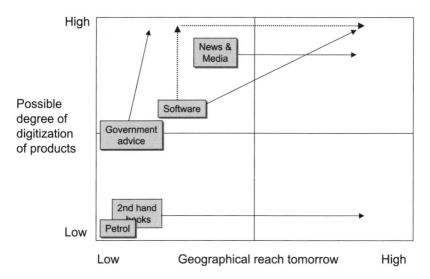

Figure 4.6   Transition towards greater globalization (with the Internet).

needs to take place, hence it is no surprise that on-line bookseller Amazon.com has bought into Bibliofind.com and is leveraging its global distribution capabilities for books and smaller parcels.

Software and music are other products that currently have medium global reach due to the need for physical distribution channels and retail outlets. The Internet offers a truly global distribution channel and there is little doubt that software will only be distributed via electronic means within the next five years. The same applies to music after the success of music sites such as mp3.com and real.com. The main challenge to the traditional music industry value chain is Napster.com. Napster is using networking software technology that allows single PCs to share files via the Internet. It is called peer-to-peer (P2P) computing and means that anyone can open their library of digitally stored music and swap it with someone else. As the host PC needs to be on-line there have been limits to P2P computing, but as broadband access is always connected it will allow such activity to take place in the background, potentially without the need for operator intervention.

This is an appropriate point to raise the question of Internet security. The adoption of all these new technologies is closely linked to issues of privacy and security. P2P computing means that you hand over access to your computer to someone else, which may not be something everyone is comfortable with. Earlier the openness of the Swedes to technology was shown to be a driving factor in globalization. However, the Swedes are also very suspicious of paying by credit card over the Internet, hence their preference for cash on delivery at the post office.

Radio is another market that is quietly being globalized. For security and technical reasons, the radio signal spectrum and reach for use by radio stations is controlled and licensed by national governments. However, by converting the broadcast to digital signals and sending them through the Internet, all of a sudden a radio station has global reach. This is great if you travel or have your roots in another country, as you can dial in to your home country radio station from wherever you are. From the advertiser's point of view this presents a dilemma. Traditionally the advertiser buys advertising space on the basis of demographics (i.e. who is listening to the station) and geographical reach (e.g. closeness to the retail outlet). If stations generally broaden their geographical reach, will they also have to change the profile of the advertiser to one with global brands and global reach? If my ear-time is capped to, let's say, driving my car and I can listen to any radio station in the world, the local stations will have lost out to a station that has no idea where I am but is potentially aware of who I am. In fact, it is possible for the radio station to know exactly where I am. Since the signal to my car is a wireless signal, the network will know in which transponder zone I am in and by cross-referencing will know my position down to the last few metres or so. Does this sound far fetched? The technology for this exists and the advertising agencies and consultants will eventually have a field day advising clients on how to master this new challenge.

Television and entertainment media are highly affected by the Internet's ability to improve transaction efficiency and deliver content on a global basis. Telecom companies offer digital subscriber lines (DSL) with access at up to 20 times the current speed of dial-up modems. Cable companies offer up to 200 times download speed and the third-generation mobile devices will have the capability to deliver up to 50 times the current download speed anywhere and at any time.

At the time of writing there is little clarity regarding which channel will deliver future digital content and market forces are compelling big companies to make large bets to ensure they participate in this new marketplace. It is estimated that the total investment in third-generation wireless licences and network infrastructure is in the region of $300 billion. It is in fact these very large investments that are going to fuel the development, while it is not at all certain that it is the first movers and those who invest in the infrastructure that will reap the profits.

If history is anything to go by, there is absolutely no doubt that technology will force the globalization of products and services that have (or can be easily converted into) a digital format. History also shows us that the speed of adoption rates will be slower than the development of new technology would suggest, but it further illustrates that the hockey stick effect is real. When the Internet was invented in 1969 it had only a few specialist uses within the US military, but had been transformed to an easy-to-use communications medium only 20 years later. Since 1989 when Tim Berners-Lee and his colleagues in the World Wide Web Consortium (W3C) created the HTTP and HTML protocols that underpin the Internet's ability to link to pages from words in another document, the Internet has developed into a colourful and innovative communication medium with over 100 million users all over the world.

A SUMMARY AND A PEEK INTO THE FUTURE

The Internet's connectivity is challenging the traditional analysis model for the forces affecting globalization. The new forces are information, network reach, culture and language and the economics of scope. All four forces will develop at different speeds in different geographical markets, but all will be fuelled by developments in technology. The counterbalancing forces are the slowness with which we as consumers or members of organizations and employees change our behaviour and our willingness to embrace change.

At the business level, the scope for developing global reach has never been more readily available. Consider that 10 years ago e-mail did not exist among the general public. Most companies in the developed world are now connected to a web of communication lines that can carry large amounts of information in the form of documents, data and video from one person's office to another across the world at the cost of only a few cents. The consequences of this have not yet been fully worked through, but it is a fair assumption that it will have a strong impact on drivers for globalization beyond traditional measures.

The most profound change will be the potential for new players taking a position in the value chain and the way we divide up the work to produce a product or a service. These new players will gain strength in the value chain if they have or control information and information flows. It could be information on customers, but probably even more valuable is information relating to products and services. In the example of Volvo, global knowledge of where every Volvo truck is, how well it is running and what it is carrying may be many times more valuable than designing and building the truck itself. Or for Electrolux to know exactly how it can design products and services around the family's central point, the kitchen, may be a hugely attractive proposition far beyond building a washing machine and not having any contact with the user for another 10 years.

The $64 000 question is how quickly these drivers will globalize new areas of the economy.

Network reach is a precursor to any of the other three forces and hence is the leading indicator. By monitoring the usage of the Internet, the type of device used and developments of useful applications etc., we can get indications of the speed of development.

Economies of scope and information are closely linked when determining the speed of globalization and are the next two forces to set the pace. Information in itself is not a sufficiently strong driver for globalization unless it is connected to a business that can use it to revolutionize its economies of scope. Economies of scope are used here rather than merely a general drive for efficiency, as the level of IT investment and organizational development requires more than gains in efficiency. The investment level requires transformation of whole value chains to offer sufficiently attractive returns. Together, information and economies of scope form a very strong indicator for globalization. The profit motive, being global number one in a market sector or forward/backward integration to capture more value will compel organizations to make the necessary investments to harness the Internet's connectivity.

The fourth force, culture and language, is the brake pad on the globalization bandwagon. There are considerable obstacles to overcome, such as local languages and habits, security concerns, telecoms infrastructure, technology adoption rates and, to some extent, demographic evolution. The areas that will change this force include investments in technology in underdeveloped areas and the evolution of generation X – i.e. our children – who switch on a computer as naturally as we switch on the light.

Culture and language changes have long timescales and are counted in tens of years rather than months. This is probably the kind of timescale we should use when trying to measure the actual evolution of an increasingly connected global village.

References

Gilder, G. (1993) *Metcalf's Law and Legacy*, www.discovery.org/gilder.

IDC (2000) The Internet Economy, Framlingham, MA, October.

Ishiguro, N. (2000) Ashridge MBA Dissertation, Berkhamsted.

Milner, Mark (2001) 'ABB to change focus', *Guardian*, January 12.

Turner, C. (2000) Ashridge MBA Dissertation, Berkhamsted.

GLOBAL
PARENTING

Marcus Alexander

CHAPTER 5

GLOBAL PARENTING

*I*n this chapter, we will be examining globalization from a particular perspective: that of the parent of a multibusiness company.

As well as individual business units, most companies have a 'parent organization'. This consists of line and staff managers who have responsibilities that go beyond a single unit, spanning different countries or different product areas. They may be located in a corporate head office, multi-unit divisional HQ or other type of corporate centre, but, importantly, their role is different from managers working within a specific business unit.

Globalization presents special opportunities and challenges for managers in the parent organization. It is principally up to them to orchestrate links between units in different countries and to decide on priorities for international expansion. They frequently have a perspective across countries and regions that individual businesses lack. But they can also act as a major constraint on effective globalization, for example by applying strong cultural influence from the centre that proves to be damaging or unhelpful in certain territories.

This chapter examines the nature and role of the corporate parent and the specific challenges that globalization poses for it. The impact of globalization is considered in four main areas:

- New opportunities for the parent to add value to its businesses.
- New risks and pitfalls that the parent must avoid.
- Changes to overall group structure and business unit definition.
- Changes required within the parent itself.

WHAT IS THE 'CORPORATE PARENT' EXACTLY?

The majority of employees in most companies work within specific businesses. They report, directly or indirectly, to a functionally integrating general manager who is profit-responsible for some more or less clearly defined business unit. However, most large or medium-sized companies, and even many quite small ones, contain more than one such business. These may be built around different combinations of products and services, focus on different types of customer or operate in different geographical areas. As a result, although they are part of the same group, they are set up as discrete profit centres. This is primarily to give them the focus and control that is needed to make appropriate trade-offs between costs, revenues and investments.

At one extreme, highly diversified groups such as General Electric or Virgin have businesses spanning many different industries. At the other end of the spectrum might be a small software company with two units focused on different market segments or countries. In between are multibusiness groups, but with some obvious form of focus. Unilever, for example, while combining hundreds of business units, is focused on food, soaps and personal products. Barclays Bank or HSBC is focused on financial services. Some multibusiness companies have more of a geographical focus, such as the Cojuango Group in the Philippines or Grupo Alpha in Mexico, covering many different business activities within their home territories.

In all these multibusiness groups, some employees are in roles that do not fit within any single business unit as such. Line managers may be responsible for a number of different businesses within the same country, for example, or for a number of businesses of a similar sort, operating in different countries. The chief executive is responsible for all the businesses in the group, but does not usually run any of them directly. Similarly, staff roles may exist at several different levels in the hierarchy above the business unit. There may be a group IT director or human resources director at the corporate centre, or a country-level finance director, or a global marketing director for a particular product group. These multiple layers of line and staff managers sitting between the business units and the shareholders or owners of the group are represented schematically in Figure 5.1.

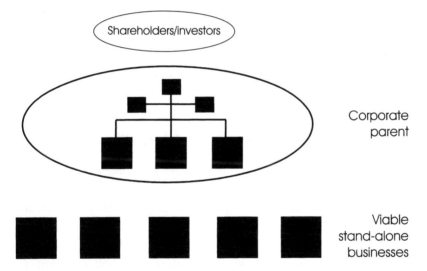

Figure 5.1 Elements within the multibusiness company.

In this chapter, we will refer collectively to all such positions that operate above and across the business units as the 'corporate parent'. We group them together because, although they may operate at different levels, their fundamental role is similar to, and quite distinct from, that of the bulk of employees, working within a particular business unit. We call them the 'parent' partly because it is a term that has been widely used, but also because it gives some useful hints as to the nature of the relationships involved. Although we may talk about the 'centre' rather than 'HQ', and although some chief executives (not many) assiduously draw the organization chart with themselves at the bottom, supporting a team that in turn supports the front-line business units and staff, the reality in most organizations is clearly different. The parent sits above the businesses and acts as an intermediary between them and the shareholders, deciding which business proposals to sanction or fund and which managers to appoint or replace. It allocates resources and judges whether they have been wisely used or not. It gives life to new units and nurtures or disciplines those that already exist. Furthermore, it tends to think of its businesses as 'one family' even if they have very different needs and characteristics, and this generally leads to greater requirements for conformity than most business managers would want. The parenting metaphor, like all metaphors, is not appropriate in every respect, but can prompt interesting insights about sibling rivalries, problem children, parental discipline and the evolution of relationships from birth to maturity.

WHAT ROLE SHOULD THE PARENT PLAY?

Over the last 12 years or so, the Ashridge Strategic Management Centre has been devoted to researching the nature and role of corporate parents around the world, trying to distinguish between good and bad practice. The starting point is to recognize something that capital markets and fund managers have only recently drawn to many senior executives' attention. This is the fact that the parent itself is in competition with other parents to be the owner of its businesses. Because the parent is an intermediary, as discussed above and illustrated in Figure 5.1, it can only justify its position by bringing something of value to the party. The parent certainly brings costs: both the *direct* costs of its own staff, offices and so on, and – far more importantly – the *indirect* costs of the business management time it demands, and the delays in decision making that it invariably brings. But what about the benefits?

Unless the parent can create at least as much additional value as its full costs, both the owners and the business managers would be better off replacing the parent, or removing it altogether. 'Additional value' is very different from overall group performance. Although hard to disentangle accurately, the impact of the parent should be distinguished from the performance that the business units could achieve by themselves. As many management buyouts have demonstrated, this performance may in fact be far better than what is achieved with the 'help' of the parent, even before allowing for the direct cost of the latter. The strategic challenge for the parent, therefore, is to demonstrate that it creates net value in its own right. That is to say, it enables the businesses to perform better than they would without its influence.

Ideally, it should not just create some net value, but more than any alternative parent would with the same business portfolio. The essence of agreed takeovers or business sales is that both parties recognize that the new parent is likely to create more additional value than the old one. A change of parenting should therefore be beneficial to all parties. The essence of hostile takeovers is that one or more external parents believes that it can add much more value than the incumbent parent, and is prepared to pay shareholders a hefty premium to have the chance. Against the backdrop of increasingly overt and direct competition between parents, it is all the more crucial for a parent to demonstrate that it is indeed creating significant value beyond what would be achieved by its businesses alone. The proper role of the parent, therefore, is not simply to preside over the various businesses and report on their progress to the owners, but to add more value to its specific businesses through its activities and influence than its own full cost and – ideally – than any other parent would. Failure in this role leads, increasingly rapidly, to replacement of the parent in one way or another.

WHAT IS REQUIRED FOR SUCCESSFUL 'PARENTING'?

Most parents, although by no means all, now recognize the importance of adding value to their businesses. This is at least a welcome start. Sadly, however, a significant proportion does not even have an impact that is net positive in practice, let alone a realistic claim to competitive 'parenting advantage'. For every example of positive intervention, at least one negative counterpart is easily found. Strategic planning reviews that are intended to focus business management thinking too often end up as remedial instruction for the parent. Budgets that attempt to create stretch targets frequently bleed the business slowly to death. Group HR policies intended to encourage consistency may actively restrict each unit from doing what is necessary in its own market. Capital expenditure reviews designed to allow rational assessment frequently build in such delay that the 'right' decision comes too late to be useful. Attempts to create exciting cross-group synergies often lead to time-wasting processes and politically charged decisions. In summary, while trying to add value, all too often parents end up causing more harm than good.

Based on our research with scores of companies over a decade or more, we have identified three basic conditions that determine whether a parent will be helpful or not. They may all seem obvious, but time and again one or more of the conditions is ignored, leading to failed initiatives, disgruntled business managers and restive shareholders.

The first condition concerns the nature and size of the opportunity for the parent to improve business management decisions or performance. Is there a clear *parenting opportunity* that explains why the business managers will not be able to achieve optimal results by themselves, and what role a helpful parent could play? Parenting opportunities are the bedrock of group-level strategy, highlighting the nature of the prize that the parent is aiming to achieve. Different businesses present different parenting opportunities and, as we shall see, increasing globalization may generate a range of new opportunities for the parent to add value.

Having an opportunity or target to aim at is a basic requirement, but the second condition concerns the parent's skills and suitability in getting at that opportunity. Does the parent possess *distinctive parenting characteristics* that are particularly well suited to exploit the type of opportunities it is targeting? If the opportunity, for example, is to help traditionally distinct businesses to share complex knowhow, is the parent any good at creating a general culture of sharing or at designing relevant transfer mechanisms that can be successfully embedded in the organization? If the opportunity is about improving global sourcing, can the parent orchestrate this without creating a bureaucracy or imposing inappropriate constraints on business choice? Recognizing an opportunity to add value to the businesses is not much use if the parent has no skills at realizing the opportunity in question. If the parent is only an 'amateur' at dealing with an important opportunity, it is highly likely that a more experienced rival parent would be better positioned to achieve it.

While the first two conditions determine the parent's ability to add significant value, the third condition concerns the risks of significant value destruction. Does the parent have sufficient feel for its businesses, or will it do things that result in a *misfit with the critical success factors* in a specific business, causing unintended damage? Quite often a parent sees opportunities to add value, and may even have superior skills at exploiting these opportunities. However, at the same time it may do other things and exert other influences that are fundamentally damaging to the health of the business.

The e-revolution, for example, has created opportunities for many parents to build new businesses that leverage existing resources such as brands, customer databases, relationships, purchasing power and so on. The new businesses often benefit from access to these resources provided by the parent. But the impact of group membership can also be severely damaging in other respects. Existing planning and control systems may move too slowly for an e-business; restrictions on recruitment and remuneration may make it impossible to attract and retain the right talent; the general culture may be quite inappropriate for the new entity and continually rub up against it, causing frustrations and ill-will. If any of these forms of misfit occurs, it will reduce, or even reverse, the benefits achieved on the positive side.

The three conditions required for good parenting are summarized in Table 5.1.

Table 5.1 Three conditions for successful parenting

- *Parenting opportunities* – There must be improvement opportunities that the business management cannot realize by itself, but that a suitable parent can.
- *Distinctive parenting characteristics* – The parent must possess skills that help to realize its targeted opportunities unusually well.
- *Avoid misfit with the critical success factors of the business* – The parent must avoid simultaneously destroying significant value in other respects.

ARE PARENTS 'GOOD' OR 'BAD'?

Because each business has different parenting opportunities and different critical success factors, it is highly unlikely that any one parent will be equally suitable for a wide range of business types. This is not to say that it cannot be a good parent of businesses in different industries, as they may share similar critical success factors and parenting opportunities even if they deal with different products or services. Globalization, as we will examine, may present similar opportunities for parents to add value in some very different industries.

Equally, 'focusing' on one industry may not be relevant at all. Within the so-called media industry, for example, financial services or even chemicals, there are many different sorts of business with radically different characteristics. To be world class, a parent has to specialize in some way. It needs to develop special, even unique, ways of doing things that are particularly suited to certain types of business. If the nature of a business changes, it is often much harder than senior executives imagine for the parent to change itself in relevant ways. The very characteristics that made IBM an excellent parent of integrated computer businesses in the 1960s and 1970s became millstones when the parenting opportunities and critical success factors in those businesses changed. Typically, therefore, at any given time the three conditions above are only satisfied to differing degrees for individual businesses in the portfolio.

The impact of the three conditions can be captured in a display mapping the parent's fit and misfit with its various business units (see Figure 5.2). The horizontal axis measures the fit of the parent's characteristics with the parenting opportunities in a business, and therefore measures the value-added 'upside' benefit. The vertical axis measures the extent of misfit between the parent's characteristics and the critical success factors in the business. It therefore gauges the downside risk that the parent will inadvertently cause damage.

It is useful to split out these two axes, because very different combinations of fit and misfit are possible. 'Heartland' businesses gain significant value from the parent's influence and are at low risk of suffering damage.

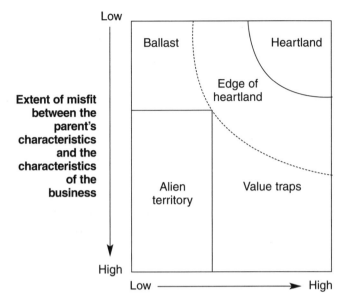

Figure 5.2 The Ashridge portfolio display.

'*Alien territory*' businesses, in contrast, gain few benefits from parental help in getting at important parenting opportunities, but are very likely to be damaged by membership of the group. Such businesses often find their way into a portfolio as part of a wider acquisition that is not sorted through. Alternatively, changes in the environment, such as extreme effects of globalization, may move even a previous heartland business into this quadrant if its parenting opportunities and critical success factors change dramatically. Also, parents are sometimes drawn to acquire 'sexy' or profitable businesses that they do not really understand. These may be good businesses in their own right, but if they are in alien territory for their particular parent, they will underperform their true potential as long as they are kept in the group. This issue is increasingly leading to spin-offs and partial flotations to reduce the parent's influence while capturing as much as possible of the business's value.

'*Ballast*' businesses neither gain much additional value from group membership nor suffer much harm. Interestingly, many businesses described in annual reports as 'core' may on closer inspection turn out to be 'ballast'. They are often large, well-performing businesses that have been around for a long time and are well understood by the parent. However, if the parent has ceased to add much value to them, it is not clear that they would suffer from being floated off and might in fact gain additional focus and accountability in the process. Like ballast in a ship, these businesses can provide weight and stability to a portfolio, but they also risk slowing it down. Every hour the parent spends with its ballast businesses is to some extent a wasted hour, deflecting attention from areas where the parent might add much more.

'Value traps' present a real dilemma. There is no doubt that they gain real benefits from the parent in some areas, perhaps technology transfer, shared branding or access to customer relationships. But at the same time they risk receiving significantly damaging influence in other areas. Key appointments may be made by the parent based on irrelevant criteria for this particular business; reporting or control mechanisms may focus on the wrong issues; or procedures may be imposed from other parts of the group where they work well, even though they cause damage in this specific context.

Finally, some businesses may lie on the 'edge of heartland', either because the parent is only partly skilled at helping with the relevant parenting opportunities, or because there are at least some significant areas of misfit.

The Ashridge portfolio display, described and illustrated above, is unlike most other portfolio displays in that it focuses attention on the relationship and fit between specific businesses and specific parents, rather than on the stand-alone health or profitability of the businesses as such. Typically, parents are much more conscious of the horizontal axis than the vertical one. They see the parenting opportunities and successes, but often underestimate the damage caused elsewhere. The business managers, in contrast, are all too often aware of the vertical axis, but may think of the horizontal axis simply in terms of access to 'cheap' capital or the use of a few specialist functions such as Treasury. Forming a measured view of the parent's impact, and how to improve it, is the essence of corporate or group-level strategy as opposed to business-level strategy.

Detailed analysis of the parent's impact takes time and involves gathering inputs from managers in the parent and the business units, as well as performance data from businesses in the portfolio. It is important to look for performance changes over time, especially in comparison with similar units in other groups, and to identify the parent's influence on those changes. Some suggestions for detailed analyses are provided in Section III of Goold *et al.* (1994). As a more rough-and-ready approach, however, readers might address the questions posed in Sidebar 1 to assess where specific businesses might sit in their own portfolio.

SIDEBAR 1: Mapping your portfolio

As a quick test of the current coherence of your own portfolio, score the following 20 questions for as many individual businesses as you choose and plot the total scores for each business on the grid in Figure 5.3. While not an 'accurate' analysis, this should provide clear indications of basic fit and misfit.

0 = statement is not at all true.
5 = statement is very clearly true.
If uncertain of response, score as 2.

Horizontal axis   **Score (0–5)**

- Managers in this business are keen to discuss their ideas and problems with members of the parent company and approach them proactively.
- Managers in this business have gained major benefits from working with colleagues in other group companies.
- Managers in this business are confident that the parent understands their challenges and is helping to address them.
- This business benefits from corporate services that are considered to provide unusually good value for money.
- Relative to competitors, performance in this business has improved significantly over the last three years and/or since it was acquired/set up.
- A number of successful managers in this business have come from other units in the group.

- Major capital expenditures in this business have been timely and value creating.

- This business clearly benefits from group resources such as brands, patents, corporate relationships or knowhow.

- Managers in this business are proud to be associated with the parent company.

- New corporate initiatives are anticipated to be relevant and useful, even if demanding.

Total horizontal score =

Vertical axis

Score (0–5)

- Decisions in this business are often delayed by requirements for head office approval.

- Over the last three years, performance has been suffering relative to competitor units in other groups.

- Corporate initiatives have seriously deflected attention from the main demands of the business.

- This business is very unlike most others in the portfolio.

- Few parent managers have worked in this business or spent a great deal of time with it.

- This business is obliged to use corporate services that are poor value for money.

- This business is often constrained in making decisions that significantly affect its performance, such as reward policy, hiring suitable numbers and quality of staff, making critical investments, developing or abandoning customer and supplier relationships and so on.

- Managers in this business devote significant time to providing the centre with inputs whose use and value they do not understand.

- Successful senior managers have often left this business to join competitors in other groups.

- Managers in this business are keen to arrange a separate listing, buyout or even a trade sale to another group.

Total vertical score =

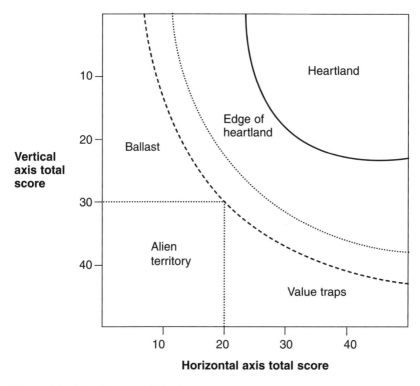

Figure 5.3 Rough-cut portfolio plot.

HOW DOES GLOBALIZATION AFFECT PARENTING?

As described elsewhere in this book, globalization can involve many different types of change concerning the impact of geography on business. On the positive side, some of these changes create exciting new parenting opportunities that may lead to considerable parental value added. In order to get at these opportunities, however, the parent will need to learn a number of new skills, which are not always easy to acquire. On the negative side, different forms of globalization may change the critical success factors in a business, increasing the risk of misfit and value destruction. The following sections provide detailed examples of these changes. For the parent as well as for its businesses, globalization is both an opportunity and a threat.

HOW DOES GLOBALIZATION AFFECT 'PARENTING OPPORTUNITIES'?

Parenting opportunities, as described above, are opportunities for a parent to help improve business unit performance beyond what would be achieved by business managers alone. They may therefore be opportunities for the parent to defend a business against threats as well as opportunities to take it into new avenues of growth or profitability. Globalization creates new parenting opportunities in five main areas:

- Access to growth opportunities in 'new' markets.
- Access to new sourcing opportunities.
- Exposure to new threats in existing markets.
- Need for networking and knowledge transfer across geographical boundaries.
- Need for global servicing of customers.

Access to Growth Opportunities in 'New' Markets

One aspect of globalization is increased access to markets that were previously closed or economically unattractive. The most obvious example in the last couple of decades has been China, and currently much attention is being focused on India. But these are only two instances of a broad shift, linked both to political and economic developments, that has recently opened up many markets in Asia, Latin America, eastern Europe and Africa to a much wider spectrum of potential suppliers. In some cases, of course, the 'change' is simply a reversion to the situation in the early twentieth century. Even so, it presents new opportunities and dilemmas with which many businesses have to wrestle.

In this context, parents are potentially valuable in a number of ways. First, the parent is often the stimulus that raises awareness of the new opportunities or pushes them up the list of business priorities. For example, seeing the potential growth in Asia generally and China in particular, ABB, a large engineering group with a strong European heritage, embarked on a major push into the region in the early 1990s. Over a period of a few years, the parent achieved a dramatic shift in resources by constantly cajoling its businesses and emphasizing the need to gain a strong presence in the region.

Second, parents can help businesses assess and select suitable new markets, as they are likely to acquire country information that is relevant to more than one business. They may also have a clearer overview of developments in a given country or region, or the resources to carry out more detailed research. Groups such as Vivendi, operating in utilities and media, have used the parent as a vehicle for exploring less familiar territories and establishing a focal point to advise different businesses about them. It may be viable, for example, for the parent to set up a local office even before any particular business commences operations. In due course, this may become a level of country or regional management spanning multiple businesses, as in ABB historically, or may melt away when individual businesses are fully established.

A third role for the parent in new markets is to help co-ordinate the activities of different units, utilizing local contacts, shared distribution channels, local alliances and so on to help each unit punch more than its individual weight. Companies such as Shell and BASF have successfully used this approach, particularly in the sort of interlinked and overlapping businesses that are common in petrochemicals.

However, as with all areas of parental involvement, good intentions do not always prove helpful in practice. While the parent may be able to acquire a better overview, it may also focus attention on the 'wrong' aspects of a new market. For example, the parent of one building products group encouraged local business developments in a number of countries that were of general economic interest, but that had very different building traditions, making many of the businesses' core products irrelevant or bad value. Similarly, one chemicals parent insisted on using the same local partner for two of its businesses with very different needs. The result was not the valuable synergy and strong relationship expected, but continual friction, leading to the eventual breakdown of the alliance.

Access to New Sourcing Opportunities

A different role for the parent concerns assistance in sourcing from countries that are unfamiliar to the business unit in question, but able to provide useful inputs. If there is already a transparent and effective market, there may be little opportunity for the parent to add value through its involvement in this area. However, this is frequently not the case. In the apparel and footwear industries, for example, several parents have established group-wide sourcing operations in the Far East or in European countries such as Italy and Portugal, to help provide for the needs of several different businesses. Pentland Group, combining a stable of highly successful sports and leisure brands such as Speedo, Kickers, Berghaus and Ellesse, as well as many others, uses its group strength and expertise in this way to provide sourcing benefits to all its individual businesses. This is particularly helpful to smaller or start-up businesses that would otherwise find it much harder to manage global sourcing cost effectively. As patterns of global trade and exchange rates shift, a skilled parent with contacts in many countries can help its businesses alter their sourcing flows rapidly to take advantage of the situation. Recently, for example, the relative benefits of sourcing from eastern Europe as opposed to Asia have fluctuated quite rapidly. Some parents, having a wider and deeper knowledge of both areas than is easy for many individual businesses to maintain, have been able to spot opportunities to gain advantage and seize them.

The benefits of sourcing from other countries are not limited to raw materials or physical goods. For example, companies such as Willis, a major player in insurance and risk management, gain significant benefit from carrying out many of their businesses' back-office operations in India. British Airways set up similar operations for many aspects of customer management, and astute parents in financial services and other industries have used companies such as Compass in Bombay to improve customer service dramatically at remarkably low cost. European call centres, combining economies of scale with multiple language capabilities, have been particularly successful in Ireland and the Benelux countries, and many parents have recently established multi-country shared service centres to gain advantages from a more global approach.

However, the parent's involvement in global sourcing is as apt to backfire, as in other areas, if insufficient attention is paid to the three conditions described above (see Table 5.1). In one record company, for example, the parent concluded a worldwide sourcing agreement with a logistics company that was very strong in the parent's own country, but relatively weak in many other parts of the world. Managers running businesses in a number of countries were outraged by the poor local service, believing that it led to lost sales and other problems that far outweighed the modest cost savings achieved from a global deal.

Exposure to New Threats in Existing Markets

Other parenting opportunities can arise from the impact of globalization on the home market of a given business. When markets open up to new types of competition, established businesses may find themselves competing with completely different business models. A skilled parent can help assess the nature of change required and facilitate developments to achieve it, or may recognize the need to retreat into a more defensible niche. These decisions are much harder for individual business managers to make, particularly given the highly disruptive conclusions that may emerge at the business level.

In Saudi Arabia, for example, the internationally astute parent of the Savola Group of food businesses realized that the arrival of Frito-Lay in snack foods, and new growth aspirations from confectionery producers such as Mars and Cadbury, were changing the basis of competition in these categories. Not only were consumer tastes shifting from more traditional snacks such as dates to potato chips and chocolate, but the sources of competitive advantage in these areas were also shifting towards expensive product development and packaging.

Simply going on competing with a business model that had proved successful in the past would no longer be sufficient. Furthermore, the parent recognized, partly from its knowledge of other Middle Eastern markets, that the value of scale in product development would increasingly favour globally integrated players. This led to parental roles both to facilitate technology alliances and to stimulate the redesign of product offerings.

Similarly, when South Africa was reopened to full global trade, companies such as Anglo American, which had diversified heavily from its base in mining, quickly realized that the previously valid 'parenting logic' of recycling cash into a broader and broader array of South African businesses would soon become inappropriate. The task of the parent was to prepare its businesses for world-class competition on a global stage. This led to a massive restructuring of the group, international development along focused product lines, such as platinum, coal and base metals, creation of a more outward-looking culture and exit from many operations that would now be worth more, and have a better future, with other parents.

Once again, however, the wrong sort of intervention by the parent may be highly destructive. For example, the response of many western European parents to global competition in their home markets, especially caused by Japanese incursions in the 1970s, was misguided 'segment retreat'. This involved pressing their businesses to abandon competition at the 'low end' of the market, where apparently unsustainably low prices were offered by Asian exporters, and to focus instead on more profitable value-added markets and applications. What many parents missed was the underlying economic link between these segments. If many of the same components, subsystems or 'building blocks' could be shared across segments, economies of scale gained in the mass market could be used to attack apparently safe positions in more specialized areas. This is a lesson that has now been fully digested by the global auto manufacturers, for example, who build variation around a small number of basic global platforms. It was much less widely understood a couple of decades ago and parallel misunderstandings are guiding the influence of many parents today.

Need for Networking and Knowledge Transfer across Geographical Boundaries

In a different guise, globalization increases the value of sharing information and knowhow across countries. In industries that have traditionally had single-country business units, this shift creates major opportunities for a parent to help create effective communication channels between the units. In the 1980s and early 1990s, for example, TI (Tube Investments as was) created significant value by linking up its different local businesses in specialist mechanical seals, small diameter tubes and aircraft systems. In each of these divisions, the parent placed major emphasis on achieving cross-country sharing, while deliberately playing down possible in-country sharing between divisions as a less valuable distraction. Similarly, in the mid to late 1990s, companies such as Redland, in roof tiles, bricks and aggregates, and Shell Chemicals, in upstream petrochemicals, shifted their organizational focus. They moved from cross-product country management to more regional or global management of individual product areas, with a strong emphasis on benchmarking and learning from global best practices.

Facilitating this sort of knowledge transfer is often a delicate and tricky task. When country managers complain, for example, that benchmarks are irrelevant to their particular business or that best practices from elsewhere would be bad practices in their territory, how should the parent react? The objections may be based on 'not-invented-here' syndrome and parochial narrow-mindedness. But they may also be based on genuine appreciation of different local market needs and priorities. After many gentler attempts to improve sharing across countries, Philips, the consumer electronics firm, concluded by the late 1990s that more radical parental intervention was required. Unilever, in contrast, remains cautious about the dangers of too centralist a view, especially in certain food products where local tastes and distribution channels are subtly different.

Each parent must assess the specific opportunities in its own businesses and also play to the cultural strengths and realities that have been built up over many years. Failure to do so will inevitably lead to problems, such as those experienced by AT&T, the giant telecommunications company, in its attempts to share international knowhow following its acquisition of NCR, a large computer business, in 1991. By not fully understanding what knowhow was suitable for sharing or what mechanisms would bring about such sharing, the parent appears to have destroyed several billion dollars of value.

Need for Global Servicing of Customers

A fifth major area of new parenting opportunities sparked by globalization concerns dealings with customers across country boundaries. As companies globalize, moving into new territories and increasing the rate of internal sharing across borders, they often expect their suppliers to provide better co-ordinated and further-flung local support. In the early 1980s, Saatchi & Saatchi popularized this growing trend, probably ahead of its time, in the advertising industry. Since then, however, pressures have clearly grown for co-ordinated global support in a wide range of professional services, including IT, process and strategy consulting, legal services and corporate financial advice. The issue is by no means confined to services, however. In white goods, for example, Emerson Electric felt obliged to set up a motor manufacturing operation in Europe to support the moves of Whirlpool, a major white goods producer and important Emerson customer in the US. Suppliers to McDonald's have often recognized the need to follow the company, sometimes reluctantly, into new territories.

One of the clearest examples of this trend is in the auto industry, where prime suppliers have been under increasing pressure to support customers on a global basis. This has led to significant changes in the parenting needs of component and system businesses, and the eclipse of parents who were least able to help. BTR, for example, was a highly successful parent of various auto-component businesses when the main opportunities were to take out costs and raise prices. As demands on suppliers changed, however, it became apparent that the rigorous financial controls and discrete business unit accountabilities so helpful in the past stood in the way of more complex cross-country co-ordination and global customer management.

Companies such as Hewlett-Packard have been leaders in support for selected global accounts, but have also recognized the costs and complexities involved. After increasing the number of designated global accounts from 26 in 1993 to 250 in 1996, it scaled back down to 95 by 1997. Other parents have been less helpful and realistic. In one consulting company, for instance, the parent insisted on a global client co-ordination system centred on a large and complex database. The initial set-up was highly expensive and the demands of 'keeping the beast fed' with up-to-date information proved so onerous that gaps quickly began to appear. Within a year the system had become largely useless and was regarded as a corporate white elephant, while the businesses themselves put in place a less comprehensive but more pragmatic solution.

WHAT PITFALLS DOES GLOBALIZATION CREATE FOR THE PARENT?

We have already seen one major globalization pitfall for parents: just because the parent sees new opportunities to help its businesses does not mean that it has the relevant skills to realize those opportunities. Attempts to wade in may be ill conceived and cause significant damage, even if the opportunity is a real one.

This, however, is by no means the only pitfall. Another cause of problems is the simplistic notion that 'globalization' is a single, homogeneous thing. In reality, it is a concept that covers a huge array of different geographically related changes. Many parents, for example, confuse the growing interdependence of economies across the world with homogenization of tastes. The increasing globalization of capital markets and trade flows mean that local economies are swiftly and significantly affected by what is going on thousands of miles away, just as individuals are now instantaneously linked, via CNN or BBC World, to events whose impact was once deflected by distance and time. This does not mean, however, that markets or individuals have suddenly become indistinguishable across the globe.

In their research and writing on this topic, Sumantra Ghoshal and Chris Bartlett (1989) have helpfully distinguished between the relative significance and value of global integration and local responsiveness. Similarly, George Yip and Andrew Campbell (see Yip, 1989; Lovelock and Yip, 1996) have emphasized the difference between the location of operations and the degree of co-ordination across them. Yves Doz and Peter Williamson (Doz *et al.*, 2001) have clarified the difference between companies directly involved in international operations and others who may not regard themselves as 'international' at all, but whose local markets are heavily influenced by other economies. All these scholars, and many others besides, are keen to break down simplistic notions of globalization into more fine-grained understanding.

Nevertheless, working out what globalization really means in a specific context is a challenging task, often misinterpreted even by highly skilled and successful parents. Disney is a case in point. Despite having some of the most globally recognized brands and characters, it has struggled to understand which elements of the Disney experience travel to different countries. The original combination at Euro Disney (a tellingly inappropriate name, subsequently changed to 'Disneyland Paris') did not work well. Despite great attention to hiring multi-cultural staff and dubbing Cinderella so that her screams would be intelligible to French children, the underlying economic model was a US one. This depended for its profitability on significant food and merchandise sales, and multi-day visits. Unfortunately, too many European visitors, especially the French, tended to come only for one day, bring a packed lunch and refrain from indulgent purchases of Mickey Mouse ears and Dumbo pencil cases. This almost bankrupted the operation until a French general manager was appointed, bringing a significant reblending of local and global elements.

Another area for parental pitfalls is a failure to recognize that some form of globalization has altered the critical success factors in a given business. International retailers, for example, have changed in their requirements significantly over the last decade, due to a mix of best practice adoption, shared systems, the search for global sourcing economies, the desire for cross-country supply and so on. Suppliers who have not changed in line with these developments have found previous sources of advantage marginalized and once-strong positions undermined. In such contexts it is not unusual for parent managers to act as a drag or constraint on change, especially if they were actively involved in a business at a different stage in its evolution.

The parent's own cultural orientation can also act as a blinker to the needs of operations in very different parts of the world. Mundane assumptions about telecommunications and transportation infrastructure, for example, can lead to major mistakes, let alone the possible impact of far more complex issues such as effective negotiation with potential Chinese or Japanese partners. While Americans and Britons may joke about being 'two nations divided by a common language', many other nations are more conspicuously separated both by language and a wider array of cultural differences. A typical parental pitfall in this regard, especially for Anglo-Saxon parents with a horror of learning 'foreign tongues', is the temptation to hire a handful of fluent polyglots and somehow assume that this will make them effective and culturally sensitive managers. Perhaps hoping to find the equivalent of a global adapter, parents frequently assume that anyone speaking several 'strange' languages will be well qualified to take on any internationally oriented challenge. They are often rudely awakened from this simplistic assumption.

Among many other possible parental pitfalls is the danger of 'conceptual geography'. This involves making dangerously sweeping assumptions about operations based in an area that has some shared label or apparent unity. At the extreme, it is typified by companies that divide their operations into two: national and 'overseas'. Americans are particularly inclined to overrate the significance of the concept of 'Europe', just as many Europeans are led astray by the broad concept of 'Asia'. As parents often have to deal with many different units and countries, they are prone to look for frameworks or structures that simplify the disturbing complexity of their worlds. This is entirely reasonable if carefully applied, but, like any simplification, may cause mistakes. The concept of 'The Americas', for example, is generally helpful in terms of broad time zones, dollar relatedness and certain trading patterns, but in other contexts may be highly misleading.

CHANGES TO OVERALL GROUP STRUCTURE AND BUSINESS DEFINITION

So far, we have primarily referred to the business units in a group as a 'given', albeit affected by globalization and the influence of the parent. In some cases, however, globalization may fundamentally change the appropriate definition of the business unit building block itself, just as changes in technology and customer behaviour sometimes can.

The most obvious change of this sort is the expansion of business scope from a single country to a region or even the world. If you run a number of retail banking units in different European countries, it is still sensible to define each one as a separate business, even if you start to make links between them. If you run a number of separate businesses making the same base chemical in these territories, you will probably suffer grave disadvantages relative to a competitor who has integrated its operations into a single unit. This is because the prime strategic orientation of nationally defined businesses will lead to suitable trade-offs in the former case, but damaging ones in the latter. Facilities will be made too small, logistics costs will not be traded off appropriately against other costs, customers will be served in a disjointed and costly way and so on.

As the significance of national boundaries wanes, increasing numbers of businesses may merit a change of scope. As we have seen above, however, in many cases there is a complex requirement to combine elements of global integration with elements of local tailoring. The parent must decide whether to set up more localized units and try to link them in various ways, or set up more global units but try to encourage suitable local tailoring inside the unit. In similar markets, Unilever has tended to favour the former approach, Procter and Gamble the latter.

Even if the fundamental business units remain nationally based, the prime line of parenting may be shifted from the geographical dimension to the product or business-area dimension. This is exactly what has happened over the last ten years at ABB, and in many companies operating in areas such as software, diverse professional services and the production of many consumer electronics.

A further issue for the parent is to decide whether changes in business or divisional definition will undermine the previous logic of owning parts of the portfolio. For example, a parent with a single-country position in a globalizing industry is generally likely to create more value from selling its one piece of the global jigsaw than trying to collect all the others. However, if no other parents are in a much better starting position, there may be an attractive opportunity for global consolidation. Even if other parents are in more advanced positions, it may be possible to form alliances to create the global network that the business now needs. These are clearly decisions that require detailed understanding of the specific case. As a general bias, however, we have noticed that even parents with a weak starting position and limited skills at alliance building or cross-country integration are tempted to move down the global expansion route. This can lead to the bidding up of prices for those businesses that can be snapped up, and often a period of depressed performance before or until a shakeout improves the new industry structure. Some mineral and mining businesses, for instance, appear to have followed this path.

CHANGES REQUIRED WITHIN THE PARENT

If successful corporate strategy is all about achieving a good 'fit' between the parent and its businesses, as argued above, it is only logical that changes caused by globalization at the business level should lead to corresponding changes in the parent. In order to capitalize on the new parenting opportunities emerging, and to support the changing critical success factors in its businesses, the parent itself may need to develop new skills and attitudes. This is often more difficult than imagined and may well involve bringing in new senior managers and changing ways of working that are culturally entrenched.

In analysing the parent organization and possible changes that it should undergo, we have found it useful to look through five 'lenses', as depicted in Figure 5.4.

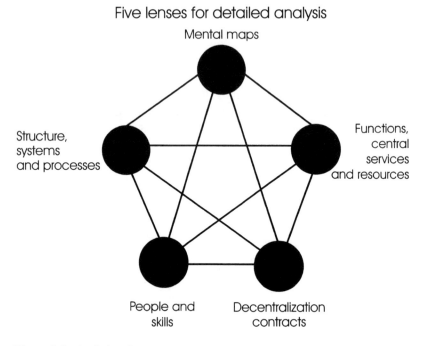

Figure 5.4 Analysing the parent.

Changes may be required in all of these areas to support businesses that are affected by globalization. Structure, systems and processes are an obvious area for change. Whether the parent creates a matrix, as ABB did, to layer global integration over local responsiveness, or changes the prime reporting direction, as Shell Chemicals did, to encourage a regional or global perspective, this is the first lever of change that most parents pull.

Functions, central services and resources are also often used as a way of reasserting a more co-ordinated or standardized global approach, although this can be seen as heavy-handed and bureaucratic in organizations used to a feeling of local empowerment and accountability.

The so-called decentralization contract is slightly more complex. This term covers the understanding between a business unit head and the parent as to who is 'allowed' to do what. In globalizing industries, there is often extreme friction between country unit heads and the parent, as an increasing number of decisions are pulled back from the local front line to one or other broader-based group. Country heads may feel that their authority is being undermined and refuse to be held accountable for performance as a result. The parent must learn to manage such changes, not only altering the unit managers' perspective, but also ensuring that complementary changes are effected at the centre. In one organization, for example, while the parent insisted on a more collegiate approach across countries to combat globally co-ordinated competition, it continued to hold each country manager brutally accountable for performance in their own patch. Hardly surprisingly, this led to time-consuming cross-country agreements that were then ignored whenever they were locally unattractive.

However, the most difficult elements to change are the last two, which are strongly linked. If the key individuals in the parent remain constant, they may develop some new skills but are unlikely to change radically, and are highly unlikely to abandon the 'mental maps' that have been built up over many years and are closely associated with their own past success. While many of us like to imagine that we are versatile and constantly changing, external assessment suggests a much slower evolution. Altering our mental maps is very different from seeing potential benefits in doing things differently. Rather like New Year's resolutions, many honest desires to change parental attitudes and behaviours founder at the first real test.

For example, parents may talk about the urgency of establishing a foothold position in certain emerging markets, but consistently reject investment proposals as too risky or close down fledgling operations if they do not turn a profit in the first year. Parents may talk about the crucial role of knowhow sharing, but baulk at the cost of three managers flying to a joint meeting. Parents may recognize the value of serving clients globally, but refuse to give up valuable pricing differentials until a competitor seizes the business. This is not to say that the 'right' answer is always clear, but that even if there is intellectual agreement as to what that answer is, the parent may still fail to implement necessary changes because they cut across enduring and deeply held beliefs.

SIDEBAR 2: Quadriga

Many of the issues discussed in this chapter can be illustrated by the case of Quadriga, a successful and rapidly growing business currently owned by Nomura.

The roots of this business go back to the 1970s and 1980s when Thorn-EMI expanded its TV and video-rental business from a largely UK domestic customer base. Expansion involved start-ups and small acquisitions in many different European countries, as well as much larger acquisitions later on in the US. Thorn Rentals had also been moving steadily into commercial markets, such as betting shops, hospitals and hotels. Around Europe, the businesses were run as largely separate entities, although with co-ordinated purchasing of the physical product to achieve economies of scale. Different countries had different brands, different pricing structures and significantly different business models, depending on the nature of local opportunities and competition. The head of each country was in many ways part of a loose federation, gaining purchasing benefits and some management guidance from the rental parent, but within a framework highly tailored to the local environment.

Over time, it became increasingly clear that the operations serving business customers had different dynamics from those serving domestic customers. Furthermore, a particular segment of business customers was opening up new service opportunities and demands. This was the hotel sector, where in-room entertainment had moved from the mere provision of a television to more complex offerings, including pay-TV, films and sometimes promotional channels for the hotel itself. Teaming up with a software company, Thorn became more and more expert in this market, creating a dominant position in the UK and strong positions in several other countries. The hotel market had much greater potential than most for adding value to the basic rental offering through technology enhancement and a detailed understanding of customers' needs.

Following the demerger of Thorn-EMI in the mid 1990s, the rental group as a whole came under some pressure and a break-up plan was put in place. This aimed to separate out the many different parts of the group, recognizing that they would be worth more as individual operations to other specific parents. Nomura, in the guise of the legendary Guy Hands, stepped in to finance and manage this complicated process. The restructuring created an ideal opportunity to group together the various hotel-serving activities, split them out from other operations around Europe and relaunch a focused new group: Quadriga.

The critical success factors and parenting opportunities for the businesses within Quadriga were very different from those in most of the other rental businesses. While purchasing of hardware was still important, other factors also loomed large and the management of shops or 'outlets' was irrelevant. Technology was critical, essentially involving software to enhance services to guests (such as interactive TV, Internet access, on-screen messaging and bill paying) and to hoteliers (such as room service scheduling, mini bar management and energy conservation). However, such technology also requires sophisticated marketing, to create product packages, usage guides and so on, and involves a complex 'consultancy' sale. All these factors encourage a much more tightly co-ordinated pan-European approach, and the parent managers at Quadriga duly established a series of new mechanisms to achieve this. As well as clustering multiple countries into more regional business units, some activities, such as product development, became more centralized and greater co-ordination was established through pan-European specialist groups, the creation of a sales school, increasingly standardized software and more frequent interactions between the business managers and parent managers as a joint team.

Meanwhile, increasing consolidation among Quadriga's hotel customers was prompting the need for stronger key account management across the whole of Europe. Furthermore, as these powerful chains expanded into new locations, such as the Middle East or Africa, they often wanted Quadriga to provide local support for in-room entertainment, even if they had not previously operated in this area.

By 2000, a typical globalization dilemma had arisen. The company had clearly moved from being a fragmented, locally focused federation to a networked, customer-focused, global (or at least regional) group – but should it become even more integrated? On the one hand, there are still significant differences between the demands of the fragmented seaside hotel industry in Italy and the concentrated corporate chains of the UK. Demand for Internet access and interactivity is far higher in Scandinavia than in France. TV programming for the Middle East is very different to that in Germany. On the other hand, global customers expect global standards. New technology investments require global scale and roll-out. Pricing differences become transparent, requiring global harmonization.

Given the above, the new chief executive has concluded that it may no longer be appropriate to run Quadriga as a group, but better to turn it into a single business. The 'parent' at this level will then cease to exist, at least until it spawns new businesses with different characteristics, although these too will quite likely be 'global'.

IMPLICATIONS FOR PRACTICE

All of the above suggests that parents should consider very carefully the implications of globalization for themselves as well as for their businesses. Because benefit only comes from suitable interaction between these parties, it is important to be realistic about both of them. Globalization in its many forms affects businesses in complex and different ways. It is essential to get to grips with the specifics of the situation rather than to talk and think in sweeping generalities. However, it is also important to recognize the characteristics of the parent, and to form an honest assessment of whether it is likely to be helpful in its chosen interventions or not.

Specifically, the parent should ask itself the following questions:

- Is globalization creating opportunities to add value in new ways to the businesses in our group? How could we help our businesses in:
  - accessing new markets;
  - utilizing global sourcing;
  - coping with new threats to established markets;
  - improving global networking and sharing;
  - developing appropriately co-ordinated customer service.
- What are the new risks and pitfalls that we must address? Are we being careful to avoid:
  - misunderstanding the specific nature of the opportunities to help our businesses;
  - addressing the opportunities in unhelpful or inappropriate ways;
  - adopting too broad-brush a view of globalization itself;
  - ignoring changes in the critical success factors of our businesses;
  - imposing narrow cultural assumptions and norms;
  - applying 'conceptual geography' and other spurious simplifications.
- Should we reconsider the definition of the basic units or structure of the corporation?
  - Is it still suitable to define some of our business units at the national level?
  - Should the reporting structure emphasize differences of product, service or customer more than those of geography?

- How much do we need to change the parent itself?
  - Do we have relevant skills to realize emerging parenting opportunities?
  - Do we need to change significantly the way we operate, behave and even think?
  - If so, are we likely to achieve this without significant changes in the key managers within the parent?

Globalization certainly creates positive new parenting opportunities, but that is a far cry from guaranteeing that the parent will be good at realizing them. Successful global parenting is as much about knowing which battles to fight as it is about fighting hard in any particular battle that crops up. For parents, as for business units, the advice of the ancient Greeks rings true: 'Know thyself.'

References

Bartlett, G. and Ghoshal, S. (1989) *Managing Across Borders: The transnational solution*, Harvard Business School Press, Boston, MA.

Doz, Y., Santos, J. and Williamson, P.J. (2001) *From Global to Metanational: How companies win in the global knowledge economy*, Harvard Business School Press, Boston, MA.

Goold, M., Campbell, A. and Alexander, M. (1994) *Corporate Level Strategy: Creating value in the multibusiness company*, John Wiley, New York.

Lovelock, C.H. and Yip, G.S. (1996) 'Developing global strategies for service businesses', *California Management Review*, 38(2), Winter.

Yip, G.S. (1989) 'Global strategy . . . in a world of nations?', *Sloan Management Review*, Fall.

MANAGING GLOBAL PARTNERSHIPS AND ALLIANCES

Roger Pudney

CHAPTER 6

MANAGING GLOBAL PARTNERSHIPS AND ALLIANCES

Alliances and partnerships increasingly have a number of major roles. For example, they can be a major strategic weapon to provide extension and growth; they can constitute a major source of collaborative learning; they can create much faster access to new market places; and they can block major competitors through the uniquely close relationships with partners. In many markets the key driver of this process is one of sheer size. The investment involved in penetrating new markets with new technologies or a new product (for example in the pharmaceutical, telecommunications and defence industries) is so significant that no one organization could do it on its own. For example, as the chief executive of British Telecom Sir Peter Bonfield said, 'Customers are demanding seamless communications to anywhere in the world at a time that suits them. The potential market is so enormous and so complex that no one company can hope to do it alone. Which is why mergers, acquisitions and partnerships are so much a feature of our industry today' (quoted in Mitchell, 1998).

Other forces driving many industries towards globalization (and opening up the possibility of alliances) include rationalization and concentration of markets, very heavy emphasis on economies of scale and search for rapid technology transfer. In the developing world particularly, the liberation and deregulation of markets often lead to incoming investors entering joint ventures with local companies (for example the Ford joint venture in India with Mahindra to manufacture automobiles). In many cases the incoming organizations' traditional marketplaces have become mature with declining profitability, which provides a strong driver to seek entry into newer marketplaces.

The trend towards seeking core suppliers and core customers globally is leading to the creation of strategic alliances between customers and suppliers on a global basis. If a customer is being driven to globalize as a result of the factors indicated above, its suppliers might have to globalize as well, which creates an opportunity for close collaboration with a limited number of major customers or major suppliers. Some of the results are remarkable – one American global consumer products company has reduced the number of worldwide suppliers of the key specialist chemical ingredient in its finished product from 30 suppliers to 2 over the last five years (Ashridge International Partnership Study, Pudney, 1996). This reduction is based on the rationale that a major customer, with a very limited number of global suppliers, receives a high level of focus on its business needs and first call on the best resources from suppliers. This is particularly important in generating joint innovation. In return, the designated core suppliers receive a substantially increased share of the customer's business with greater security of supply. They can therefore take a more strategic view of the customer's business and cost benefits should arise because the supplier can now process a greater volume with similar overheads. The global automotive industry is steadily increasing its use of various forms of collaboration between companies.

As a side issue, the automotive industry has recently been strongly characterized by acquisitions and mergers, which raises the question of whether it is better as a global strategy to acquire or to take the alliancing route. Historically, and on average, acquisitions and mergers have not been characterized by high success rates. There is increasing evidence that organizations that have learnt to be skilled in alliancing and joint venturing can in fact achieve good rates of return from these

CASE STUDY – Global partnerships and alliances in the automotive industry

One example of a global industry with a huge increase in collaborative relationships is the automotive industry, both at OEM (original equipment manufacturer) level and that of major suppliers. The industry is heavily cyclical and it is not unknown for it to experience several years of global losses followed by several years of heavy profit, although regional variations in this pattern may be significant. For many years the industry has operated a high level of co-operation in the various levels of the supply chain:

- backwards from the manufacturers, through the 'tier' system of component and raw materials suppliers;
- at OEM level with co-operation between manufacturers.

The result has been to create, over time, a remarkably complex patchwork of global collaboration. Because individual manufacturers and suppliers have long faced such strong competitive pressures, one of their responses was to seek competitive advantage and risk sharing from collaboration. The average number of suppliers to each European car manufacturer was 1250 in 1988 and is currently below 400. Most analysts predict that this process of reduction will continue, not least because of the continuing consolidation at OEM level through mergers (DaimlerChrysler and the GM co-operation with Fiat for example). Many analysts predict that before long there will be no more than six major OEMs globally in the industry.

There are now signs that the industry is moving towards new business models, for example by creating Internet-based purchase networks on a global scale. OEMs are also shifting the content of vehicles significantly to suppliers through outsourcing the engineering and manufacturing of large elements of the car, often in the form of modules and systems. A further trend is the 'downstreaming' of activity within the industry. The initial sale of the vehicle accounts for around only 25 per cent of the lifetime revenue stream from the vehicle and, faced with heavy pressure on real prices at consumer level, OEMs are now trying to increase the amount of revenue from downstream activity such as distribution, retailing, servicing and insurance. In its own right, the retailing part of the industry is experiencing a global change, notably driven by the Internet and the accessibility of market information on pricing and delivery times to individual car buyers.

The industry is also profoundly affected by the fact that there is over 30 per cent overcapacity of manufacturing production in Europe, whereas the major growth in world demand is predicted to come from markets such as Brazil and China. This has led, paradoxically, to a huge increase in the productive capacity being built in those marketplaces. Once again, these operations are often in conjunction with local partners, for example Volkswagen's major joint ventures in Shanghai and elsewhere in China with local Chinese partners.

In our work with various suppliers to global OEMs in the automotive industry, we see an interesting dichotomy between those manufacturers that have moved strongly towards using collaborative alliances as a way of building competitive advantage globally, and those that are more embedded in traditional patterns of treatment of suppliers. Historically, the industry has been based largely on the exercise of power by OEMs over major suppliers, even very substantial organizations such as Delphi, which until recently was part of GM. There remain significant differences within the industry between organizations that still attempt to dominate supplier relationships themselves and those that are more typified by the following quote from a former chief executive of Chrysler: 'When you start to see your suppliers as the experts then they become valuable partners instead of a switchable commodity. You have to have some technique other than just bludgeoning to get efficiency out of them' (Stallkamp, 1993).

collaborative ventures and, for these companies, strategic alliances may be a less risky route to global expansion than acquisitions. Indeed, they also offer the opportunity to work with a potential acquisition candidate before finally committing to a merger or acquisition.

One example of this would be the long-standing relationship between ICL, the British computer manufacturer, and Fujitsu, who worked closely in collaboration for ten years before Fujitsu finally acquired ICL in 1990. The learning process involved in the first ten years was critical to the success of the organization post-acquisition and to the close integration of the two companies. A similar example would be the long and carefully managed process between competitors Electrolux and AEG in the white goods market. Here Electrolux took a minority stake in AEG and operated a close partnership with cross-supply agreements in various markets, before finally taking a majority stake as a key part of its globalization strategy. In many markets, companies looking for access have little choice but to go into collaborative ventures because there is a shortage of acquisition candidates, either because of sheer lack of availability or because of local legislation.

We believe that those organizations that have learnt to use alliances to build competitive advantage will have a significant advantage in expanding globally. For example, the French automotive component supplier Valeo is dominant in nearly all its seven key target product segments. Based on its very close historical relationship with Renault in Europe, Valeo is now using Renault's purchase of a minority share in Nissan to extend opportunistically into the Asia-Pacific region, and benefiting from the consolidation in the industry as well its previously developed skills in building partnerships with major manufacturers (Merrill Lynch, 1999).

WHAT DISTINGUISHES SUCCESSFUL FROM UNSUCCESSFUL ALLIANCES IN GLOBAL BUSINESS?

In the past six years, the author has led a practical research study on partnerships and strategic alliances. The primary purpose of this research has been to identify how organizations are achieving competitive advantage from partnering. This Ashridge International Partnership Study has involved over 80 companies worldwide, primarily in western Europe, North America and Asia-Pacific (including Japan and Australia), and to a lesser extent in Latin America, eastern Europe and Africa. It has included detailed interviews and a significant number of consulting interventions, partnering workshops either for individual companies or joint workshops with two or more partners present. The output has been outlined in a number of publications and is summarized in the remainder of this chapter (Pudney, 1996; Pudney, 1998; Pudney, 2000). The collaborations that we studied take many forms: with or without an equity involvement, based on a local regional or global geographical spread, with a single partner or many partners in a network. They can be based on manufacturing, distribution, R&D,

marketing collaborations or combinations of several of these, and a significant number are with competitors. A further category is acquisitions and mergers, which in essence are an attempt to create added value from bringing together previously separate companies. This research on success and failure in international alliances indicates strongly that there are a number of key guidelines that companies need to address if they want to make the best use of strategic alliances.

Before outlining the factors that improve the odds of success, it is worth providing a working definition of what makes the difference between a high-performing alliance and an ordinary alliance. We use the term 'partnership' to describe a high-performing, genuinely mutual relationship producing significant added benefits to all parties involved. Partnerships can include customer–supplier relationships, joint ventures (with equity share and usually the establishment of a separate legal entity), extensive strategic alliances (which can be any of the above), internal alliances between parts of the same company, as well as mergers and acquisitions (where the basic rules for success are broadly the same). The term 'partnership' therefore describes the high quality of the relationship. There are a very large number of strategic relationships in operation in the business world, but only a much smaller number truly deserve to be called partnerships.

WHAT IS IT THAT CREATES A TRUE PARTNERSHIP? THE SCOPE MODEL

From our work with a large number of organizations worldwide, we believe that the key to really high performance and the creation of genuinely innovative ways of working together lies in the understanding and management of five categories of interlinked factors. Together these make what we call the SCOPE model of successful partnership. This model is an acronym for a combination of these sets of factors, where inadequate performance on one or more of the categories of factors may well severely inhibit the formation of a high-performing partnership (see Figure 6.1).

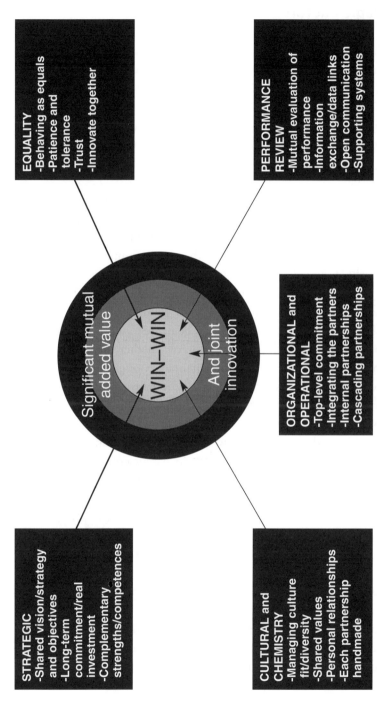

Figure 6.1   What makes partnerships successful? The SCOPE model.

Source: Ashridge International Partnership Study.

Strategic Factors

The first group is strategic factors, for example having joint and long-term objectives that are rigorously reviewed together, real investment in terms of time and money and complementary strengths and competences. Because partnerships are highly demanding relationships involving considerable investments of time, senior management attention and resources (particularly technical and financial), it is particularly important in global partnerships to clarify the strategic objectives at the earliest possible stage.

As one example of the importance of this, in the telecom industry British Telecom was heavily engaged in the process of pooling resources with AT&T to create a new international telecom joint venture (Concert) owned 50:50 by the two companies. This was particularly designed to cater for the needs of the two companies' largest global customers, with joint responsibilities shared for the top 300 accounts. The two parties spent six months in robust dialogue hammering out how the alliance could be made to work to best advantage, particularly discussing the question of whether their strategies for the global joint venture were complementary enough. In simple terms, complementarity means that both or all the partners (in the case of a more complex arrangement) bring something specific and different to the party that overlaps with whatever is provided by the other partners. In this alliance, the companies put a particular premium on the autonomy of the joint venture from the two parent companies. The BT director of alliances is quoted as saying, 'We have to rebuild BT and AT&T behind it [the alliance]. We have new commercial relationships between ourselves and our global venture. This is a complex thing to do – only to be attempted when you believe you have a real need. We think that it is a great solution but it is a tough thing to do' (Lewis, 1999).

Unfortunately, we see many attempted alliances where hardly any thought is given to the strategic rationale behind the alliance and the potential difficulties of implementing it in a global marketplace. Within the issue of complementarity, the question of core competences is very significant. These are defined as those elements in a company that

UNIVERSITY OF WOLVERHAMPTON
Compton Learning Centre

ITEMS ISSUED:

Customer ID: 7605444748

Title: Globalization : the external pressures
ID: 7622589481
Due: 14/10/2010 23:59

Total items: 1
07/10/2010 14:08
Issued: 4
Overdue: 0

Thank you for using Self Service.
Please keep your receipt.

Overdue books are fined at 40p per day for
1 week loans, 10p per day for long loans.

provide major differentiation from competitors and major value to customers, and that can be leveraged into the creation of substantial new businesses (Prahalad and Hamel, 1990).

Within this area of strategic factors, one of the keys to success in partnering is focus, which comes in a number of different ways:

- Focus on making the best use of the overlapping core competences of the partners in the alliance.
- Strategic focus within the global sphere of operations on key markets (whether country or segment based) and key joint opportunities within those markets.
- Focus on a small range of the most appropriate actual and potential partners.
- Tight focus on the joint key objectives for each partnership.
- Focus on identifying and resolving the priority issues that need to be addressed to ensure the sustainable success of the alliance.

Many organizations fail to meet their objectives and expectations in alliances because of a failure to ask fundamental questions at the outset about the real focus of the alliance. This can lead to months, if not years, of frustrating and often bad-tempered attempts to make the alliance work, while key opportunities slip by and are picked up by competitors.

Cultural and Chemistry Factors

The second group of factors in the SCOPE model is to do with culture and chemistry. This should start with a real understanding of each other's cultures and with genuine attempts to identify the level of diversity and to respect and value it within the alliance. There should be a good overlap between the philosophies, values and belief systems of the partnering organizations and a whole series of strong personal relationships (from the top of the organizations downward), producing genuine innovation at many levels within the partnership, including the strategic level.

In terms of value systems, Figure 6.2 is a very simple model developed from our research into alliances and showing a continuum from adversarial to collaborative relationships. Alliances that fail almost invariably exhibit more of the characteristics closer to the left-hand side (adversarial) of the continuum and are often based on older cultural mindsets. These can be closely linked to 'command-and-control' approaches where the main objective appears to be to direct and dominate the partner. The prevailing climate in these relationships is a series of negative values and emotions, for example aggression, fear, resentment, blame and single-minded protection of each organization's self-interest, without giving any thought to the interest of the partner. A completely different set of values features under the right-hand side (collaborative) of the continuum. These involve the building of genuine understanding, trust and respect between the partners.

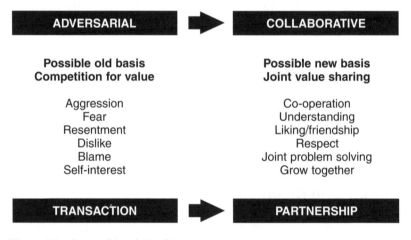

Figure 6.2 Partnership relationships.

Critically, the issue in terms of culture is that of managing the fit rather than having the same cultures in the two partners. As one senior manager involved in a global alliance in the chemical industry said during an interview with the author, 'You don't have to like your partner but you do have to respect them if you want the alliance to succeed.'

CASE STUDY – Partnership – joint value sharing

As an example of what is meant by 'joint value sharing', two major companies involved in the pan-European food industry, one as a manufacturer of consumer products and the other as a supplier of basic cooking oils, transformed their relationship from what had been primarily a 'transaction' where the supplier supplied its ingredients and the food manufacturer bought them without any development of a close working relationship. Indeed, real problems had been created over many years by a continuing fight between the two organizations for more margin (or value) on both sides. The relationship reached a point of no return where the supplier was not achieving the margins necessary for future sustained investment in supplying the customer and was prepared to withdraw. Both parties agreed that this would be a bad option and decided to try to seek another solution.

This was to put together a joint 'reengineering' team from both companies involving sales, marketing, financial, operations and IT people. They pooled financial cost and margin information and analysed all of the processes that took place between them and within their supply chain from the supplier to end customer. They assessed which of these processes actually added value to the end consumer (and which were subtracting it). As a result of this close and open collaboration, they were able to remove a great deal of unnecessary cost from their joint processes, to improve the quality of the finished product at lower cost and to increase the margins of both players in the alliance.

The close collaboration continued to the point where the partners jointly built an econometric model of the market to predict future demand, cost and profit trends. As a result, they were able to understand very clearly how much each of them needed to invest and take out from the relationship in terms of financial value (but always driven by a strong focus on end-user satisfaction). As a major side benefit, in the words of one of the partners 'The two partner managers on both sides of the relationship are now acting as effective change managers in their own companies.'

Organizational and Operational Factors

The third element in the SCOPE model is what we call organizational and operational factors. In simple terms, this means close integration of the partners at the appropriate points necessary for the successful performance of the partnership. Organizationally, it means multi-level and multi-personnel links based on strong personal relationships between the opposite numbers or networks of individuals in the various partners. The key factors here are top-level commitment in all the partners to the joint success of the alliance – without this, in our view, the alliance is doomed to failure or at best to indifferent performance in its marketplace. Equally, in terms of cascading the partnership philosophy through the organization, there is a clear need for empowerment of the individuals involved in the partnership at all levels and education of many of these in the partnership philosophy and approach.

In terms of integration, one simple analogy is to think of the partners as the opposite sides of a ladder indicating the hierarchy on both sides, with the 'opposite numbers' indicated (see Figure 6.3). It is important to get clarity on which are the key relationships in each of the component parts of the alliance, and therefore this diagram is one of a series found within the alliance. It is important to note that on each side of the ladder there are individuals designated with a title such as 'partner manager' or 'partner liaison manager'. These individuals, who need to be of high calibre, have overall responsibility for co-ordinating and facilitating the performance of the alliance and will report at a higher level inside their own organizations. Interestingly, we see a strong correlation between highly successful alliances and the use of a competent and empowered individual in this role in each of the partners. In a number of examples of global alliances with which we have worked, these individuals are given more authority (to acquire resources, for example) than their status or grade within the organization would in fact justify. This flexible approach avoids a perceived mismatch between the level of authority in people who are co-ordinating one or other side of the partnership (which can be a major source of frustration in alliances). Figure 6.3 obviously illustrates the fit between two companies with traditional hierarchical structures. The same analogy holds true for organizations with matrix or network structures, since the key issue is to get 'multi-point linking' between the partners.

A more detailed analysis of the key interfaces in the alliance can be shown by another analytical approach. In Figure 6.4 this is shown as a

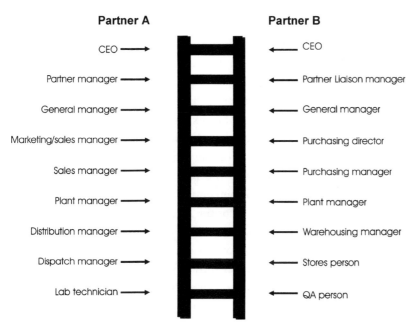

Figure 6.3 Partnership: multi-point linkage ladder.
Source: Ashridge International Partnership Study.

Partner A

	Partner manager	Purchasing	Marketing	Quality control	R&D	Planning	Operations	Senior management
Partner manager	■■	■■■	■			■■■		■■
Sales support	■	■■	■			■		■
Field sales			■					
Technical	■							■
Marketing			■■					
Distribution						■■■		
Operations		■		■■				
Senior management								■

■■■ Good   ■■ Average   ■ Poor/limited   Blank = Non-existent

Figure 6.4 Mapping the quality of partner relationships.

relationship map, which is a simple but powerful technique for identifying the key boxes in the matrix of relationships between (for the sake of simplicity) two partners, evaluating the current health of those two relationships and assessing their future ideal state. This is particularly important as a way of prioritizing key relationships as a strategic target. It is worth noting that the role of key figures on the matrix may shift in terms of importance over time. For example, this has happened during the exploration, extraction and commercialization phases of major projects in alliances in the oil and mining industry.

The method used to map the relationships is a joint discussion between the partners on their perceptions of the strength of individual relationships and agreed action for the future development of particular relationships. Inherent in the process of integration is the role of top management. Without exception, in our experience, alliances do not become high-performing partnerships unless there is full and consistent support from the top management of all the partners involved. Nevertheless, good top relationships are not a good enough basis for a successful partnership – we have encountered a number of examples where top management felt they had a real partnership with their counterparts in the other company. However, management further down the organization saw no partnership, because the linkages had simply not been made in enough places down through both organizations and across between the two.

As can be seen from the SCOPE model, one of the key outputs from partnerships that leads to significant competitive advantage is a high level of joint innovation. Clearly, the amount of learning that is transferred between the partners will have a major impact on the level of innovation achieved. This type of tight, interlinked network of relationships naturally plays a key part in transferring learning between the partners, which is notoriously difficult to do in global organizations (let alone in an alliance). Within a globalization strategy, the ability to learn from partners requires first the recognition that a great deal of organizational development and advantage can be gained from working with other organizations on clearly defined common objectives. One Japanese electronics company, for example, describes some major customers as *sensei* or 'teacher' customers in recognition of the learning that takes place in the relationship (Ashridge International Partnership Study).

Traditionally, many organizations would have rejected out of hand the idea of learning from competitors or suppliers, whereas today such an attitude would be severely damaging to an organization's ability to compete globally. The first mental attitude to abandon in global competition is the idea that 'we have all the answers and don't need anyone else to help us'. As one example, Britain's prime grocery retailer Tesco is managing its South Korean expansion through an alliance with Samsung – a long way from traditional British retailing.

The idea of cross-border learning brings with it the interesting issue of the 'borderless organization' (Bartlett and Ghoshal, 1999; General Electric, 1994) or the 'extended enterprise' (DaimlerChrysler, 1999). This is a key concept in building effective strategic alliances and using them to expand globally. Increasingly, alliances are not about extension of global territory, since in many markets the idea of place is being rendered irrelevant by such developments as the Internet, but about global collaborations using combinations of competences held by the partners in the alliance. In successful examples, therefore, the idea of the defined firm becomes irrelevant, because it is increasingly difficult to see where one partner ends and the other begins. Indeed, Peter Drucker is quoted as saying that the idea of the Fortune 500 group of companies will be irrelevant before very long, since companies will operate as networks of collaboration with many other organizations rather than as individual corporate entities (Harari, 1998).

Doz and Hamel (1998) in their work on successful learning in alliances, stress the importance of learning as a reinforcement of the original conditions of setting up the partnership and as a lead into continuous re-evaluation and constructive adjustments, which take place by agreement within the alliance (see Figure 6.5). In this process, we believe there is a very strong link between the quality of the initial set-up of the alliance – involving factors such as the degree of cultural difference, the level of openness between the respective partners and the clarity of the alliance's objectives and mission – and the eventual amount of learning that takes place. What is particularly critical appears to be the employment as a natural and continuous process of the classic 'learning organization' approach of rapid Plan–Do–Review cycles. In high-performing partnerships there often appears to be a tremendous amount of joint and more or less continuous development work done in the middle of the partner organizations. After the initial phase of working together, the two parties realized that they could work extremely productively and add to each other's knowledge and learning.

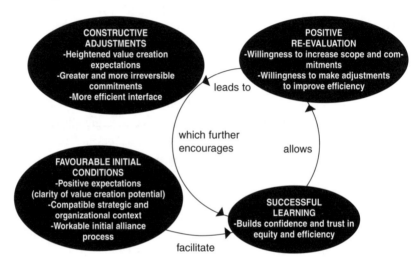

Figure 6.5 A typical successful learning cycle.
Source: Doz and Hamel (1998).

In one of these relationships in the textile industry, a managing director in Courtaulds said, 'We work so closely with our partner and on such a continuous basis that it is difficult to say who initiates projects – there is a totally continuous development cycle' (interview with author). Needless to say, output from this kind of relationship based on learning tends to result in significant amounts of competitive advantage for the partners.

One significant quote on the subject of learning comes from the director of strategic alliances at UPS, the global package-delivery company: 'The making of global alliances has opened us up to new ways, new cultures and new learning. We used to think the UPS way is the only way but this doesn't work in a global business. The outside world

---

CASE STUDY – Transferring learning in alliances

One example where a major global company has set up an effective process for transferring learning in hard-to-manage major alliances is a global oil company. On a major project anywhere in the world (because of the nature of the oil industry and the need to spread risk these invariably involve partners, including local governments and national governments), its project managers can ask for a 'peer assist conference'. At this event, other project managers who are experienced in running similar multinational projects and alliances in other regions of the world will come together in the form of a short workshop in order to share their key learning from their own projects and help apply this to the conference initiators' project.

---

of alliance partners has changed us for the better' (Conference Board, 1997). As an organization, UPS has expanded from being present in three countries in 1985 to over 200 countries currently. Alliances have been critical to this expansion. The typical approach has been to appoint a small private carrier as a local agency; if this agency relationship is satisfactory, over time UPS takes a minority share in a joint venture with the local company and eventually (again subject to success) moves to acquisition. The whole approach is designed to allow the companies to understand each other well and to manage the risk of choosing the wrong partner. Naturally, UPS also has significant alliances with major Internet search engines such as Lycos and Yahoo! to provide package tracing and tracking for its clients.

The final point to be made under this organizational and operational factor heading relates to internal partnerships. Very simply, organizations who are trying to build global alliances, (which in itself is a very difficult thing to do) should first look carefully at the levels of partnership across their own organization. The strong evidence is that, as a senior vice-president of a major global advertising agency said during our Partnership Study, 'If you are having trouble partnering externally, you can be very sure that the problems will lie in your own organization.'

Organizations that are primarily run on a divisional, functional, country or regional 'silo' basis often have poor levels of collaboration and learning across their internal boundaries. When they attempt cross-border external strategic alliances, these problems will quickly manifest themselves to the partner and often lead to frustration and lack of trust. One of the critical roles of the partner managers is to by-pass and neutralize this problem and drive internal partnership in their own organizations.

One example of very good awareness of this potential issue is the international furniture manufacturer and retailer IKEA (now operating with stores in 29 countries). It believes firmly that its partnership with its major suppliers is important in maintaining future growth. Product life cycles in its industry are shortening, which puts a premium on the responsiveness of the customer–supplier relationships and the ability of the alliances with suppliers to move quickly to protect competitor advantage. However, in the view of a senior director within the European operation, the critical issue is to ensure internal partnership between the country and regionally based purchasing offices around the world and the central product line management function in Scandinavia. Without this, it would find the development of external partnerships much more difficult. The company has therefore given considerable attention to improving the quality of its internal partnerships.

Performance Review Factors

Performance review factors are the fourth category in the SCOPE model and include two types of activity: communication/transferring information between the partners and mutual evaluation of performance. In high-performing alliances, increasingly effective use is being made of electronic ways of communication to download key information automatically to the partner. This was originally done through EDI (electronic data interchange), but this approach is now merely part of much more extensive Internet-based communication activities between partners in alliances. Communication issues are always crucial in partnerships, particularly in global alliances where the sheer problems of communication are magnified by geographical distance and the complexity of these alliances. In a Swiss speciality chemicals company working in strategic alliances with its major customers across the world, a top alliances manager said during our study: 'Even something as simple as getting our strategic customers to share and use our electronic mail system globally has been very important in building our relationships.'

Review systems, processes and metrics are often a weak area in alliances. As back-up to their review process, strong alliances have good information exchange and data links between the partners and open and frequent communication channels. Poor measurement of the performance of alliances can severely inhibit their conversion into highly successful partnerships. An Andersen Consulting (now Accenture) study suggested that only 51 per cent of alliances used formal performance measurement and that only 20 per cent of executives considered these measurements as reliable predictors of success (Andersen Consulting, 1999). In our experience the best partnerships agree early in the relationship on a tight, mutually acceptable and mutually reviewed process, which measures not only the financial performance but also the softer issues involved in the partnership. This 'Balanced Scorecard' approach (as pioneered originally by Kaplan and Norton, 1993) is effective in partnerships where the alliance partners jointly agrees the nature of the scorecard to include financial measures, customer-related measures, measures of effectiveness of the business processes and measures of the organizational learning in a partnership. This core scorecard of measures should reflect the key indicators and predictors of partnership success in its marketplace. The process of agreeing the scorecard therefore becomes an important phase in the establishment of the alliance, since the partners are committing to be measured themselves by the indicators that they agree for the scorecard. This does not prevent each of the partners from having separate measurements peculiar to their own businesses, but the key issue is that the partners will agree to be bound by performance on the scorecard measures. This process can itself drive a very thorough review of the partnership development process by clarifying the key strategic objectives and partners' views of the outputs that will constitute success in their own minds.

As mentioned above, it is important that due attention is paid to the critical softer factors as well as the hard. Examples of scorecard factors from actual alliances in our Partnership Study that have adopted this approach include growth in profit, number of tenders won, growth in economic value added, market share growth in developing markets, percentage of revenue from innovation between the partners, trends in levels of trust, trends in levels of constructive challenge within the alliance, measures of the degree of personal development of managers in the alliance and the amount of progress made in managing the cultural fit between the partners.

As Callahan and Mackenzie (1999) have pointed out, any metrics should be simple and clear, both for the alliance manager and joint decision making. They should not depend on complex data that is difficult to obtain, should be easy to evaluate and should above all be actionable by the partners. Equal in importance to the metrics is the review process that takes place between the partners. Needless to say, because they are attempting to build the alliance into a high-performing partnership, the process has to be entirely mutual and based on equality of voice in the relationship. It should agree how often review meetings need to be held, what preparation is required for them, who attends, how long they last, where they take place, and the action that follows a typical review meeting.

As an example of a highly effective process, in one alliance across South-East Asia between an Australian company and its partner, the two companies meet every quarter with both parties holding preparatory internal meetings to discuss the issues between the partners. After the joint meeting, the supplier and partner both have their own follow-up meetings to identify specific actions to be taken during the next three months and beyond to build the partnership further. There is a very significant focus in this relationship on future development rather than historical assessment. As an agreed part of the process, the partners also review at each meeting the effectiveness of key relationships between the people in the respective companies. This is an area that is very often dealt with cursorily in partnership review. It may require some difficult conversations and coaching or transfer of individuals who are not performing together because the chemistry is not right. In

this particular partnership, the assessment of the relationship is manda-
tory, not optional.

In another example relating to a pan-European alliance, the two
partner managers prepare for their major six-monthly review meetings
(which also involve their chief executives) by jointly visiting each of
the two organizations in all the key countries where the alliance operates, thereby avoiding any filtering process of the key issues raised by
people further down in the alliance.

In the particular case of joint ventures, great care needs to be given
to the metrics that are used to assess their health, since some parent
organizations have performance targets and required rates of return that
are unachievable in a start-up joint venture. This may lead to a short-
term killing off of the joint venture whereas, with more realistic long-
term targets, it might have been a considerable success. Naturally, the
length of time that the parents should allow for assessing whether the
joint venture will work or not will vary depending on its marketplace.

Equality Factors

The final category of factors in the SCOPE model is equality factors,
which include crucial behaviour areas such as patience and tolerance,
the process of building and keeping trust, and above all a belief in
valuing the partner as an equal, irrespective of the relative size, shareholding or power of the organization. A vice-president of the US
company Corning Glass, which has over 40 major equity participations
in strategic alliances around the world with a very high success rate in
joint venturing, is explicit on this point: 'Corning's emphasis on
equality has been a key factor in its success rate in alliances', and
similarly, as a great believer in equal shareholdings in ventures, 'management should not underestimate the symbolic value of a 50:50 venture to make co-operation work' (Weber and Barrett, 1999).

One example of the problems generated by failing to treat your
partner as an equal is the significant attempted alliance between
Johnson & Johnson and Amgem Inc, a Californian biotech company.
The alliance was designed to market the blood treatment

erythropoietin (EPO) and has been in place for some 15 years. The relationship has resulted in legal action and arbitration, and has a record of what one pharmaceutical analyst called 'continual disagreement throughout their history' (Weber and Barrett, 1999). The underlying problems have been described as very strong competition in the marketplace, amplified by high levels of mistrust between the partners, reputed arrogance on both sides and unforeseen market changes. Commentators regard one of the root causes of problems as the partners' failure to treat each other as equals, even in the set-up of the alliance. Instead of agreeing to share the gains evenly, Johnson & Johnson had a disproportionate amount of the $3.7 billion sales generated by the alliance. Johnson & Johnson's version of the product was sold to the chemotherapy market and other substantial therapeutic markets, while Amgem was left with the relatively smaller dialysis market.

Following this issue and the problems engendered by it, the companies could not see eye to eye on collaboration for follow-on products, which is a clear indicator of a partnership that is not succeeding. After arbitration in 1998, Amgem won the right to sell a chemically similar medicine that is in fact superior to the current formula in terms of being used weekly instead of daily. The arbitration process agreed that this new formulation was different enough to fall outside the licensing pact between Amgem and Johnson & Johnson. It is worth mentioning that both companies have separately managed to create very successful partnerships with other partners, which makes the point that each separate strategic relationship needs a great deal of individual care, crafting and attention before it can be turned into a true partnership.

THE PARTNERSHIP DEVELOPMENT PROCESS

So far in this chapter we have outlined our view of the critical factors (summarized in the SCOPE model) that seem to lead to success in building alliances. However, it is also worth outlining the partnership development process that successful alliancing companies have followed in building their partnerships. From our research, we believe that the key is to adopt a simple but potent common-sense process with a number of clearly defined stages. This is followed by both partners initially in parallel and in later stages together. The process can significantly help the establishment of successful alliances. The key stages of the partnership development process are outlined in Figure 6.6.

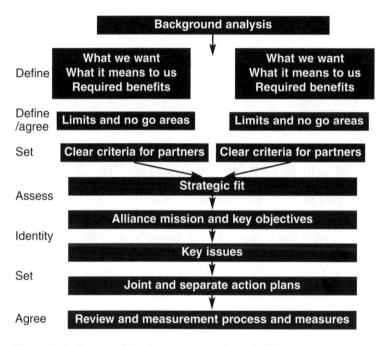

Figure 6.6 Process of developing partnerships and alliances.

Background Analysis

This should analyse the marketplace, customers' needs, competitive situation, trends in the business environment and other factors to the point where there appears to be a clear business (or value-creation) opportunity that needs to be accessed by some form of alliance.

Define What You Want from the Alliance, What it Means to You (Where it Fits into Your Overall Strategy) and What Benefits it Will Produce for Your Organization

This sounds simple, but the divisions in one major European service company currently cannot answer these questions because their parent company has not clarified the global core strategy. Contrast this with the response of the CEO of a major company in an interview with the author. To paraphrase his words: 'Our market is mature and highly competitive. In five years' time I want at least one major alliance in each of six additional chosen target business areas. These alliances will have an ROI significantly above our current core business and in total will account for at least 30 per cent of our profit. Alliances are therefore crucial to our future growth.'

Clarify the Limits and No Go Areas in the Alliance

Actual examples of these that we have encountered are confidential information that will not be transferred to the partner, ownership of intellectual property rights, geographical limits, barring direct access by the partner to the customer database (in the case of a big European mail order company) and areas linked to control or board representation. For example, for its joint ventures in emergent markets such as India, Ford prefers majority shareholding but insists on operating control.

Develop Clear Criteria for the Kinds of Partners with which You Wish to Partner

For example, UPS has clear criteria for what it calls 'strategic partners'. These are superb reputation, broad scope of services, compatible style/ culture and core strengths similar to (but not the same as) UPS.

Hewlett-Packard, which has more than 300 major alliances worldwide, is actively seeking partners in its e-services business. Its approach to attracting them includes outlining on its website the benefits of partnering with HP in this area ('Sharing risk, sharing knowledge, technical access and connections'). It also describes in short vignettes some of the key alliances in which it is involved (for example with Cisco Systems), as a way of clarifying their requirements from prospective partners.

At this point, the partners should separately have clarified their thinking about the alliances and, crucially, shared these views with each other (unless one partner is assessing an alliance candidate without having made contact). They can now go to the next step.

Assess the Strategic Fit Between Them

Here the partners are looking at the compatibility of their rationale for the alliance, highlighting any major conflicts between their views and checking whether they can really work together closely to produce added value from the relationship. At this point it is worth discussing in more detail three key elements of fit:

- attitudes to power and equality;
- cultural differences;
- willingness to build trust.

As mentioned earlier, the issue of exercise of power can be dramatically inhibiting to the development of partnerships. Possibly the most damaging aspect is any attempt to dominate the relationship. As a vice-president of a major US telecommunications company said, 'If people come to feel they are junior partners at the table it can be absolutely devastating to the sense of partnership, mutual commitment and mutual risk taking.' Indeed, even the use of terms such as 'junior' or 'senior' or 'lead' partner in conversation with a partner or prospective partner can be damaging.

In some industries where, historically, the prevailing management styles have been regarded as fairly macho (perhaps automotive, oil and defence), this change in behaviour may be difficult for many managers, even at senior level. We have been involved in one example in the defence industry where there has been an attempt for several years to form a strong partnership between two successful global players. The strategic rationale is excellent for the two companies (who are competitors) to work together and should lead to major new business and significant competitive advantage for both. However, one organization is naturally much more collaborative than the other, which has a much more autocratic and 'command-and-control' culture. The behaviour towards the 'softer' partner that this hard culture has generated has been a major blockage to substantial development of the partnership during its attempted life. Perhaps more seriously, the partners did not discuss these issues until relatively recently (after several years of attempted collaboration). To their credit, they have now initiated the painful conversations necessary to deal with the issue and move forward in commercial terms.

A key part of the philosophical approach to partnership should be a genuine interest in understanding the partner and their needs and concerns, as indicated in the partnership development process. Where the two partners have compatible cultures (this does mean compatible rather than the same), the personnel in the two organizations seem to understand each other and the ways in which their companies can operate together more quickly. This in turn leads to faster development of openness and mutual trust between the key individuals in the relationships. The reason for stressing that a culture should not be the same is that both partners should bring something different to the party. There should therefore be enough difference between them to create real synergy from the relationship. Several companies have found that too close a fit between the partners can create a lack of urgency in innovative approaches to the future and eventually to some complacency in the relationship.

Sharing of some common values can give strong continuity to a partnership by supporting the development of personal relationships. Examples could include commitment to a global approach, quality and customer service, integrity in commercial dealings and valuing the development of people in organizations. Naturally, in global strategic alliances, the alliance partners not only have to face different organizational cultures but will also have to deal with different national and sometimes regional cultures.

CASE STUDY – Overcoming cultural differences

In one long-standing (over 15-year) alliance between a Japanese pharmaceuticals distributor and an American pharmaceuticals manufacturer, the strategic rationale for the alliance was very strong, with one partner providing access to distribution channels in a new market for the other partner who brought excellent products to the relationship. However, the initial years of the partnership were very difficult because of major cultural differences, primarily caused by the unwillingness of the US partner to adapt to or even understand the difference in business approaches adopted by the Japanese partner. After a great deal of patience on the part of the Japanese company, it eventually had to request that the US parent provide a new management team for the partnership. This was done and a whole series of new actions and mechanisms were put into place, with a strong emphasis on mutual understanding of the two businesses and the ways in which they preferred to operate. The actions included long-term secondments of personnel between the two companies, rotating the location for the reviews of the alliance performance and other genuine attempts to bring the two partners closer. Following this watershed, the performance of the alliance improved significantly and has remained strong in the more than 10 years since. It seems obvious that the alliance could have made a much faster and more productive start if the simple question of cultural difference had been prioritized at the outset.

How is it possible to identify the issues within the partners' cultures? One approach that appears to help is for the partners first to describe their own perception of cultures separately, then to share this with their partners and map the cultural values on a common scale. An example is shown in Figure 6.7, where the framework used is based on a common technique employed in psychometric testing, known colloquially as the 'spider diagram' (Bronder and Pritzl, 1992)

The real example in Figure 6.7 shows an attempted joint venture between a major long-established financial services company and a much younger but nevertheless substantial dotcom organization. The purpose of this joint venture is to open up new cross-border market access to both partners using their genuinely complementary skills.

The map scores each partner against a series of cultural orientations that they have agreed will be important to the success of the joint venture

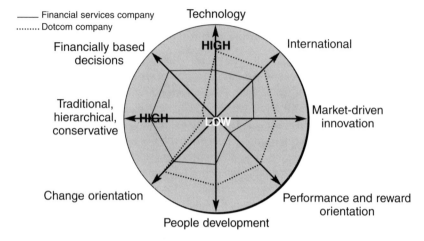

Figure 6.7 Cultural profile.

in international markets. A high rating means the partner gives high importance (in reality not just intention) to this variable in its own culture.

As can be seen, the two profiles show some areas of correlation (international and technology), but marked differences in other cultural variables (traditional attitudes, performance and reward, the importance of finance in decision making). They will see the world through different mindsets and this could lead to major problems in the alliance. Given the amount of divergence, they will need to pay urgent attention early on to managing these cultural differences. The main key to this is to understand and value the diversity that each provides to the joint culture.

A key part of the management of the softer issues in alliances needs to come from the initial building of the vision or common purpose for the alliance, the values or 'ground rules' under which it operates, and the mechanisms for implementing these in a variety of locations in the global alliance. There seems to be almost universal agreement that the building and sustaining of trust are central to success in alliances, as the following quotes during interviews with the author may indicate:

- 'You can't build anything if there is no trust between the partners' (senior partnership manager at Electrolux).
- 'Trust is the basis of everything' (DHL senior manager).

- 'If one partner is considered too strong, trust can't be built' (European MD at Unilever).

This, however, begs the important question of how partners build trust in their alliances. The keys are perhaps contained much more in behaviour than in harder considerations such as systems, percentage ownership in joint ventures, and the legal agreements reached by the parties forming the alliance. Bechtel, a US construction company that is involved in complex construction projects all over the world, often in alliance with local governments and several other construction companies, believes strongly that 'an alliance is a collaborative process and not a transaction. We need to approach the negotiations and the entire alliance from the standpoint of how do we grow this business together. We must persuade not command.'

Similarly, when British Airways' director of alliances was referring to the One World alliance with a number of major airlines, which operates in 138 countries and involves flights to over 600 destinations, he commented, 'Consensus rules. It does not build a bureaucracy and we deliberately do not build a strong centre. The fact that we are forced to move in a different way than a command and control environment is actually of benefit' (Lewis, 1999). A critical element in this alliance, in his view, is the ability to swap best practice between the partners across the world. This requires a more subtle and flexible approach than the traditional operating methods of the partners.

Table 6.1 Partnership and alliances

Building trust:
Shared sensitive information
Shared understanding of roles/accountabilities
Clear mutual review process
Share concerns (real and perceived)
Open access to partners
Meet promises
Avoid dominant behaviour
Welcome constructive challenge
Open to learning from partner
Admit mistakes

The key elements of building trust are shown in Table 6.1, which underlines a number of key ways of cementing the relationship. It is worth highlighting the view of some companies that an important way to build trust early in the alliance is to share key information, particularly on the strategic objectives of the partners. Since the alliance is presumably intended to be a long-term strategic development, this should be regarded as an essential part of the process of alliance set-up. A senior executive in Levi-Strauss's European operation said, 'A critical way to build trust quickly is through the carefully controlled sharing of sensitive information and we don't mind going first because that is part of our culture' (Ashridge Partnership Study). The clarification of relative roles and accountabilities in the partnership is critical, particularly to avoid misunderstandings and duplication of key input areas. The critical point is that any process should be genuinely mutual between the partners, irrespective of the percentage ownership in a joint venture, for example.

Other factors in building trust include a whole cluster of related issues such as the following:

- Sharing concerns (whether real or perceived), since they may be very strongly held and involve significant emotion that could damage the partnership.
- Avoiding the command-and-control type of dominant behaviour.
- Being open to constructive challenge of the ideas being put forward by the partner.

A senior executive at Corning Glass said, when referring to the company's approach to building partnership and joint ventures, that it always tries to say to its partners, 'If you are unhappy, let's sit down and talk about it – don't just walk away' (Cauley De La Sierra, 1995). It is worth noting that Corning has a remarkable record of creating successful joint ventures since its initial alliances in the late 1930s with companies like Owens–Illinois, which gave it entry into the glass fibre industry. One of its key criteria for the health of the partnership is whether the partners feel they can raise issues comfortably with each other. The final comment in Table 6.1 is the conclusion reached by many companies that in order to build trust, you have to be prepared to give something up.

CASE STUDY – Giving something up to build trust

One remarkable example of this was in a long-standing alliance between two global manufacturing companies in nine European countries. The strategic rationale for the alliance was always very strong and over the more than 10 years of its existence it has outperformed competitors in the specific marketplace. A critical moment early in the development of the alliance related to building trust. In the alliance agreement, there was provision for adjustment of cost and prices due to changes in certain key exchange rates. At one point in the early days of the alliance the exchange rates moved strongly in favour of one of the partners, who therefore, as specified within the terms of the alliance, could have received significant windfall profits. Instead, the partner refused to take the short-term currency gains, because it saw the alliance as strategic and designed to build strong, normal profit growth for both partners. It did not therefore want to benefit in this way from an abnormal event early in the life of the alliance. This attitude created a very strong surge in the levels of trust built within the alliance, and significantly accelerated development of the relationship into a high-performing partnership.

Can alliances be set up in ways that minimize issues of governance and improve the chances of resolving conflict? The evidence from a very large number of existing alliances of all sorts, including joint ventures, R&D collaborations, marketing agreements, licensing agreements and mergers and acquisitions, is that it is not possible to draw a strong correlation between one particular type of organization structure or governance set-up in alliances and the success of the alliance. In essence, the reason seems very simple, namely that the people involved in the alliance have to make it work and therefore the personal chemistry in co-operation between individuals at various locations and at various levels is the crucial element. What does appear to be very clear, however (as mentioned by Reuer and Zollo, 2000), is that where the partners have prior significant experience of working together, and therefore understand each other's routines for managing collaborative processes, issues of governance are less likely to arise. Equally, with this level of knowledge of each other, any adjustments to the type of governance being used or the alliance structure are easier to manage.

One of the critical ways to reduce the likelihood of conflict in alliances is through prior negotiation at the time of forming the alliance of a pre-nuptial agreement or an exit strategy for the partners. This sounds counter-intuitive, since one is forming a long-term relationship. One interesting case is the Autolatina joint venture between Volkswagen and Ford in Latin America, where the merged company that was 50:50 owned by the two partners operated successfully from 1989 to 1995. At its height it produced 700 000 vehicles a year with a considerable record of prof-itability. With hindsight, however, the two companies had not given sufficient weight to alternative scenarios for the future of the major mar-kets in Brazil and Argentina, and to predicting the life span of the joint venture. When these markets deregulated by lowering the tariff barriers considerably, much of the strategic rationale for the alliance was by-passed, since the market was now open to much more competition from more advanced imported models. In this situation, and in the absence of a detailed pre-nuptial agreement for separation, the parties found the process of negotiating the separation and redistribution of assets to be time con-suming and arduous before the alliance's conclusion in 1996.

A degree of scenario planning at the point of formation may well change the way in which the alliance is set up, with longer-term benefit to the parties involved. This could include a clear date for termination (or expansion) of the alliance, subject to a later review.

Referring back to Figure 6.6, after assessing the level of strategic fit, the partners need to decide whether to take the alliance further. This partnership development process can be applied both to prospec-tive alliances and those that have already been formed. Indeed, we have worked with a number of alliances that applied the process because the attempted partnership seemed to have problems between one and three years into its life span. The analytical process then led to the conclusion that the alliance would never be high performing and should either dissolve or be treated as a straightforward transaction.

Assuming the fit is good, the next stages are:

- *Set the alliance mission and key objectives.* This process is done jointly and should lay out clearly what the alliance is intended to become and by when. Key objectives will be quantified (sales, profit, market share, or Economic Value Added, for example) and dated. Naturally, this stage has a strong link to measuring the performance of the alliance.
- *Identifying the key issues* that need to be managed by the partners to achieve the alliance's mission and key objectives.
- *Set joint and separate action plans* for dealing with the individual key issues.
- *Agree the review and measurement process and procedures*, as stated earlier in the chapter. This last stage is critical to high-performing partnerships, but is often omitted or done superficially. When done properly with joint agreement of a tight set of critical review procedures and methods, it acts as a tangible joint commitment to the future of the alliance.

This process of partnerships appears obvious. In practice, however, it is often not rigorously applied. Seduced by the idea of collaboration, companies leap into trying to implement alliances before they are properly formed, which increases the risk of failure and loss of the investment involved. The evidence indicates that carrying out a basic partnership development process similar to that described above reduces these risks significantly. This does not need to be a lengthy operation, but instead should pose and answer the key questions quickly.

HOW DO PARTNERS ESTABLISH WHETHER THEY HAVE A HIGH-PERFORMING ALLIANCE?

From our Partnership Study, we have developed a simple set of acid-test questions, shown in Figure 6.8. Roughly anything over ten ticks is a strong partnership, between six and nine ticks has the potential to be a strong relationship and five or below indicates either a newly forming relationship or one that is unlikely (without a major change in approach) to reach partnership. In practice, each alliance should create its own tailor-made set of acid-test questions as a health check.

✔ or ✗ acid test of partnership:

☐ Does it feel like joint ownership?

☐ Do you treat each other as equals (even if you're not)?

☐ Do you keep trying to extend the partnership's scope in the future?

☐ Can it survive a major restructuring by either partner?

☐ Do you never/rarely look at the contract?

☐ What happens when a major mistake is made? Do you solve the problem together (✔) or just apportion the blame (✗)?

☐ How do you behave when times are bad: support (✔) or retrench (✗)?

☐ Do you regularly and jointly evaluate its performance and set future plans?

☐ Are you willing to expose your weaknesses to each other?

☐ Do you evaluate the relationship itself?

☐ Are your people fighting to work in this partnership?

☐ Do your competitors find it impossible to break in?

☐ Is it producing really innovative approaches? Are you outside you comfort zones?

☐ Would you do this again if you were starting now?

☐ Is it great fun?

Figure 6.8   Acid-test questions.
Source: Ashridge International Partnership Study.

In summary, we believe that strategic alliances are a successful major weapon in the globalization strategies of a large number of organisations and this trend shows every sign of continuing to develop. These relationships are not easy to build into high-performing partnerships in global businesses. This is particularly because of the significant issues of managing cultural differences, managing communications, and agreeing tough but effective review processes. However, the evidence is that the great majority of the factors that create successful high-performing partnerships are basic common sense, with a particular emphasis on 'front-end loading' the set-up and initial phases of the development of the partnership. It is particularly important to clarify objectives, respective roles and contributions in the early stages to avoid later high levels of frustration, delay, non-performance and actual loss of competitive advantage, which can be very expensive in an attempted global relationship.

In the simplest terms, successful partnerships are built and sustained by careful management of both the hard and soft factors together. It is worth recalling, however, the comment of a former chief executive (now president) of PepsiCo, that 'the soft stuff is always harder to do than the hard stuff. Human interactions are a lot tougher to manage than numbers and P and Ls. So the trick is to operationalize it' (*Fortune*, 1995) and particularly to measure it. In Figure 6.9 the importance of managing both hard and soft factors in alliances is summarized under the heading 'partnership thinking' (Feurer *et al.*, 1995). As can be seen, this includes not only strategic approaches but also, crucially, attitudes towards the partners and the alliance, notably flexibility and openness to learning. We believe that building high-performing innovative partnerships, which generate real competitive advantage for the partners, can only take place if the partners think and behave predominantly with a 'whole system' approach rather than a 'separate unit' state of mind.

One successful and experienced global alliance manager recently summarized his views on building true partnerships as, 'Know exactly what

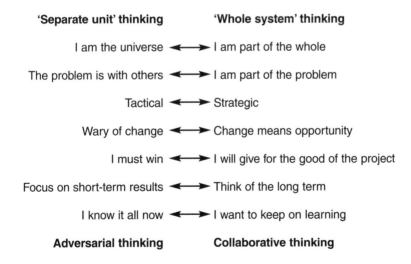

'Separate unit' thinking   **'Whole system' thinking**

I am the universe ⟵⟶ I am part of the whole

The problem is with others ⟵⟶ I am part of the problem

Tactical ⟵⟶ Strategic

Wary of change ⟵⟶ Change means opportunity

I must win ⟵⟶ I will give for the good of the project

Focus on short-term results ⟵⟶ Think of the long term

I know it all now ⟵⟶ I want to keep on learning

Adversarial thinking   **Collaborative thinking**

Figure 6.9 Partnership thinking.
Adapted from Feurer *et al.* (1995) by permission of MCB University Press.

you want and then really listen to and really talk to each other. Be prepared to unlearn and let go of your past. That's all – the rest will follow.'

References

Andersen Consulting (1999) *Dispelling the Myths of Alliances: The new successful alliance management*, Anderson Consulting, London.

Bartlett, C. and Ghoshal, S. (1999) *Managing Across Borders: The transnational solution*, Random House, London.

Bronder, C. and Pritzl, R. (1992) 'Developing stategic alliances', *European Management Journal*, 10(4, Dec.), 412–21.

Callahan, J. and Mackenzie, S. (1999) 'Metrics for strategic alliance control', *R&D Management*, 29(4), 365–78.

Cauley de la Sierra, M. (1995) *Managing Global Alliances*, Addison Wesley, Reading, MA.

Conference Board (1997) *Proceedings of Strategic Alliances Conference*, Conference Board, London.

DaimlerChrysler (1999) *Annual Report*.

Doz, Y. and Hamel, G. (1998) *Alliance Advantage: The art of creating value through partnering*, Harvard Business School Press, Boston, MA.

Feurer, R., Chaharbagi, K. and Wargin, J. (1995) 'Analysis of strategy formulation and implementation at Hewlett-Packard', *Management Decision*, 33(10), 4–16.

Fortune (1995) 'How tomorrow's best leaders are learning their stuff', *Fortune*, November 27, 64–72.

General Electric (1994) *Annual Report*.

Harari, O. (1998) 'Transform your organization with a web of relationships', *Management Review*, January, 134–142.

Kaplan, R.S. and Norton, D.P. (1993) 'Putting the balanced scorecard to work', *Harvard Business Review*, Sept.–Oct.

Lewis, J. (1999) 'The science of alliance', *Personnel Today*, 24 June, 25–6.

Merrill Lynch (1999) *The Global Automotive Industry: Fighting the cycle*, December.

Mitchell, A. (1998) 'Marriage à la mode', *Marketing Business*, March, 40–45.

Prahalad, C.K. and Hamel, G. (1990) 'The core competences of the corporation', *Harvard Business Review*, May/June, 79–91.

Pudney, R. (1996) 'Dancing partners', *Directions – The Ashridge Journal*, March, 4–9.

Pudney, R. (1998) 'Working partners', *Directions – The Ashridge Journal*, November, 10–15.

Pudney, R. (2000) 'Creating competetive advantage from partnerships and alliances', *White Space Review – The Post Office*, August, 18–21.

Reuer, J. and Zollo, M (2000) 'Managing governance adaptations in strategic alliances', *European Management Journal*, 18(2, April), 164–72.

Stallkamp, T. (1993) 'Chrysler's man of many parts cuts costs,' *Wall Street Journal*, 14 May, p. 7.

Weber, J. and Barrett, A. (1999) 'Volatile combos', *Business Week*, October 25, 72–6.

GLOBAL MARKETING

H. David Hennessey

CHAPTER 7

GLOBAL MARKETING

*I*n this chapter, which draws on work in Jeannet and Hennessey (2001), we will examine the complex opportunities a company faces when it markets products or services globally. This begins with the examination of global opportunities. How do you evaluate all the opportunities in every country in the world? Then, what global strategies are appropriate? Finally, how is the global marketing strategy implemented through the marketing mix?

Historically most companies have entered the markets of other countries because a potential customer from another country asks to buy their product, or a current domestic customer expands in another country and asks for supplies. As firms become more sophisticated they learn about other potential benefits of global expansion, such as exploiting different economic growth rates, diversifying geographic position, or pursuing the market potential in other markets. For example, as Anheuser-Busch's share of the US beer market reached over 40 per cent, it entered global beer markets, which offered significant potential growth. It has since launched several brands in Japan and China. While consumption per capita is still low in China, the total volume of beer consumed is higher than in Germany and is expected to exceed the size of the US market in a few years.

The world marketplace is large and complex. A global company needs systematically to evaluate the entire world market on a regular basis to be sure that company assets are directed towards the countries with the best opportunities. The basis for an evaluation of countries should be a comparative analysis of different countries. Certain ones may be unsuitable because of their unstable political situation, and others may have little potential because their population is small or the per capita income is low. The screening process gives the firm information about market size, competition, trade regulations and distribution systems that will form the basis for the development of a market strategy. As international firms evaluate different consumer, business and government market opportunities, they must be aware of the nature of the differences between countries.

After selecting which markets to participate in, a firm is faced with the decision of developing a marketing strategy. The strategy may be different for every market a firm enters or there may be possibilities of developing strategies that leverage the company's assets and knowledge in multiple geographies to better serve its customers. In some business-to-business (B2B) markets, customers may require the same product and pricing in different countries. In some consumer markets, it may be more cost effective to serve similar market segments with the same positioning and advertising. For example, Citibank serves the same target market in much of Asia, with a premium positioning targeted towards the aspiring professional. While the advertisements are tailored to the local culture, they all use similar creative thinking and positioning, therefore Citibank has lower marketing and advertising costs for each country.

Finally, after selecting a marketing strategy, it must be communicated to the customer in terms of the product offering, the channels of distribution, pricing and the promotional message. The chapter will explain the unique aspects of the use of these tools in a global marketing context.

GLOBAL OPPORTUNITY ANALYSIS

Assessment of market opportunities is an important aspect of global marketing. The process of evaluating worldwide opportunities is complicated for a number of reasons. First, there are over 200 countries and territories in the world; second, given the number of countries and resource limitations, the initial screening process is usually limited to the analysis of published data. Third, many possible markets are small, with little data available about specific consumer, business or government needs.

Screening Process

The assessment of global marketing opportunities usually begins with a screening process that involves gathering relevant information on each potential country and filtering out the less desirable countries. The overwhelming number of market opportunities makes it necessary to break the process down into a series of steps. Although a firm does not want to miss a potential opportunity, it cannot conduct extensive market research studies in every country of the world: the *World Bank Atlas* includes 210 countries and territories.

The screening process is used to identify good prospects. Two common errors of country screening are ignoring countries that offer good potential for the company's products; and spending too much time investigating countries that are poor prospects. Thus, the screening process allows an international company to focus efforts quickly on the most promising market opportunities by using published secondary sources available in most business libraries and on-line.

Screening with macroeconomic variables

The first stage of the selection process uses macroeconomic variables to discriminate between countries that represent basic opportunities and countries that represent limited opportunity or excessive risk. Macroeconomic variables describe the total market in terms of economic, social, geographic and political information. Often macroeconomic statistics indicate that the country is too small, as described by the gross national (or domestic) product. Possibly the gross national product seems large enough, but the personal disposable income per household may be too low. Political instability can also be used to remove a country from the set of possible opportunities.

Screening for market size

In the second stage of the selection process, variables are used that indicate the potential market size and acceptance rate of the product or similar products. Often proxy variables are used in this screening process. A proxy variable is a similar or related product that indicates a demand for your product. For example, if you are attempting to measure the potential market size and receptivity for a palm-held communicator, possible proxy variables may be the number of telephone lines per person, personal computers per person, or cellular telephone usage per person. The number of telephone lines and cellular phones indicates communication needs, and the number of personal computers indicates a propensity to use advanced technologies. For example, the number of phone lines per 1000 people is 644 in the US, 575 in France, 556 in Finland and 304 in Hungary. Personal computers per 1000 people are 407 in the US, 175 in France, 310 in Finland and 49 in Hungary. This indicates that Finland may be more receptive to the personal communicator technology than France (*World Bank Atlas*, 2000: 50–51). The year-to-year growth rates and the total sales of similar or proxy products are good predictors of market size and growth. Other factors in the second stage of the selection process can also be used to screen out countries, such as the stage of economic development, taxes, and duty requirements. If you do not plan to manufacture locally, a high import duty may eliminate a country from consideration in the second stage of the screening process.

Screening with microeconomic variables

The third stage of the screening process focuses on micro-level considerations such as competitors, ease of entry, cost of entry and profit potential. Micro-level factors influence the success or failure of a specific product in a specific market. The number of households with televisions indicates the potential market size for televisions if every household purchased a new television. Depending on the life of the average television in use, one can estimate the annual demand. Although the actual consumption statistics may not be available for a certain product category, often the consumption of similar or substitute products is used as proxy variables. For example, in determining the market size for surgical sutures, marketers may use the number of hospital beds or doctors as a proxy variable.

At this stage of the process, marketers may be considering only a small number of countries, so it is feasible to get more detailed, up-to-date information from your home country's department of commerce or department of state about other companies currently operating in these potential countries. Your embassy in the chosen countries may have a commercial attaché who can provide information and contacts for many markets. Also, customs brokers and freight forwarders may possess knowledge that can help at this stage of the process.

Screening for profitability

At this stage of the screening process, the focus switches from total market size to profitability. For example, based on the current and potential competitors, how much would you need to invest to gain a particular market share? Given the prices currently charged in the market, what margin can your company expect? Given the cost of entry and the expected sales, what is the expected profit? This stage of the analysis focuses on the quantitative profit expected, but many subjective judgements are made to arrive at the expected profit. For example, an Israeli manufacturer of pipe insulation found that the market price in the UK was $10 per kilo versus $6 per kilo in the US, whereas its manufacturing cost was $5 per kilo. This indicated a more favourable profit potential in the UK if the company could gain access to the market.

This fourth stage of the screening process is an evaluation and rank ordering of the potential target countries, based on corporate resources, objectives and strategies. For example, although South Africa may have the same expected potential as Venezuela, Venezuela may be given a higher priority because successful entry there can later be followed by entry into Colombia and Bolivia.

Sources of information for screening market opportunities

In almost every country, embassies employ commercial attachés whose main function is to assist home companies entering that foreign marketplace. Embassies of the foreign country being investigated may also be able to help marketers in their analysis. For example, a US company investigating the competition for farm implements in Spain can call or write to the Spanish embassy in Washington, DC, and secure a list of manufacturers of farm implements in Spain. In developing countries U.S. AID (United States Agency for International Development) is a very good source of information.

The World Wide Web has opened up a number of sources of global market information, such as the following:

Stat-USA	http://www.stat-usa.gov
UK Department of Trade and Industry	http://www.dti.gov.uk
National Trade Data Bank	http://iserve.wtca.org/ intro_ntdb.html
Global business opportunities	http://www.usaid.gov/ procurement_bus_opp/
Is-Trade	http://www.i-trade.com
Index of free services	http://www.123link.com/ 1stglobal/
Market your company	http://www .globalbusinessinternet.com/
International Trade Administration	http://www.ita.doc.gov
Worldwide market reports and business information search	http://www.market-reports.co.uk

Information directories   http://ciber.bus.msu.edu/busres/
                             Static/Other-Indexes-
                             International.htm
                             http://gats-info.eu.int
                             http://www.sice.oas.org
                             http://www.pangaea.net

Other sources of competitive information vary widely, depending on the size of the country and the product. Many of the larger countries have chambers of commerce or other in-country organizations that may be able to assist potential investors. For example, if you were investigating the Japanese market for electronic measuring devices, the following groups could assist you in determining the competitive structure of the market in Japan:

- US Chamber of Commerce in Japan
- Japan External Trade Organization (JETRO)
- American Electronics Association in Japan
- Japan Electronic Industry Development Association
- Electronic Industries Association of Japan
- Japan Electronic Measuring Instrument Manufacturers Association

Country visits

The final and usually most expensive way to assess the market is to go to the country of interest and interview potential customers and competitors to determine the size and strength of the competition. As a trip to a potential market is always required before a final decision is made, it should not be overlooked as an important part of the screening process. If you are well prepared in advance, two to three days in a country talking to distributors, large buyers and trade officials can be extremely valuable in assessing the competitiveness of the market and the potential profitability.

Market Groupings

The nature of the world marketplace has changed as a result of the development of major regional market groups. The economic integration of a number of countries offers great opportunities to companies. Many national markets, such as those in Europe, that are small individually become significant when combined with other countries. By locating production facilities in one country of a market group, the international company has access to the other countries with little or no trade restrictions. The market groups also increase competition. Local producers who for years completely dominated their national markets thanks to tariff protection now face competition from many other member countries.

The development of these market groups can also have negative effects on international companies. If a company is unable or unwilling to build a manufacturing plant in a certain market group, it may be unprofitable to export to that market. There are often more regulations between market groups, making it more complicated and expensive to move goods from one group to another. Also, the market group does not necessarily reduce the complexity of consumer and cultural differences. For example, while Germany and Spain are both in the EU, the marketing programmes, products and strategies for success in each market may differ.

The success of market groups formed after the Second World War, particularly the EU, indicates that such groups will continue to grow. The potential entry of some eastern European countries into the EU, as well as the expansion of NAFTA to include other Central or South American countries, supports the growth of market groups and the growing interdependence of trading partners. International companies need to monitor the development of new groups and any changes in the structure of current groups, because changes within market groups will result in changes in market size and competition.

The largest business markets for goods are in countries that have a sophisticated industrial infrastructure, such as the US, Canada, Japan, Germany, France and England. These countries have a large industrial base, a strong stable financial base and a good transportation network. These countries are also large importers and exporters of goods and services. Developing countries offer a different type of market opportunity. They have specific economic needs that must be met with limited financial resources. In these situations, the government is likely to get involved in the purchase process, offering concessions to obtain the correct product or agreement. In many cases, the government will be the decision maker.

GLOBAL MARKETING STRATEGIES

To many, discussion of global marketing strategies often suggests that the same marketing strategy should be duplicated around the world. This is a very limited view of global marketing strategies, which are based on studies of marketing decisions by executives working across geographical markets. These show that certain elements of the marketing programme, like brand name, product characteristics and intermediary roles, tend to be highly standardized across different countries, while media allocation and pricing are less standardized across countries (Sorenson and Wiechmann, 1975). A global marketing strategy represents the application of a common set of strategic marketing principles across most world markets. It may include, but does not require, a standard product and/or standard advertising. A company that pursues a global marketing strategy tends to look at the global market in its entirety and not on a country-by-country basis.

Standardization deals with the amount of similarity that companies want to achieve across many countries with respect to the marketing strategy and marketing mix elements. Globalization deals with the integration of many country strategies and the subordination of these country strategies to one global framework. As a result, it is possible for a company to have a globalized approach to its marketing strategy but to leave many of the details of the marketing plan to the local subsidiaries. Few companies want to globalize all the marketing elements, but would rather adapt to local needs and local competitive threats. The specific type of global logic will tend to determine the choice of an appropriate global strategy.

Customer-based global logics include global customers with the same needs in all markets, global information that is available and used by most customers, and global purchasing logics where customers have centralized purchasing for their global needs. For example, DSM, a Dutch chemical company that makes elastomers used for automobile door seals, found that in order to serve the research and manufacturing functions of global car manufacturers, it needed to be located in the US, Europe, Asia and Latin America. In B2B markets, it is important for suppliers to know that the globalization plans of their customers especially when they include centralized purchasing for their world-wide needs. These customer-based logics tend to influence marketing variables such as product, branding and communications.

Industry-based global logics include global competitors, global industry or global size. These industry-based logics tend to affect the integration of manufacturing, logistics, distribution, research and de-velopment. For example, pharmaceutical companies have merged dur-ing the 1990s based on a global size logic, which is based on the premise that a larger merged pharmaceutical company with more pro-jects in the pipeline will be more likely to have success in new products than a smaller company.

Global customer and industry logics can be used to classify mar-keting strategies. In a business where both customer and industry logics are low, companies tend to operate multidomestic strategies.

Multidomestic Strategies

A multidomestic strategy is normally developed and implemented on a local geographical level, with little thought given to integration across different geographic business units. As a result, the organizational struc-ture is geographic and the profit and loss responsibilities are on a local subsidiary basis. When using a multidomestic strategy, some key deci-sions such as which products, technology and geographies the company will support are decided centrally, but the development and implemen-tation of the marketing plan are done locally.

A large number of firms use multidomestic marketing strategies. For example, Nestlé, one of the world's largest food companies, uses a multidomestic approach to marketing strategies. With operating companies including Rowntree, Carnation and Alcon Labs, it has practised a decentralized approach to management. Local managers, who are thought to be much more in touch with local market needs, are given the freedom to develop locally tailored marketing programmes. In the food business, where considerable differences exist between countries in terms of cultures and consumer habits or competition and market structures, decentralization was judged to be the best approach. Like many other companies using a multidomestic marketing approach, Nestlé has begun to centralize some aspects of its marketing in order to leverage some of its many experiences around the globe.

Procter and Gamble, a US-based consumer products company, has used a multidomestic marketing approach for years, replicating in each country all the home office functions at the headquarters in Cincinnati. In the 1980s P&G began to centralize its technical functions. In the late 1990s it started to centralize many of the marketing functions under the leadership of Dirk Jager, hoping to speed up new product development, increase sales growth and reduce overall marketing expenses. This change was not well received by many of the local operating companies, however, and the transition process was slowed down. Dirk Jager resigned in mid-2000 when P&G results continued to be flat.

Regional Strategies

Regional strategies focusing on similar strategies for North America, Europe, Asia or Latin America represent a mid-point between multidomestic strategies and global strategies. The regional strategies are not global because the co-ordination is only for a single region, such as Europe or Asia. On the other hand, regional strategies do cut across a number of countries, usually located close together. Pan-European strategies have received a great deal of attention since the significant drive in 1992 for European integration among the (then) 15 EC countries. While not a global strategy, a regional strategy requires more global thinking, with management considering what is best for Europe, rather than what is best for each country.

The conversion to the euro will continue to support the development of pan-European strategies as consumers in the 12 Eurozone countries adopt one currency. Unilever, an Anglo-Dutch company in detergents, and Electrolux, a Swedish white goods manufacturer, have both moved to a regional strategy to reduce the number of offerings across Europe and to support common positioning and advertising for pan-European brands. Similarly, with the passing of NAFTA, more companies are treating the North American market of the US, Mexico and Canada as a single market. The recent growth of Mercosur in Latin America and ASEAN in Asia has also supported the development of pan-Latin American and pan-Asian marketing strategies, although the country-to-country differences in consumer income levels, consumer needs and market structures have hindered some regional marketing approaches.

Toyota and Honda have both developed pan-Asian strategies. They have used their strong base in Japan to develop a pan-Asian car, which is based on using local parts and labour to develop a low-priced car such as the City by Honda and the Soluna by Toyota. Both cars have been successful in lower-income Asian countries.

Global Strategies

The concept of global marketing strategies was initially thought to be one of a single strategy for all markets. As marketers gained more expertise, they found that there are many types of global marketing strategies that focus on co-ordinating only a part of the global marketing strategy, leaving the rest to be tailored to local markets. These variations give most marketers the opportunity to identify components of the marketing strategy that require a global approach and components that necessitate local adaptation.

Few companies are facing a single marketplace where a totally integrated strategy will be able to be used around the globe. In order to use a totally integrated single marketing strategy, a company must face both a global consumer and an industry that operates the same in all markets. Coca–Cola has an integrated marketing strategy, which covers most elements of the marketing programme, including market segmentation, positioning, branding, distribution, promotion and more. This globally integrated strategy is supported by similar consumer needs, global competitors such as PepsiCo, and industry structures based on a syrup sold to bottlers in each market, with the cola companies doing the consumer marketing to end-users. While there are opportunities for integrated global marketing strategies for luxury watches, high-priced perfumes, long-distance airline companies and a few other products, most companies will use a global marketing strategy that is adapted to fit the consumers, competitors and industry they face worldwide. There are a variety of different global strategies, which leverage some part of the marketing programme worldwide, while leaving other parts do be developed locally.

Global product category strategy

A global product category strategy is a marketing strategy where a company focuses on a set of product categories in all markets. This is one of the least integrated global marketing strategies. A company using this strategy will leverage its research and development and technology across the world by focusing on a few product categories. However, the specific product formula, market segment, positioning, brand name, pricing, advertising and distribution may vary from market to market. P&G reorganized in 1999 around seven categories worldwide, giving profit and loss responsibility to a single executive. Unilever has developed a similar approach based on 14 main categories. Many times a global segment strategy is the first step as a company moves from a multidomestic to a global strategy. This approach starts the process of executives seeing additional opportunities to globalize elements of the marketing programme globally.

Global segment strategy

A global segment strategy occurs when a company finds that it can or does serve the same segment globally. Using a global segment strategy, a company develops an in-depth understanding of the selected segment of a market. This accumulated knowledge is used to develop a unique offering to the segment, while allowing for different product, pricing, brands and advertising, although some standardization may accrue. This is used most often with B2B companies, who find that segment needs are similar across countries. For example, in explosive and heavy equipment industries, the global segments of road construction, deep drill mining and surface mining were similar worldwide, therefore the companies serving these sectors could leverage experience with products, positioning and sales efforts. Citibank, the recently formed consumer group of CitiGroup, has developed several segment strategies for the major segments of private banking clients.

Electrolux, a Swedish white goods manufacturer, made over 100 acquisitions between 1975 and 1985, which resulted in over 20 brands in 40 countries. Large markets such as Germany and the UK had as many as six major Electrolux brands each. In some cases, the exact same brand was positioned as a premium product in one country and as a low-priced option in another market. Theses differences were the result of the country managers positioning the products based on the market offering and competitive situation. A study by Electrolux found a convergence of market segments across Europe, with the customers' need for 'localness' being primarily in terms of distribution channels, promotion in local media and use of local names instead of product design and features. From this analysis, Electrolux developed a strategy with two pan-European brands and one or two local brands in each country. The Electrolux brand was targeted to the high-prestige, conservative consumers, and the Zanussi brand was targeted to the innovative, trend-setting consumers. The local brands were targeted to the young, aggressive urban professionals and the warm and friendly, value-oriented consumers. This new strategy allowed Electrolux to use its extensive knowledge of the product category to reduce the number of different brands and models, while leveraging pan-European opportunities and continuing to serve the local consumers with local brands (Bartlett and Ghoshal, 1992).

Global Marketing Mix Elemental Strategies

Global marketing mix element strategies occur when a company uses a global approach for one or more of the marketing mix elements such as product, price or distribution. These partially global strategies allow the company to use a local approach for the other elements of the marketing mix. The globalization effort must be supported with a strong element of global logic. A company facing a strong global purchasing logic may adopt a global account management programme, as discussed in Chapter 8. A firm facing global information logic may decide to have global communications and or global pricing. Every element of the marketing mix can be globalized, depending on the strength of the supporting global logic. The most common forms of global marketing mix strategies are global product strategies, global branding strategies and global advertising strategies.

Global product strategies

A global product strategy is when a company globalizes the product offering, having the same or a similar product for all markets. For this to be possible, the consumer needs the product use conditions and the required product features to be almost identical in all markets. The firm that pursues a global product strategy will be able to leverage all its investments in developing and manufacturing a product, therefore yielding increased economies of scale.

This approach may not require the exact same product in each market, but key aspects and modules must be the same. For example, Ford Motor Company has transitioned to a global product strategy. In the past, the company was structured around a geographic profit centre. Although the same model was sold in both the US and Europe, they were different products, therefore yielding little leverage over the total volume. Ford has reorganized around global models, therefore producing global cars to replace the Escort and Mondeo (Contour in the US). It invested $6 billion in developing the Mondeo series, including two assembly plants and four engine plants, but it saved millions based on its economies of scale. Other companies with homogeneous products have also developed global product strategies. For example, in hand-held mobile phones, the manufacturers produce the same products except for adaptation to local telephone standards.

One of the most significant changes in product development strategy has been the move towards modularity. This involves the development of standard modules, which can be combined with other modules to increase the variety of products offered while maintaining low production and development costs. The challenge faced by companies is that cost pressures force them to standardize, while market pressures force them to customize. Global firms will need to standardize the core of their products to achieve the economies of scale that are their advantage over smaller firms.

A platform strategy allows for a maximum number of different configurations while maintaining a stable base product and therefore reducing basic development costs. Different firms will have different levels of standardization: shifting from 0 per cent modular to 20 per cent modular may be a significant advantage as well as the maximum standardization desirable for that product. However, if a firm focuses entirely on the differences from market to market, it may miss the opportunity to develop a standard module. The result of modular thinking has led many global firms to develop standard platforms for use in many markets, with each country or region adding the features needed in their market. This global product approach is only possible if a company has a clear, coherent, well-planned global product development concept.

While global products with worldwide volumes will reduce manufacturing costs, a number of situations limit the ability of a company to develop a single global product. For example, most of the world uses metric measurements while the US continues to be non-metric and the UK uses some metric and some imperial measurements. Physical size needs can vary as well. Watch makers must make watchbands smaller for Japanese consumers who have smaller wrists. Italian shoe makers have found that different countries have different size and shaped feet. For example, Americans have longer toes and smaller insteps than Italians. Size can also be affected by physical surroundings. US manufacturers of large household appliances found that their refrigerators would not fit through many Japanese doorways. Paint companies find that they must modify the paint formulas for different climates.

Some markets have different required standards, which affect product design. For example, the noise standards in Europe required Murray Manufacturing, a lawnmower producer, to reduce the blade speed and change the exhaust and bagging system. Of course, if Murray had considered the different world standards when developing its products, it may have been able to develop a single product for the world market. Most countries have local standards for many products. Groups such as the Canadian Standards Association, the British Standards Institute and the American National Standards Institute all develop standards for product design and testing, which can vary from country to country. The International Standards Organization (ISO), located in Geneva, Switzerland, is co-ordinating the development of world standards. ISO 9000 has become one of the most widely accepted worldwide standards (it is a quality standard, which ensures that an organization consistently delivers a product or service that satisfies customer requirements).

Global branding strategies

Global branding strategies consist of using the same brand or logo worldwide. Companies tend to use a global branding strategy to leverage the substantial cost of developing a brand name in each market. Global brands tend to be used where the product users travel to different countries and/or the consumers use global information. For example, Reebok spends over $140 million on the worldwide development of its brand, consolidating all of its advertising at the Leo Burnett advertising agency. Reebok wanted to become the leading sports and fitness brand in the $12 billion athletic shoe market. While the target market of athletic shoe buyers may not travel extensively to many countries, they do tend to watch sports often held in different geographical markets. A UK golfer may be watching a PGA match held in Spain, where the Reebok advertising is shown on golfers' clothing or on posters. In Europe, where cross-border television advertising is found on MTV, CNN and other channels, there are obvious benefits of a global branding strategy. Global brands such as Kodak, Fuji, Coca-Cola, Pepsi, Sony, Marlboro, Swatch and Benetton all benefit from strong consumer recognition and a clear image of higher perceived quality. The funds spent on these global brands help the consumer make decisions more easily and quickly.

Global branding also benefits the company because everyone in the organization has a clear understanding of the brand and what it means, therefore it is simpler and faster to make decisions, as they must all be in alignment with the brand values. One of the biggest brand success stories is at Intel. After losing its trademark case to protect the '386' name, Intel launched the 'Intel Inside' campaign through its own and co-operative advertising with PC manufacturers. The awareness of Intel's chips went from 20 to 80 per cent in two years. Intel has also been able to migrate this brand equity over to its Pentium chip.

Selecting a brand name is an important and complex process when done on a global basis. Generally, a brand name is based on a single language, which if used in other markets will have different meanings. Ideally, companies would like a brand name that evokes the same meaning around the world. From years of experience and advertising, consumers have become aware of what to expect from Coca-Cola, IBM, Häagen Dazs and Sony. When selecting a new brand name it is impossible to have a brand that will have the same meaning in all markets because of the different languages. Branding in Asia, especially China, is very difficult because a brand name has to be translated into Chinese characters. Good examples include Coca-Cola, which means 'tasty and happy' in Chinese characters. Mercedes-Benz's Chinese name means 'striving forward fast,' and Sharp means 'the treasure of sound'.

Given the infinite possibilities and the potential misunderstandings in different languages, global companies must spend a considerable amount of time on selecting a new global brand name. Some companies use a word that has no meaning in most languages, such as Lexus, others pick a name that means something in a few languages, but will mean nothing in the other languages, such as the nappy brand Pampers. Other companies rely on a set of symbols that may have no meaning, such as 3M.

As many companies start in a single country and then go global, they are faced with the challenge of a brand name that does not travel well. Federal Express found it needed to change to FedEx as it went global, as federal meant government or military in many markets. Colgate-Palmolive acquired the leading toothpaste brand in South-east Asia, called Darkie, which had been successfully marketed since 1925. Because of pressure from the US, it did an extensive search to find a less offensive name that would still have meaning to consumers. It changed the name to Darlie, which migrated its substantial market share only with extensive marketing support.

Interbrew, the world's fourth largest brewer, had for years acquired strong local beer companies and increased its product quality and positioning, with a goal of having the top two local brands in each market. In 1998, it decided to launch Stella Artois as a global brand, therefore serving the affluent beer drinker who was exposed to global media such as CNN, MTV, Eurosport and international magazines. With 81 per cent of Stella Artois's volume in the UK, France and Belgium, Interbrew saw a big potential for its global brand in the US, New Zealand and Australia using a single global positioning and similar advertising (University of Western Ontario, 2000).

Global advertising strategies

Global advertising strategy is when a firm uses the same advertisement or advertising theme in most countries. The advantage of a global advertising strategy is that the same creative talent can be used once for all countries. Also, all or part of the actual advertisements may be used for multiple countries. This allows the company to spend more money on a high-quality advertisement, which can be used in many markets. For example Patek Philippe, the luxury watch maker has developed a global TV and print advertising campaign using the theme 'You never actually own a Patek Philippe. You merely look after it for the next generation.' The campaign has been successful in the US, Europe, China, Taiwan, Japan and Singapore.

While there are obvious benefits to a global advertising campaign, it requires a great deal of consistency in terms of the brand name, the target market, the desired positioning and the cultural acceptance of a specific concept. For example, Pringles potato crisps was successfully able to use the theme 'once you pop, you can't stop' in most countries, although the advertisements had to use local actors and be adapted for local flavours. Taco Bell, a US-based, Mexican restaurant chain, found it could not use the talking Chihuahua dog that was successful in America in Asia, where dog was a delicacy, or in Muslim countries, where it is taboo to touch a dog. Global advertisements with strong visuals linked to the brand have the benefit of being universally understood and less likely to be culturally specific. British Airways, BP, Heinz, Hewlett-Packard, Volvo, Sony and L'Oréal have all used global campaigns successfully to support their brands.

Global pricing strategies

As international companies deal with market and environmental factors, they face two major strategic pricing alternatives. Essentially, the choice is between the global, single-price strategy and the individualized country strategy.

To maximize a company's revenues, it would appear to be logical to set prices on a market-by-market basis, looking in each market for the best combination of revenue versus volume yielding maximum profit. This strategy was common for many firms in the early part of their international development. For many products, however, noticeable price differences between markets are taken advantage of by independent companies or channel members who see a profit from buying in lower-price markets and exporting products to high-price markets. For products that are relatively similar in many markets and for which transportation costs are not significant, substantial price differences will quickly result in the emergence of a 'grey' market. Grey markets exist where the price for a given product is widely different between two countries. Aware of the price difference, consumers begin to purchase in the low-priced area and move products into the high-priced area. As the markets become more transparent, the information flows more efficiently; and as products become more similar, the trend away from market-by-market pricing to a co-ordinated global pricing strategy will continue.

Managing pricing policies for an international firm is an especially challenging task. The international marketer is confronted with a number of uncontrollable factors deriving from the economic, legal and regulatory environment, all of which have an impact on how prices are established in various countries. Although these influences are usually quite manageable in any given country, pricing across many markets means coping with price differentials that evolve out of environmental factors working in various combinations in different countries. Managing these price differentials and keeping them within tolerable limits are major tasks in international pricing.

McDonald's, the leading US fast-food chain, has taken the route of pricing its products according to local market conditions. Its key product, the Big Mac, priced at $2.43 in the US, ranges from $1.19 in Malaysia to $3.97 in Switzerland. The cost of a Big Mac in each country divided by its cost in the home market gives the implied purchasing power of the local currency. When compared to the actual exchange rate, you can see which currencies are overvalued or undervalued based on the Big Mac; for example, the Swiss franc is overvalued by 64 per cent, whereas the Chinese yuan or Malaysian ringgit is undervalued by 51 per cent (*Economist*, 1999).

Employing a uniform pricing strategy on a global scale requires that a company, which can determine its prices in local currency, will always charge the same price everywhere when the price is translated into a base currency. In reality, this becomes very difficult to achieve whenever different taxes, trade margins and customs duties are involved. As a result, there are likely to be price differences due to those factors not under the control of the company. Keeping prices identical, aside from those non-controllable factors, is a challenge. Firms may start out with identical prices in various countries, but soon find that prices have to change to stay in line with often substantial currency fluctuations.

Although it is becoming increasingly clear for many companies that market-by-market pricing strategies will cause difficulties, many firms have found that changing to a uniform pricing policy is rather like pursuing a moving target. Even when a global pricing policy is adopted, a company must carefully monitor price levels in each country and avoid large gaps that can then cause problems when independent or grey market forces move in and take advantage of large price differentials.

One of the most critical factors affecting price levels is the foreign exchange rate. Today, managers find currencies moving both up and down, and the swings have assumed magnitudes that may substantially affect competitiveness. Understanding the factors that shape the directions of the foreign exchange market and mastering the technical tools that protect firms against large swings have become required skills for the international marketer. To the extent that a company can make itself less vulnerable to exchange rate movements compared to its competitors, it may gain additional competitive advantage.

Because the relevant factors that affect price levels on an international scale are always fluctuating, the international pricing task is a never-ending process in which each day may bring new problems to be resolved. Whenever a company is slow to adapt or makes a wrong judgement, the market is very quick at adapting and at exploiting any weaknesses. As long as uncontrollable factors such as currency rates and inflation are subject to considerable fluctuations, the pricing strategies of international companies will have to remain under constant review. The ultimate goal is to minimize the gap between the price levels of various markets.

Global distribution strategies

To be successful in the global marketplace, a company needs market acceptance by and access to the potential customers. Effective distribution systems can give it access to potential customers, while marketing communications may be used to gain market acceptance. Generally, the current companies in a local market have a close relationship with the wholesalers, distributors, agents and retailers, making access to the existing channels of distribution problematic. With substantial differences between countries on both the wholesale and retail level, a global company must choose the most suitable members of a channel to distribute its product. Given the current market structures, it may be difficult to get access to the best possible channel members, so global marketers are forced to use other options. A proper global distribution effort accounts for the different buying habits, culture, regulations and structures in each country. These country-to-country differences may cause a company to use different distribution strategies in different countries.

To enter a blocked channel, a global marketer has several options. First, the company can look for a way to circumvent the current channel members. For example, when American Standard attempted to enter the Korean market, it found that all the distributors were controlled by local plumbing manufacturers, therefore they were not willing to carry American Standard products. American Standard found that one of the local retailers, Home Center, was willing to buy direct from it, therefore circumventing the locked distributors.

A second option for a global firm is to acquire an existing local company. For example, when Merck wanted to enter the Japanese market, it acquired 51 per cent of Banyu, a Japanese pharmaceutical manufacturer.

A third option is to set up a joint venture with a local manufacturer. For example, when Budweiser wanted to enter the Japanese market, it established a joint venture with Kirin Beer, the largest local manufacturer, to gain market access. When Asahi wanted to launch its Super Dry beer in the US, it developed a joint venture with Miller Brewing Company.

Fourth, a company can use a local original equipment manufacturer to enter a market. For example Hewlett-Packard (HP), a global leader in Internet servers, sells its equipment to NEC, who resells them under the NEC name to local companies. This gives NEC access to the latest server technology and HP access to the Japanese market.

Finally, a company can use the Internet as a vehicle to go directly to potential customers. When easyJet, a low-cost UK-based airline, wanted to enter Switzerland, the Netherlands and Spain, it used the Internet as a distribution channel. This distribution strategy reduced the cost of distributing its ticket sales through travel agents. In addition, using the Internet reduces the cost of distribution, as fewer reservations staff are required. By January 2001, 80 per cent of easyJet's sales were via the Internet.

Global distribution has seen significant change over the past five years. There is a trend towards fewer but larger retailers, which is supported by an increase in the number of homes with cars, the number of refrigerators and the increased number of working women. For example, the growth of superstores in the UK has significantly reduced the number of medium and small stores. In the Netherlands, while total food stores have decreased by 22 per cent, the number of superstores increased by 33 per cent. There are a number of globally active retailers, who have expanded beyond domestic markets. These expansions are through both opening new stores and acquisitions. Wal-Mart, IKEA, Carrefour, Benetton, Aldi, the Body Shop, Toys 'R' Us and Starbucks have all become global retailers. These firms have developed strong retail formats, which can be translated into other countries. The global expansion of retailers has not been without difficulties, however. Marks & Spencer, a UK-based food and clothing retailer, had difficulty in France and Asia. Some argue that its international expansion and acquisition of Brooks Brothers in the US caused the company to lose focus in its home market. Therefore in 2001 it decided to sell Brooks Brothers and Kings Supermarket chains in the US and close its continental operation. Dutch clothing retailer C&A found that its concept and product range were no longer successful in the UK, so it had to exit that country in 2000.

Direct marketing has grown rapidly as an international distribution channel. Catalogue sales and direct door-to-door sales have been successful in many markets. Paul Fredrick Menswear, a US clothing company, used a catalogue to penetrate the Japanese market for men's shirts and ties. Catalogue sales are also successful in France, Brazil and Russia. Companies such as Avon and Amway have been successful in many parts of Asia with a direct door-to-door selling format.

On-line distribution is the fastest-growing global channel of distribution. Amazon, Bertelsmann and Barnes and Noble are growing the on-line book-retailing market globally. While consumer markets have received much press coverage, the real growth in on-line distribution will be in the B2B marketplace. For example, General Electric Plastics launched the Polymerland website, which sold over $100 million in 1999. By March 2000, Polymerland was selling $2.0 million on-line daily! Enron Corporation launched EnronOnline as a global Internet transaction system for wholesale energy. In its first six months the site handled $35 billion of wholesale transactions, or 45 per cent of the company's wholesale business. While it is too early to tell which on-line buying groups and on-line auctions will be successful, there is no doubt that on-line distribution will be a major channel of distribution in the B2B market.

CONCLUSION

Any company engaged in global marketing is faced with a number of strategic decisions. These decisions are based on the level of globalization a firm has decided to pursue. While many firms are currently using multidomestic strategies, the growth of global logics is forcing most firms to look for opportunities to leverage their global assets and knowledge to remain competitive. Once the decision is made to look at the world globally instead of country by country, a firm must decide where and how to operate.

A global firm operates differently from a multidomestic firm. A global marketing strategy begins with a global view of the world, understanding the global logics and identifying the company's strengths across markets. This does not mean that a global company must standardize all of its marketing programmes on a global scale or even operate in all markets in the world. A global company is aware of the value of global size and global market share, which will influence the decision of which markets to enter. Rather than viewing each market independently, the costs of serving a market can be shared across many countries, with the objective of global profit maximization. This may mean that a company chooses to operate in a less profitable market to monitor a competitor or to be aware of new technologies. This approach resembles a chess game: different pieces having different values, but to win a player must use all the pieces appropriately. This approach requires new skills.

Globalization is not a new term for something that has existed in the past; it is a new competitive game, which will continue to change. Leading companies will need to adjust and learn new ways to play. Survival will depend on how well a company can continue to learn.

References

Bartlett, C.A. and Ghoshal, S. (1992) 'What is a global manager?', *Harvard Business Review*, September-October.

Economist (1999) 'The hamburger standard', *The Economist*, April 3.

Jeannet, J.-P. and Hennessey, H.D. (2001) *Global Marketing Strategies*, 5th edn, Houghton Mifflin, New York.

Sorenson, R.Z. and Wiechmann, U.E. (1975) 'How multinationals view marketing standardization', *Harvard Business Review*, May–June.

University of Western Ontario (2000) 'The Global Branding of Stella Artois,' case number 9B00A019.

World Bank (2000) *World Bank Atlas*, World Bank, New York.

MANAGING
GLOBAL
CUSTOMERS

H. David Hennessey

CHAPTER 8

MANAGING GLOBAL CUSTOMERS

*I*n this chapter we will be examining the key aspects of developing and managing global customers. At the outset, it is important to define a global customer as an account that is strategically important to a supplier, operationally active on multiple continents and globally co-ordinated in its purchasing. This clearly excludes accounts that operate in one area of the world, as well as those that operate in multiple areas but think and buy locally.

The globalization of many industries has created a unique opportunity for co-ordinated client interaction on a global basis, which is different to the normal approach to handling national or key accounts. This chapter examines the following areas of managing global customers:

- What factors are driving customers to become global?
- How can the potential of global account management be evaluated?
- What is a global account management programme?
- How can a company determine which customers to serve globally?

- What do customers want from global suppliers?
- How can a global account plan be developed?
- What are the barriers to a successful global account programme?
- What is the impact of the new economy on global account management?
- What is considered best practice in global account management?

Examples from leading companies will be used to describe global account management practices and experiences.

A global account management programme co-ordinates the global offering to a company. Customers with operations around the globe want to receive the same service, product and pricing wherever they are doing business. This standardization reduces acquisition costs, improves quality and supports global products. Companies such as HP, IBM and Lucent as well as global advertising agencies or global accounting agencies have found it very useful to establish a global account management programme. Global account management requires an in-depth understanding of the customer's industry, their position in the industry and their overall strategy. For example, why is the biggest connector customer building a factory in China? Why is the automotive customer converting from hydraulic power steering to electronic power steering? Why are your automobile component manufacturers establishing a trading marketplace? The experience and training of the global account managers, along with multi-person high-level contact at the customer level, will allow managers to answer these questions and better identify ways to meet the future needs of global customers.

Global account management requires a high level of executive commitment and support, to influence national account managers around the world to do things that may not be in the best interests of the global account. National account executives and country managers with different metrics may pursue actions beneficial for that country and not the world. Global account management is also supported with a global information system, which provides all the information necessary to best serve a global customer.

WHAT IS DRIVING CUSTOMERS TO BECOME, THINK AND OPERATE GLOBALLY?

Macroeconomic Factors

On a macro level, the reduction of trade barriers and the growth of the World Trade Organization have facilitated the growth of cross-border trade and the opening of markets. For example, as China prepares to enter the WTO, it has needed to open its major domestic markets to foreign companies such as Siemens, Mercedes and Procter and Gamble.

Regionally, the growth and influence of trading groups such as NAFTA, Mercosur and ASEAN have reduced trade barriers and encouraged trade. Likewise, the anticipated expansion of the European Union (EU) and the transition to a single currency (the euro) will encourage many companies to consider pan-European approaches to manufacturing, marketing and logistics.

Driving this trend we find that slow growth within a company's current markets, such as the US, Germany or Japan, has caused many firms to consider higher-growth markets such as Asia or Latin America. Especially large opportunities are available in the heavily populated countries of China, India and Brazil. This strategy can be seen in Wal-Mart, as sales approached $100 billion in the US and it began to expand into both Europe and Asia. Procter and Gamble has found that 40–45 per cent of its current growth comes from its global customers (Napolitano, 1999: 11).

Industry Factors

In some cases, the actions of specific companies in an industry have caused the entire industry to operate globally. For example, when Electrolux entered the US market through the acquisition of White Consolidated, an American white goods company, Whirlpool countered by entering the European market though the purchase of Philips' white goods business. Similar competitive actions have happened in the automotive, pharmaceutical, retail, chemical, beverage and computer industries.

The global expansion of firms in an industry can also be explained by the desire to achieve economies of scale. Economies of scale may be found in new product development, a very expensive aspect of the pharmaceutical industry, in manufacturing start-up costs, a common activity within the automotive industry, or in brand development costs. Developing brands in consumer markets can be very expensive. Danone, the French yogurt, bottled water and biscuit company, has expanded into eastern Europe, Latin America, Asia and the US in order to leverage its brand. While economies of scale are often based on R&D, manufacturing or branding, they can also be based on other sources of competitive advantage such as the processes of logistics, customer service, trade financing or business planning. An in-depth understanding of a customer's source of competitive advantage and economies of scale is important to serve a global account, more effectively.

In turn, the development of any global industry can drive the suppliers of that industry also to become global. For example, Corning, a US maker of optical fibre and components, found that it needed to set up operations in Europe, Japan and China to serve large telecommunications companies such as Nortel. Given the need to support your current customers and the reduced risk of expanding with current customers, rather than growing using entirely new customers, experts recommend leading or accompanying major customers into new geographical locations. Once established with them in these new territories, a shift towards attracting new customers located in the new area is appropriate (Valentine Pope and Brown, 1999: 33).

Technology Drivers

The growth of the Internet has made it possible for suppliers and customers to share information and interact on a global basis, with limited impact from geographical distance or time zone differences. Sophisticated software such as enterprise resource planning (ERP), customer relationship management (CRM) and supply chain management (SCM), in conjunction with the Internet, now allows suppliers to interact and co-ordinate purchasing globally while reducing transaction and supply chain costs. Finally, the impact of e-business sites, including marketplaces, exchanges and auctions, has driven suppliers and customers to identify opportunities that leverage strategic relationships. With any potential customer only two clicks away via the Internet, this will clearly have an impact on customer–supplier relationships globally.

These factors and drivers of globalization are affecting most industries and companies to varying degrees. There will be cases where these forces start to result in global products or global brands in such markets as soft drinks, luxury watches or motorcycles. However, in many industries we will continue to see the delivery of 'local' products or services.

Global sourcing of raw materials is often the first step companies take in globalizing their practices, but more and more companies want to leverage assets, knowledge and experiences across many countries for competitive advantage. In fact, a final driver of globalization is the importance that firms are giving to customer focus as a successful business strategy. As companies evaluate their potential global relationships, an important decision will be whether to start a global account management programme.

HOW CAN THE POTENTIAL OF GLOBAL ACCOUNT MANAGEMENT BE EVALUATED?

With all the factors that are driving customers to become more global and therefore request and value global suppliers, it is important to evaluate the strategic implications of the decision. While becoming a global supplier should provide more volume, it is usually expected that there will be some associated price decrease for the customer. It is hoped that the increased volume will offset the price reduction. However, the increased revenue may not cover the increase in costs incurred in serving a global account.

For example, the customer will want local supply and service for all plants. The global supplier will need a sophisticated customer information and supply management system. In addition to these costs, the global supplier may have the additional costs of both global and local account managers. While there can be significant value created by an effective global account management approach to serving customers, this value will be shared by both the supplier and the customer. Given the balance of power between the supplier and the customer, the benefits may tend to favour the customer.

DSM Engineering Plastics reports that some of its large customers who have limited co-ordinated purchasing, place great value on the information that DSM can provide about what their company is doing in different parts of the world. The potential of a global account approach will be significantly influenced by the success of implementation. The implementation will be affected by the balance of power between the local management and the global management. For the global approach to be successful, the global account manager must be able to leverage the existing marketing efforts and local sales in a co-ordinated fashion without incurring the cost of a totally new organization. This infers that the balance of power must favour the global organization, while the local organization continues to be critical for delivering value. The decision to establish a global account management system is not easy. The costs and benefits are difficult to estimate, but in some cases the customers will demand such a system.

WHAT IS A GLOBAL ACCOUNT MANAGEMENT PROGRAMME?

The elements of a global account management programme vary between suppliers and in some cases can even vary between accounts. However, the main elements of the programme fall under the general areas of: co-ordinated supplier–account interactions; co-ordinated supply chain interactions; co-ordinated product–service development; co-ordinated terms and pricing.

Co-ordinated Supplier–Account Interactions

Global account relationships serve complex companies with many functions, many locations and in some cases even many businesses. The functions could include global purchasing, local purchasing, marketing, manufacturing, logistics, accounting and sales. For example, Gillette operates in 200 countries, with 50 factories and 37 000 employees, therefore an advertising agency, computer supplier or plastics supplier could potentially have hundreds if not thousands of contacts with Gillette. Any company that elects to serve Gillette globally would need to co-ordinate the overall relationship and manage the interaction process. This would usually include a global account manager as the main point of contact, who would co-ordinate the interactions across functions, geographies and business units. Speaking to the customer in one voice is a major potential benefit of a global account management system.

This single-point methodology would also include facilitating senior management interaction at a corporate level. Initially, when Van Leer Industrial Packaging, the largest worldwide supplier of steel drums, set up global account management it appointed a respected salesperson as international account co-ordinator. This approach was unsuccessful, as the geographically based business unit managers would not yield to the suggestions of the international account co-ordinator if they were at cross-purposes with their own objectives. Later, Van Leer decided to assign global account management responsibilities to the business unit manager in the geography where the global account was headquartered. As each business unit manager managed between one and three of the company's global accounts, they became aware of the need to compromise to serve global accounts.

Earnest W. Davenport Jr., Chairman and CEO of Eastman Chemical, reports:

> It is essential that a Global Account Manager has access to the CEO and senior management at a company and I make sure that is the case at Eastman Chemical Company. The CEO must champion the global account managers. We assign accounts to all our senior executives including the CEO, and expect relationships to be established with senior management at all of our major customers. Without global account management we could not do business effectively with our global customers. We're now building a resin plant in China to serve the adhesives industry because one of our global accounts decided to move into China. Without global account relationship we would not have had the opportunity to follow this customer into a new market. (Davenport, 1999: 15)

To support the global account manager, a company must have a worldwide information technology and communication system to support rapid and accurate exchange of information on the account and the hundreds of associated interactions. Van Leer found that it was also very helpful to have four global account support centres around the world to handle any global customer questions, requests or problems. Given the location of these support centres, there was 24 hour a day support for all global customers. Eastman Chemical invested millions into a SAP ERP system to manage information about its global customers in real time. This has helped Eastman better serve its global customers.

Co-ordinated Supply Chain Interactions

Every supplier relationship with a global account relies on the processes of predicting demand, ordering materials, manufacturing products, controlling quality and delivering logistics on the supplier side, and ordering, receiving, manufacturing and payment on the customer side. These activities, which make up the supply chain, include multiple opportunities to reduce cost, reduce inventory, reduce manufacturing costs and reduce transaction costs.

One of the key reasons that companies are reducing the number of vendors and selecting global suppliers is to reduce the supply chain costs. Global customers may have access to a supplier's production planning process or inventory management system to facilitate supply chain efficiencies. Conversely, a supplier may be electronically linked to the customer's sales function so that, as specific products are sold, the supplier can adjust its production as necessary on a real-time basis. These linkages were electronic data interchanges (EDI) in the past, but today tend to be via the Internet.

Co-ordination of the supply chain is also supported by an advanced information technology system and senior management involvement and support. Initially, a global account relationship will require supply chain management skills and funding to make the necessary changes in technology and process.

A longer-term benefit of co-ordinated supply chain activities is to increase the switching cost of a global customer to another supplier.

Co-ordinated Product–Service Development

Global accounts will usually require some product or service development. At first this may include product standardization for the purposes of reducing the variety of products being used. This will help to reduce supply chain costs. As a supplier and a global account work together, they will often establish joint development teams to improve the final product performance, to reduce total product costs through improved manufacturability or to develop new products. These collaborative teams will require dedicated budgets. The product and service co-ordination may also include value-added services. For example, Van Leer developed special services to handle drums after use that were carrying hazardous chemicals.

Co-ordinated Terms and Pricing

Any discussion of global accounts usually moves quickly to the issue of pricing and the belief that global customers are looking for low uniform prices in exchange for the global relationship. However, in a study of 191 global companies, uniform pricing was found not to be one of the most important items for global customers. Much more important were consistency in quality and services and standardization of products and services (Montgomery *et al.*, 1999: 25).

For example at Xerox, if an account requests to become a global account and the account manager thinks the motivation is to receive uniform low prices worldwide, Xerox will not grant the account's request. The company operates through four separate pricing contracts for Asia, North America, Europe and Latin America. Within those regions global accounts are guaranteed uniform prices.

A major risk of a global account management system is the potential demand for global pricing. While the volume benefits of a global relationship may outweigh the price reduction, this can be a slippery slope. It is critical to be able to quantify the value added of the global account relationship to maintain adequate margins. It is also critical to have accurate cost and volume information when negotiating pricing to achieve global account maximization. Hewlett-Packard's installation of a global account management programme resulted in a 20 per cent sales growth and a reduction of sales cost from 47–50 per cent to 38–41 per cent (Yip and Madsen, 1996: 38).

It is common for global accounts to prefer standard terms and conditions worldwide. As with pricing this can also be a complicated area, as customers want the best possible terms for all locations while some locations will be small volume. Given the costs and risks of serving global customers, the process of deciding which accounts should be treated through a global account management programme is very important.

HOW CAN A COMPANY DETERMINE WHICH CUSTOMERS TO SERVE GLOBALLY?

While many companies operate in multiple geographies, this is not sufficient to be selected as a global account. The company must be of a current or potential size to be considered strategic. While most companies consider current or potential size to be critical, other considerations such as technology leadership, growth rate, profitability and technology synergies are used to identify potential global accounts (Wilson *et al.*, 2000: 11).

For example, regarding technology, the majority of HP's global customers operate in countries with high computer usage such as Japan, US, Germany, Sweden and the UK. DSM Engineering Plastics has selected its global customers based on total dollar profitability, which includes both volume and profit margin.

It is also helpful if the customer has a global strategy that is executed consistently in its different geographical markets. This makes it much easier for a company to work with the customer on a global basis. In addition, it is critical that the customer is co-ordinating its purchasing globally. Without some form of global co-ordination, the primary result of having a global supplier may merely be lower prices. Van Leer attempted to serve French oil company Total on a global basis, only to find that headquarter purchasing at Total could not influence its different country subsidiaries to purchase from a specific supplier.

The number of global accounts is small compared to the total number of accounts served. This means that accounts are selected on some combination of the above criteria. For example, IBM selects its Selected International Accounts based on revenues, demand for IBM products, installed base at each location and degree of control the client's head office has over local purchasing (Yip and Madsen, 1996: 31–2).

Hewlett-Packard selects its global accounts based on a minimum of $10 million in HP product/service purchases across two or three continents, the account being in an industry that HP predicts will grow globally, and the account must provide HP with an opportunity to develop a defensible position. To develop a defensible position in a global account, it is important to understand what the customers want from a global supplier.

WHAT DO CUSTOMERS WANT FROM GLOBAL SUPPLIERS?

Every customer is different and therefore may have different expectations from a global supplier. Even within a particular customer, different people throughout the organization will have different expectations. Recognizing the requirement to understand a customer in detail and understand how as a global supplier you can add value to the customer, there are some common needs found in many global customers. Specifically, global customers desire a single point of contact and single voice from a global supplier. This assures customers that they can ultimately go to one person to make decisions, to resolve differences and to determine how the two firms will work together.

Sufficient Resources and Management Attention

Global customers want sufficient resources to be devoted to their firm in a co-ordinated manner. These co-ordinated resources can be used to achieve the desired objectives of the customer and to avoid wasted resources, working at cross-purposes. Chemical companies often find that they could have three or four business units serving a single global customer, such as Ford Motor. It is often possible that these different business units would be attempting to sell different materials for the same application.

The other possible benefit of co-ordinating the activities of a global supplier is that in the previous example the customers could communicate a single global strategy to the global supplier through the global account manager, who would relate it to the appropriate people in his or her organization. This reduces the need for multiple people to be explaining the business to multiple salespeople from the same supplier, sometimes with inconsistent messages.

Global customers also want to have sufficient engagement with senior management of the global supplier. This assures the global customer that they are important and will get sufficient resources allocated to their needs. It also provides some assurance of continuity of supply. Senior management engagement and support also assure the customer that sufficient attention and weight will be given to solving the challenges of managing a complex relationship.

Pricing Consideration

Global customers want some price consideration in exchange for their volume of business. In some cases this may be a uniform global price, a regional price or a specified price in each market. Differences in prices are often related to the different cost structures of different markets. However, it is expected that global customers will be examining these differences to identify opportunities for more uniform prices. If a supplier is offering the same standard product in each market, customers may see this as an opportunity to buy from the least expensive location (including logistics costs). This issue of pricing will be affected by the new economy. As some products will be purchased through exchanges, marketplaces and auctions (to be discussed later), it is expected that there will be some shift to more uniform global pricing.

Consistency

According to David Macaulay, vice-president information and communications global accounts at Siemens, the primary challenge in serving global accounts is delivering consistency. Siemens finds that the primary requirement of its global customers is consistency in logistics, support, advertising, service quality, pricing and ease of doing business. To deliver consistency, Macaulay recommends a focus on co-operation, contacts, communication and culture. Co-operation is required across the supplier organization so that all individuals and functions understand the needs and roles of the global accounts. Suppliers must also focus energy on involving and compensating their local organization through contracts to support the on-going global account business. Communication requirements are magnified twenty times when dealing with a global customer operating in many geographies. Both formal and informal communications are important and can be significantly affected by language differences. Culture adds to the language hurdles and can be one of the most underestimated components of a global account programme. Suppliers need cultural empathy for the local operations, to understand if they support the global strategy, to understand if yes means yes, and whether the global account manager can help align the local needs with the global needs (Macaulay, 2000: 21).

HOW CAN A GLOBAL ACCOUNT PLAN BE DEVELOPED?

The process of developing a global account plan begins with an understanding of the account and its potential. After the account has been selected to be a global account, a detailed understanding of the industry must be undertaken. The industry analysis starts with understanding the macro business system, from raw materials, to components, to manufacturing (or assembly), to distributors, to retailers, to consumers. To better understand how to create value for a global customer, it is necessary to understand what potential changes may affect the macro business system.

For example, the automobile industry over the past ten years has been heavily influenced by consumer and government desires to reduce fuel consumption and carbon dioxide emissions. These needs have driven car manufacturers to reduce car weight, modify body styles to be more aerodynamic and change engine design to reduce emissions. In the future, industry observers predict that consumers and governments will want cars to be more recyclable. This will mean that the car must be easily broken down into materials that can be reused. In turn, chemical companies providing material to component manufacturers may benefit from research to make their materials more easily recycled. Another change in the automobile industry is the consolidation of the number of car manufacturers from approximately 25 to 6 major car companies due to the benefits of economies of scale. To leverage design and manufacturing assets further, car companies will be delivering multiple car brands on common platforms. In addition, as customers use the Internet to research car choices and in some cases to purchase cars, the traditional role of the dealer may change.

This level of industry knowledge helps a global automobile component supplier or system supplier understand the new pressures facing its customers. This integrated understanding also helps the supplier anticipate how its customer's key success factors may be changing. For example, given the reduced number of car manufacturers and the trend towards similar aerodynamic exterior designs, car manufacturers may be putting increased efforts on using the interior of the car and the customer interfaces for product differentiation. Seeing this possible change in the industry, car seat manufacturers may look at a new seat design that uses sensors to respond to the passenger's height, weight and size to adjust the seat for maximum comfort and driver visibility. As a supplier understands all the things a customer must do to become successful along with the potential changes in the macro business system, it will provide a number of options in which the supplier can contribute to the customer's success.

This level of understanding will lead to an account strategy that adds significant value to your global customer. The global supplier can focus internal resources in its account plan to identify and support these new opportunities. This may require a research and development project or possibly a joint effort with the supplier and customer. A clear account strategy will support the detailed plan, which determines what actions need to be taken and what resources are needed to support these actions.

WHAT ARE THE BARRIERS TO A SUCCESSFUL GLOBAL ACCOUNT PROGRAMME?

Supplier Barriers

Serving customers globally is a complex process, because in addition to the difficulty of co-ordinating and operating across countries, business units and functions, a global account programme must be aligned with the strategy, people and cultures of the supplier and customer. On the supplier side, most difficulties arise from conflict between the local and global perspectives. The conflicts are the result of a variety of possible misalignments. For example, if the supplier does not have a clear global strategy that is effectively communicated to all managers, local managers will focus on serving customer needs entirely based on local conditions and practices. Of course, it is necessary to have a product that conforms to local needs, but the product is only one part of the total offering. When thinking globally a supplier is likely to offer a similar package globally, with some local variation, thus leveraging the knowledge of the global relationship to a greater degree than operating entirely on a local basis. Also, if the compensation system is based totally on local performance rather than supporting the global strategy, priority will be given to local rather than global customer needs. Finally, if the management organization structure is totally geographical and senior management support is inconsistent, local managers will give little support to global customer needs.

Customer Barriers

On the customer's side, the ability to appreciate and gain value from a global relationship is a function of the customer's ability physically to accept a global offering. This will often be the concern where the customer does not have a global strategy or does not have any global co-ordinating structures, and therefore focuses mostly on obtaining the lowest price. Without the necessary organization and perspective, a customer cannot appreciate the value of a global supplier. A European supplier to the semiconductor industry, for example, decided that given the global nature of semiconductors it should serve its five largest semiconductor companies by having global operations with global accounts. After two years, the company determined that none of the firms had significant global behaviour. In the end, these customers did not appreciate the efforts of the global account teams. The three accounts that were buying regionally were returned to the regional sales organization and the two accounts buying locally were returned to the local country management (Senn, 2000: 43).

While global account management is appropriate for some customers, it is not the best alternative for all large customers. With the growth and strength of trading blocs such as NAFTA, Mercosur, EU and ASEAN, for many companies it may be better to think about regional account co-ordination as a first step to global account management.

Alignment of Objectives

Ultimately, organizations consist of people, so for a global account approach to work there need to be sufficient systems for the people to communicate effectively. Barriers to this ability to communicate would include a lack of an efficient supplier–customer communication system, a misalignment of geographical locations, a language barrier or a lack of cultural understanding.

A survey of 159 companies with global account management programmes revealed that the following major difficulties were experienced by global account managers: 69 per cent experienced conflicts of interest between global and local businesses, 61 per cent had difficulty with regional or local implementation, 50 per cent had problems because they lacked an integrated IT system and 44 per cent had problems managing and co-ordinating multinational teams (Wilson *et al.*, 2000).

A common thread running through this survey is the difficulty of aligning global with local or regional deliverables. Asea Brown Boveri (ABB) has a dedicated global account management programme that has operated with a clear focus on local, regional and global levels for over a decade. Where appropriate, ABB operates regional account programmes (e.g. European Union) and national account programmes (e.g. US or Germany). These different account programmes are linked through the global key account manager who co-ordinates the various ABB activities and ensures that the total business potential is known by the local ABB companies. ABB, which has only 20 global accounts, has 15–20 people on a worldwide customer team led by the global key account executive. This approach ensures that the local and regional account managers are actively involved in the process of managing the global accounts operating in their regions (Senn, 2000: 7).

WHAT IS THE IMPACT OF THE NEW ECONOMY ON GLOBAL ACCOUNT MANAGEMENT?

The Internet has reduced the effective size of the world so that it is just two or three clicks from any supplier to any buying organization. The Web allows companies to search, compare and buy almost any product or service from anywhere around the globe. Globalization and e-commerce are discussed in detail in Chapter 4.

What this means to executives is that they need to understand how to use the Internet to reduce costs and increase value for their customers. Jack Welch, chief executive of General Electric, told shareholders at the company's annual meeting in 2000, 'Any company, old or new that does not see this technology as literally as important as breathing could be on its last breath.'

As the digital world facilitates product and price transparency, it may make it hard for customers to differentiate products or services. Companies with regional or global brands will be able to afford the cost of constant innovation and brand promotion to differentiate their products. Customers may rely on brand image to help decide, but will also be looking for value-added services such as shipment tracking, quality certification, superior logistics, tailored solutions and so on when choosing between similar offerings.

The Internet will allow easy point-to-point transactions, which in some industries will reduce the need for distributors, wholesalers, agents and retailers. Point-to-point communications between buyers and sellers will allow global marketers to understand more about the needs of each customer and become more customer focused. Using the latest information, sellers can tailor their offering to specific needs. For example, booksellers can feature recent books on global strategy to the business executive who has bought similar books in the past. The Internet and point-to-point communications offer companies new ways to communicate with customers. Specialized industry websites allow marketers to advertise directly to their target audience.

The Internet, the euro and the interdependence of major world economies are all supporting the opportunity for companies to serve the global marketplace. Large and small companies can serve customers around the globe. First, given that any customer can reach a company in two or three clicks, it will become common to sell books, art, travel, market information, music, shares of stock, hardware, machinery, planes, trains, automobiles and many other items over the Net. Along with reduced trade and geographical barriers for many products, there will be few limits to what products and services can be sold globally over the Web. Second, the Internet eliminates time zone restrictions and speeds up information exchange. Third, it allows for two-way interaction so each customer can receive products only when required (JIT), eliminating inventory, warehousing and obsolete stock.

Given the large volume of Internet sites and trading marketplaces, a key role of global marketers will be to attract and keep customers at their site. Attracting customers to your site requires agreements and alliances with search engines and non-competitive sites that serve your potential customer base. Through search engines, advertising and links you will be able to get customers to your site. However, the site content must give customers perceived value on each visit or they will not return to the site. This perceived quality and value determines how long a customer will stay on the site or how often they return.

The Internet and e-mail raise the issue of the global account manager, as the need to provide product information, negotiate prices and track shipments may be better handled by technology. In some industries where the global account manager's primary role was to facilitate transactions, that person will no longer be needed. In other industries, the global account manager's role will be to monitor the customer's industry and work face to face with the customer to add value. This new role will require global account managers with new skills to assimilate industry information and identify new ways to add value for customers. The global account manager will work closely with marketing to identify and create innovative, value-added products and services.

The new world of global marketing will require significant e-commerce skills for global account managers. At first, these skills involve using the electronic point-to-point capability of the Internet to reduce costs and improve customer value. The digital world provides an amazing variety of new ways to serve customers. One of the biggest growth areas in global marketing will be the use of e-mail to communicate with, inform and provide value to current and potential customers. Second, global account managers will be faced with the challenge of co-operation. Companies will be working directly with competitors in trading marketplaces to reduce purchase costs.

For example, 11 of the world's leading retailers have set up the Worldwide Retail Exchange, a business-to-business on-line exchange for buying, selling or auctioning goods and services. This group includes Casino and Auchan of France, Safeway and K-Mart of the US, Kingfisher and Marks & Spencer of the UK, and Royal Ahold of the Netherlands. The exchange follows the establishment of the GlobalNetExchange set up by Carrefour of France and Sears of the US and joined by Metro of Germany, Sainsbury of the UK and Kroger of the US. These new exchanges will require new skills to obtain the best results while still remaining differentiated in the marketplace. It is expected that governments may question some of these new arrangements, which is why in many cases the exchanges are operated by a separate company. For example, a computer component exchange including HP, Gateway, Compaq, Hitachi, NEC, Advanced Micro Devices and others will be operated by an independent company, yet to be named.

The future of global account management is difficult to predict in the wired world. Barriers to trade will continue to fall, currency risk and currency conversion costs will decline and geographical borders will become less important, all leading to an increase in world trade. To keep up in this new world will require new skills and vision. The winning companies will be those who have the vision and can switch to the new approach without being burdened with legacy information technology systems and methods. Most major firms will need to restructure and redefine themselves.

WHAT IS CONSIDERED BEST PRACTICE IN GLOBAL ACCOUNT MANAGEMENT?

The Strategic Account Management Association hosts a global forum of seven companies, ABB, Cable & Wireless, Dun & Bradstreet, IBM, Reuters, Xerox and Young & Rubicam. The group meets every two months and shares best practices for global account management. Recently, they presented the top seven best global account management best practices, as follows:

1 *Get an executive champion.* Each global account management programme needs high-level executive support. Executive commitment is required to provide the global account effort with sufficient resources, give authority to the global account team, provide access to the global customer and the global account team, and support the long-term strategic benefits of a global account approach.

2 *Measure customer satisfaction and act on the findings.* Customer surveys should be conducted by an outside firm to assure accurate and unbiased results. The survey should include questions relevant to global accounts and not be attached to the normal customer satisfaction survey. The results of the survey should be acted on. The attributes for global customers would include information quality, global account manager knowledge and consistency of customer service across geographies. Dun and Bradstreet makes its investment decisions based on the areas needing improvement and communicates the results of the survey to its global customers indicating planned improvements.

3 *Global account management training.* The Global Forum agreed that the global account team members and their support people should receive on-going training and tools to help them better understand and serve customers. The content of the training may come from the global customer satisfaction survey and/or from direct customer involvement in setting the training requirements. Van Leer held a one-week programme for all business unit managers, sales managers and global account managers. DSM holds a four- to five-day global account management programme, which focuses on understanding the global customer's industry, understanding the customer's key success factors and determining how DSM can create value for the customer. The week ends with global account teams presenting their global account plan incorporating the learning for the week.

4 *Make account planning a priority.* Global account team members operate around the world and therefore need a common electronic platform to communicate and collaborate 24 hours a day. Global account teams need to meet and agree on a consistent account plan for the account to be implemented around the world. Dun and Bradstreet has an annual three-day meeting of all account team members, of which one and a half days are devoted to account planning. The account plan puts heavy emphasis on a value-based approach, which has been included in previous training sessions.

5 *Establish consistent, rational pricing and contracts all over the world.* Global customers of the seven companies in the forum have

expressed dissatisfaction with pricing and contract procedures. The best practice was to implement umbrella agreements with global customers, which includes country-specific terms. Dun and Bradstreet uses an umbrella contract, which establishes a consistent discount policy based on the global volume. The umbrella agreement sits on top of the local agreements. Dun and Bradstreet is also designated as the preferred global supplier, which supports a business partnership rather than just a buyer/seller relationship.

6   *Set up incentives that reward global selling.* The compensation of the account manager needs to be tied to the performance of the account globally, not just in a single region or country.

7   *Constant communication is key, internally and externally.* The value of the global account management programme is its strategies, goals and successes. These need to be constantly communicated to customers and internal co-workers. Dun and Bradstreet touches its customers at least 10 times a year with a variety of communication vehicles that focus on the D&B value proposition, how the discounts work and the special services available to global accounts. D&B also communicates with 500 internal associates who are involved with and support the global account effort. Special emphasis is put on the value of the Global D&B Brand and its linkage to the overall strategy (Anon, 1999: 15–19).

CONCLUSIONS

Global drivers are forcing many companies to explore the potential value of developing global strategies. As your customers globalize, some will ask you to serve them globally. Implementing a global account programme requires a radical change for most organizations, which can involve changing the organizational structure, the measurement systems, the compensation systems, the order processing interfaces and much more. If a company is not prepared to make these changes, it runs the risk of developing a global account management programme that increases costs without delivering significant value to its global accounts. This will reduce profit and cause some customers to move to other suppliers who are better suited to serve their needs. While some customers may continue to demand a global approach, there will be limited long-term payback for the supplier because it will incur the additional costs with little or no payback. It may be better for a firm to continue serving customers regionally or locally until there is sufficient leadership to support all the changes necessary to build and implement a successful, global account management programme.

References

Anon (1999) 'How Dun and Bradstreet global implemented lessons learned from a world class benchmarking consortium', *Velocity, Journal of the Strategic Account Management Association*, Fall.

Davenport, E.W., Jr. (1999) 'The formula for global account management success', *Velocity, Journal of the Strategic Account Management Association*, Summer.

Macaulay, D. (2000) 'Consistency in global accounts: Fulfilling your commitment', *Velocity, Journal of the Strategic Account Management Association*, Summer.

Montgomery, D.B., Yip, G.S. and Villalonga, B. (1999) 'Demand for and use of global account management', Marketing Science Institute Working Paper No. 99–115.

Napolitano, L. (1999) 'The state of SAM in Europe', *Velocity, Journal of the Strategic Account Management Association*, Spring.

Senn, C. (2000) 'Operating globally: Not without the regional and local level', *Velocity, Journal of the Strategic Account Management Association*, Spring.

Valentine Pope, A. and Brown, G. (1999) 'Three Cs of GAM: Customer, Customization and Competitive Advantage', *Velocity, Journal of the Strategic Account Management Association*, Summer.

Wilson, K., Croom, S., Millman, T. and Weilbaker, D. (2000) *Global Account Management Study Research Report*, Strategic Account Management Association, April.

Yip, G.S. and Madsen, T.L. (1996) 'Global account management: The new frontier in relationship marketing', *International Marketing Review*, 13, 3.

THE GLOBAL
PHARMACEUTICAL
INDUSTRY

Malcolm Schofield

CHAPTER 9

THE GLOBAL PHARMACEUTICAL INDUSTRY

*I*n this chapter, we will take a snapshot close-up of global factors, influences and behaviours within a twentieth-century industry. From humble origins in traditional medicine, through 100 years of chemical influence and the synthesis of a multiplicity of drugs, the pharmaceutical industry (pharma) presents a combination of the characteristics of other more mature industries. There are the technological complexity, future uncertainty and long-term investment time frames of the energy industry but, in contrast, the new product development challenges and pressures resemble more those of the consumer goods industries.

The industry is therefore a suitable global example within which to identify and discuss the trends and perspectives explored in other chapters. The maturity of the industry will be examined from its historical origins to its present international structure with a longer-lens perspective on its likely form and function in 2020. The nature of globalization and its significance as an influential factor in the pharma industry's growth and development are considered from the following perspectives:

- Historical milestones and evolutionary trends.
- Corporate parenting roles and global/local tension.
- Consolidation/convergence through mergers, acquisitions, partnerships and alliances.
- Parallel global influences in commerce and communications.
- Product development, branding and life cycle management.

HAS THE PHARMACEUTICAL INDUSTRY COME OF AGE?

> By the first decade of the new century, biotechnology could pave the way to a new era in healthcare. (Naisbitt and Aburdene, 1988: 237)

Good health and a happy life are still a distant dream for the substantial majority of the world's population. The extent of this unfulfilled need now fuels and energizes the growth of many global industries grouped and labelled conveniently as life sciences, healthcare and disease management. Within this industry cluster sits pharmaceuticals and the provision of remedies designed to prevent, ameliorate or cure hundreds of discrete diseases, from flu and the common cold to AIDS and the Ebola virus. They are aided and abetted by some new pretenders, in particular biotechnology, genetics and even foodaceuticals. They may or may not transform the industry in the twenty-first century.

It all began just 100 years ago. Felix Hoffman's curiosity created the pharmaceutical industry. Adding a cluster of carbon and hydrogen atoms to a willow bark extract, he produced acetylsalicylic acid and aspirin was born. Germany and Switzerland, the Rhine connection, led the way. Bayer began it. Antecedents of Novartis in Basel and Aventis in Berlin expanded the fledgling industry, a spin-off from bulk chemical manufacture. Progress was slow. While other new industries had moved into global mass production by 1930, drugs still consisted primarily of medicinal compounds, galenicals first formulated by the Greek physician Galen in the second century AD. The chemotherapeutic revolution began seriously with early anti-bacterial substances, Prontosil (Farber) and M&B693 (May & Baker) revolutionizing the practice of medicine.

There have been many significant milestones since in the growth and early maturity of a global ethical drugs industry worth an annual $300 billion by the turn of the twenty-first century. These are summarized below:

1930–45	Anti-infective compounds and penicillin developed. US industry (less disrupted by the Second World War) discovers and markets broader-spectrum antibiotics (Pfizer and Cyanamid). Economies of scale were an essential factor, particularly in the use of the fermentation process.
1945–60	Traditional galenic (organic) and bulk chemical (inorganic) companies create the new synthetic research-based and transatlantic pharmaceutical industry, concentrated in the US, Germany, France, Switzerland, Italy and the UK.
1960–80	Early consolidation through merger or acquisition and increase in cross-competition collaboration through licensing. Global marketing becomes essential as the cost of new drug development escalates. Concern for public health, following serious thalidomide side effects, prompts the establishment of regulatory authorities and in particular the Food and Drug Administration (FDA) in the US. Japan joins the six innovating countries as both a major market (almost as big as the US) and a potential large-scale innovator.
1980–2000	The battle lines are drawn. Sales in excess of $200 billion per annum are shared between over 100 global competitors. Drug development costs rise twentyfold over the period, to in excess of $600 million for each successful drug launched. Cost, growth rate and margin pressures focus both the corporate mind and the business intent. Regulatory authorities rule. Governments intervene in the face of rising healthcare expenditure. The global healthcare burden increases as life expectancy in the advanced industrialized countries rises. Powerful local buyers emerge, health insurers, health services and health

maintenance organizations (HMOs). Decisions are obligatory for all the major providers. What business are we in? Life sciences, healthcare or pure pharma? Modest acquisitions and divestments are overshadowed by mega-mergers. The good fortune of a blockbuster drug provides both the resource and the impetus for the urge to merge. The process becomes cyclical, fad and fashion following form and function. While the industry consolidates, new industries and new specialisms emerge. The major players prefer a focus on pharmaceuticals. Interests in agro-chemicals and animal health are sold or merged with competitors to form bigger independent companies. Origins are forgotten as the industry comes of age. Biotechnology and genetics arrive as seductive investments or potential partners. The industry shows few signs of convergence, consolidation by the few pharmaceutical giants matched by the proliferation of the new science start-up companies.

From early growth in mid-century, 50 years later the industry displays the complex symptoms of dynamic maturity. Eight countries and 20 or so companies dominate the development and marketing of patented drugs with a classic three-way global market split. North America represents one-third of the world market ($100 billion annual sales). Japan and South-East Asian sales now account for between 20 and 25 per cent of the world market ($50–75 billion). Europe accounts for between 25 and 30 per cent ($75–90 billion). The rest of the world, largely concentrating on off-patent derivative products or generics, contributes just one-fifth or so to the total ethical pharma market, tempting only to those blockbuster drugs whose profit and return are already guaranteed elsewhere.

That the market is mature is confirmed by its lack of growth in the later years of the twentieth century. That it is dynamic is evidenced by the scientific and technological revolution sweeping through the pharmaceutical industry (*Economist*, 1998). The industry has blurred boundaries. It is a borderless world in principle, although the sheer size of the American market, European fragmentation and the insularity of the Japanese have made it easier for US industry to grow and prosper. A foothold in America and a global presence are mutually inclusive. As Kenichi Ohmae observed a decade ago, 'national borders have effectively disappeared and, along with them, the economic logic that made them useful lines in the first place. Not everyone however has noticed ... the critical activities of drug discovery, screening, and testing are now virtually the same among the best companies everywhere in the world' (Ohmae, 1990: 21).

IS FOCUS INEVITABLE?

Life sciences are the orthodox foundation for a corporate parent providing and seeking synergy for a healthcare subsidiary, as can be seen from Figure 9.1. Aventis and Bayer both possess such conventional upbringings, even though one has merged recently and the other has more or less stayed with the same broad-based corporate strategy for a century. In contrast, Johnson & Johnson and GlaxoSmithKline balance their ethical portfolios with strong over-the-counter (OTC) business divisions.

There are other strategic choices for parents to make, although few so far have been tempted vertically into a seamless healthcare service. Merck is the exception, with its steady growth by acquisition into managed care. The post-merger preference more recently is the desire for a concentrated focus around pharmaceuticals. Pfizer, GlaxoSmithKline, AstraZeneca and Novartis have a declared strategic intent to limit their parental hierarchy to this single tier or generation. Relinquishing an OTC business is a different issue. Early rationalization initiated by such parent boards, as Glaxo did, favours a pure ethical business intent. The value of global brands as a counterweight to off-patent blockbuster product decline may discourage future parents from the easy divestment of such businesses.

Recent mergers and steady organic growth have produced a number of industry giants. Table 9.1 lists the industry top 20, of which eight are American, eight are European, one is mixed and the last three are

New opportunity industries			
biotechnology, genetics, alternative therapies			

Established industries

Life sciences (bio-sciences) Agrochemical
Animal health
Human health = healthcare, see below

Healthcare disease management
Including hospital/home-managed care, surgery and non-drug therapies
Therapeutics and drug-based treatment, see below

Therapeutics and drug-based treatment
1 Diagnostics
2 Delivery systems
3 Devices
4 Drugs--------------------
Consumer products (OTC)
Over the counter (non-prescription) **Annual global sales $40bn**
Ethical products = pharmaceuticals, see below

Global market for pharmaceuticals, sales $300bn*

North America $100bn	Europe $85bn		Asia $60bn	Other $55bn
USA $95bn	Germany $ 15bn France $ 14 bn Italy $ 9bn UK $ 9bn	Rest of Europe	Japan $55bn	Latin America $20 bn

Figure 9.1 The industry and global market context.
* Pharmaceutic sales of prescribed drugs and estimated market sizes in 2000.

Japanese. Market dominance is very evident. The market share percentage held by the top 20 companies (full merger is assumed and calculated retrospectively) has increased from 36 per cent in 1990 to an estimated 69 per cent in 2000. However, only one of the top 20 features in the Fortune all companies Global Top 100. Merck is in at number 100, dwarfed by such industry leaders as General Motors who generate five times Merck's parent company revenue of $32.7 billion, less than half of which, $17.5 billion, is pharmaceutical sales. Similarly Wal-Mart, ranked second to General Motors, generates revenues of $167 billion, seven and a half times the pharmaceutical sales of the most focused company, GlaxoSmithKline. Europe's largest company,

DaimlerChrysler, is five times the size of its near geographical neighbour Bayer, whose pharmaceutical sales ($5.3 billion) account for only one-fifth of its total annual turnover.

The major US companies shown in the table have more than doubled their market share from 14 per cent in 1990 (39 per cent of the

Table 9.1 The pharmaceutical league table

Year		1980	1990	1995	1999/2000		
Total market size $ billion		226.0	266.0	286.0	304.0		
Rank and region	Global organization	Annual sales $ bn	Annual sales $ bn	Annual sales $ bn	Market share %	Fortune 500 global ranking	
1 EUR	GlaxoSmithKline	12.0	18.7	22.2	7.3	125	
2 USA	Pfizer/Warner-Lambert	5.6	9.5	20.5	6.7	115	
3 USA	Merck	6.1	11.3	17.5	5.8	100	
4 EUR	AstraZeneca	4.0	8.0	14.8	4.9	237	
5 EUR	Aventis	10.2	13.2	14.8	4.9	362	
6 USA	Bristol-Myers Squibb	5.8	7.8	14.3	4.7	206	
7 EUR	Novartis	8.3	10.5	12.6	4.1	192	
8 US/ EUR	Pharmacia Upjohn/ Monsanto	4.4	5.2	11.2	3.7	500+	
9 EUR	Roche	4.5	8.0	11.0	3.6	239	
10 USA	Johnson & Johnson	4.1	6.3	10.7	3.5	126	
11 USA	Eli Lilly	3.6	6.0	9.5	3.1	485	
12 USA	American Home Products	4.1	7.0	9.5	3.1	358	
13 USA	Schering-Plough	2.6	4.3	8.0	2.6	500+	
14 USA	Abbott Laboratories	3.5	6.3	5.7	1.9	372	
15 EUR	Sanofi-Synthelabo	3.0	4.0	5.3	1.7	500+	
16 EUR	Bayer	3.6	4.6	5.3	1.7	117	
17 EUR	Boehringer Ingelheim	2.5	3.8	5.0	1.6	500+	
18 JAP	Takeda	2.6	3.5	5.0	1.6	500+	
19 JAP	Sankyo	3.0	4.4	4.0	1.3	500+	
20 JAP	Yamanouchi	2.8	3.6	3.5	1.2	500+	
Total top twenty		96.3	146.0	210.4			
US organizations %		39	42	51	35.0		
European organizations %		52	50	43	30.0		
Japanese organizations %		9	8	6	4.0		
% total market (top twenty)		36.0	51.0		69.0		

Source: Scrip magazine annual reviews, 1995–2000; company annual reviews and their official websites.

top 20 share) to 35 per cent in 1999 (51 per cent of the top 20 share). A greater preoccupation with merger and acquisition activity among the major European companies appears to have distracted them from such steady organic growth over the same period. Their share of the global market increased by only 11 per cent, from 19 to 30 per cent (43 per cent of the top 20 share). The Japanese, challenged by domestic market difficulties, have grown their market share by only 1 per cent, to 4 per cent over the same period, while losing a 3 per cent share among the top 20.

Many industry observers have argued that in spite of apparent major company dominance, consolidation is far from over. Excess capacity still costs the industry almost half total annual turnover (Pursche, 1996). The pattern at the turn of the century does illustrate the emergence of a super league, the top five doubling their market share to nearly 30 per cent, the bottom five adding only 1 per cent to just over 7 per cent.

The first consolidation wave took place in the 1980s, SmithKline with Beecham and Bristol-Myers with Squibb. Increased scale was the rationale. The primary synergies were revenue based. The second wave in the middle of the 1990s was primarily cost based and included such mergers as Glaxo and Wellcome, Hoechst, Marion Merrill Dow and Roussel, Pharmacia and Upjohn. The first wave arose from a desire for greater physician and geographical coverage; the second from a need to reduce capacity in terms of products, sales teams and headquarters overheads. The most recent wave appears to be a third distinct initiative where the parental intent appears to be the pursuit of growth-based synergies. This means aiming for a lead position in specific therapeutic areas (TAs) or disease states.

Corporate parent agendas in any of the top companies, striving to build or protect their interests in pharmaceuticals, are once again dominated by a felt need to merge. To be significantly bigger is a catch-all response to the current dilemmas of contained health expenditures and low market growth, escalating drug development costs and the diminished prospect for blockbuster product launches. If merger is the preferred strategic option, the following is the key question for the corporate parent.

WHAT SORT OF BUSINESSES ARE WE AND HOW WOULD WE AIM TO BE DIFFERENT IN FUTURE?

It is no longer fashionable to be positioned on the extreme, in chemicals or in drugs. Life sciences, disease management, healthcare and pharma have been more popular business definitions. Within these definitions, only GlaxoWellcome, of the top 20 'healthcare/life sciences' companies, can claim dedication to a single cause, with 100 per cent pharma sales. Its merger with SmithKline Beecham raises the corporate issue once again of whether to retain and build or divest the significant consumer product interests of its new partner. Pfizer is intent on the same aim, reducing its non-pharma activities from 50 per cent of sales in 1990 to less than 10 per cent by 2000, while at the same time trebling total revenues to $20.5 billion. For Pfizer the post-merger issue is the same, to build on or dispose of the Warner-Lambert OTC portfolio.

Many others defined their first-tier business as life sciences, their second tier as healthcare and their third tier as pharma (see Figure 9.1). Aventis (life sciences, 67 per cent pharma) Merck (healthcare, 58 per cent pharma) were bigger in 1999 than either Glaxo or Pfizer in total annual sales. AstraZeneca (70 per cent pharma) – 'a winning combination' – claimed to have similar science-based cultures, management philosophies and a shared vision of the pharmaceutical industry. Yet Zeneca held other interests, Salick Health Care, which perhaps encouraged it to aspire to be a healthcare company, and its £100 million agrochemical business, which placed it in the life sciences galaxy of companies. Legal battles with Monsanto over glyphosate-tolerant soya beans, spreading the debilitating conflict, like an allergic rash, over a number of states in the US, were a frustrating distraction. In 1998 Zeneca announced the possible divestment of Zeneca specialities (other than Marlow Foods). So where was AstraZeneca heading, healthcare or life sciences or pure pharma?

The requirement to undertake global restructuring within the pharmaceuticals business has not deflected the executive team from its objective of converting

AstraZeneca from a bio-science business into an essentially pure healthcare company. (1999 Annual Review)

Some of its businesses have been sold or merged, for example Syngenta was created in a joint venture with Novartis to grant independence to its agrochemical and seed businesses. Merck, Eli Lilly and SmithKline Beecham (SB) had originally chosen to extend their activities in the direction of healthcare, buying pharmacy benefits management (PBM) firms in the US. Yet in 1999, SB chief executive, Jan Leschly announced the sale of their interests at a loss of $1.6 billion, equivalent to more than its annual investment in R&D ($1.3 billion). Four years earlier Eli Lilly had invested and lost the equivalent of two years R&D in its similarly fated venture into PBMs.

Does such corporate activity arise from parental concern or just plain interference and lack of trust? Managing the transformation through a period of global uncertainty and change seems to give purpose to the responsible parent. *The Economist* recently commented that 'one of the latest ideas to come unstuck is the life sciences company – no surprise to cynics who saw it as a pretty label' (*Economist*, 2000a). 'Sticking to the knitting' seems to be the core philosophy behind current corporate positioning. The definition of the 'knitting' for pharma companies is probably 'fighting, treating and preventing human disease through drug-based therapies'. Perhaps then there is some wisdom in avoiding close association with plants and animals. There is a convincing case to be argued for higher expenditure on drugs, devices, diagnostics and delivery systems, for both life-threatening and life-limiting conditions. Such higher expenditure could lead to a lower overall expenditure on healthcare. The case is evidently more difficult to argue for lifestyle therapies – erectile dysfunction, obesity etc.

All three sectors conventionally subdivide into a discrete number of therapeutic areas, the popular top 10 of which are shown in Table 9.2. These form the essential business building blocks of a pharma company. The degree of interest in pharmaceuticals is the fundamental stage in the knitting process – choosing the fibre. The changes are both the perspective and the spectrum of expertise available at corporate board level. The dedicated companies would claim such focused expertise already:

- GlaxoSmithKline avoids the broader-based potential conflict of interest by aspiring to discover breakthrough medicines that fight asthma, migraine, HIV and other diseases that affect people's lives.

- Novartis chooses to pursue new skills in the science of life, and within pharma is focused in several therapeutic categories, including transplantation, central nervous system disorders, cardiovascular/endocrine/respiratory diseases, dermatology, oncology/haematology, rheumatism/bone and hormone replacement therapy.

- Roche offers a family of pharmaceuticals, diagnostics, vitamins, fine chemicals, fragrances and flavours as a healthcare group.

- Eli Lilly addresses people's urgent and unmet medical needs in neuroscience, diabetes, cancer, cardiovascular diseases, infectious diseases and women's health.

- Pfizer's chairman and chief executive, Bill Steere, made no secret of his single aim – to beat Merck in the USA drugs market, in total sales, by 2001. He is quoted as saying, 'mergers in this industry are done out of weakness; we're not weak' (Woolley, 1999). Yet even he changed strategy unable to resist the allure and acquisition of Warner-Lambert's marketing capabilities and the possibility of then falling into rival hands. Where rivals had previously frittered away energies on mergers and acquisitions and other distractions, Pfizer had hitherto intensified its spending in the laboratory and in detailing (salesforce coverage).

WHO FEATURES IN THE 2000 LEAGUE TABLE OF STRATEGIC INTENT?

The current league table, compiled from sales volumes, R&D expenditures, company annual reports and website statements, is shown in Table 9.2. The 10 therapeutic areas (TAs) identified represent two-thirds of total pharma sales. The 20 companies also account for 69 per cent of the industry's $300 billion sales. Each company has been allocated a ranking that represents its current presence and future prospects within each TA. Three credits and above suggests market leadership, depending on the size of the TA and the competitive position.

Table 9.2 Strategic focus and intent in the pharmaceutical industry

Therapeutic area	Skin	Anti inf	Anti vir	CV	CNS	GI	End	Onc	Res	WH	Other
Area size $billion	10	25	20	35	30	10	25	15	20	10	
Global organization											
GlaxoSmithKline	0	0000	00	0	000	00	00	00	0000	0	0
Pfizer/Warner-Lambert	0	000	0	0000	000		000	0	0		0
Merck	0	00	00	0000	0	00	00	0	0	0	0
AstraZeneca				00	00	0000	00	000	00		00
Aventis	0	00	00	00	0		00	00		0	00
Bristol-Myers Squibb	0	00	00	00	00		00	00		0	0
Novartis	00	0	00	00	00		0	00	00		0
Roche	0	00	00	0	00		0	000	0		00
Johnson & Johnson	00	00	0		00	00	0				0
Eli Lilly		00		0	000		00	00		00	
Pharmacia Upjohn		00	0	0	0		0	00	0	0	0
American Home Products			0	0	0	0		00	0		00
Schering-Plough	0	0		0			0	00			0
Abbott Laboratories		0	0		0	0	0				0
Sanofi-Synthelabo				00	00		0				0
Bayer		0	0	00	0		0	0		0	0
Boehringer Ingelheim		0		0			0	00			
Takeda				0	0		00				0
Sankyo				0			0				0
Yamanouchi				0			0	0		0	0

Key: Skin = Dermatology; Anti inf = Anti-infective; Anti vir = Anti-viral; CV = Cardiovascular; CNS = Central nervous system; GI = Gastroenterology; End = Endocrinology; Onc = Oncology; Res = Respiratory; WH = Women's Health.

0 = active global market presence/pipeline products
00 = strong global market position in the medium term
000 = market leadership in sales revenue/new product development
0000 = dominant position sustainable in the longer term

Source: Scrip magazine annual review, 1995–2000; company annual reviews and their official websites.

Dominance could possibly be claimed by GlaxoSmithKline in respiratory and anti-infectives, AstraZeneca in GI and Merck and Pfizer in the largest market, cardiovascular. Conversely, nearly 90 of the TA subsectors show only a modest presence for the company concerned. Such weak representation should be subject to regular corporate review, as candidates for either withdrawal or for strengthening through merger, alliance, joint venture or acquisition.

Merger alone rarely brings a perfect synergy. The key strategic question for the hunter to address is which prospective partner would best suit each of the chosen and targeted TAs. A BMS/Novartis merger would offer potential dominance in four TAs. A potent Roche/Novartis Basel-based link-up could bring about dominant positions in three TAs, with strength elsewhere. It would, however, take a mega-merger of the three to achieve and strive to retain a double-digit market share. The partner-seeking and match-making game is simplistic at this level, but nevertheless forces the issue of where the ideal terrestrial marriages are. The ideal search should be initiated at the TA level. While this makes practical sense, in political terms it is unlikely. Parental guidance rather than parental choice should be the more appropriate role relationship for corporate HQs. Joint development ventures and co-marketing agreements are useful introductions to potential merger partners. The neater the fit, the clearer the intent, the more quickly the sought-after growth should materialize. The better the motives behind the merger, as perceived by all the stakeholders, the greater the motivation of all concerned.

Strategic initiatives aimed at business growth should ideally then emerge out of therapeutic area strategy teams rather than life sciences, healthcare or even pharma boardrooms. Merger is just one way of responding and a mega-merger is unlikely to provide the perfect reply. Better a combination of modest acquisitions and alliances with hand-picked smaller companies, whose focus and dedicated competencies enable the new venture to secure stronger TA positions. At that level, the new working relationship is more likely to be one of equals and both parties positively charged towards future growth. It is easy to argue for the ideal. The reality is still more likely to be parental initiatives, targeting mergers with other large organizations, particularly if the intent arises from concern about the future profitability impact of other more mature interests such as agrochemicals.

WHO ARE THE MORE FOCUSED OF THE MAJOR PLAYERS?

Where do companies aim to be number 1? Do the advantages of knitting a simple pattern from a single fibre (pharma by organic growth) outweigh the advantages of a multifibre complex pattern (life sciences or healthcare + acquisition)? These are important questions for the corporate parent. The issue is the extent to which they offer the right specialist knowledge and visionary skills in order to make the right choices and allocate resources accordingly. Do they add or diminish value as they modify or vary their strategic aims and intent?

Market dynamics, growth rates, complexity and the ease and cost of access to customers determine the degree of focus found in any industry. Fast-growing markets, requiring modest development expenditures, never force the issue of choice. Mature markets/industries force the pace of consolidation. Present market conditions, with healthcare expenditure globally contained to a single-digit annual increase and development costs heading towards $0.75 billion per successful drug launched, make focus the essential discipline for all in this industry. Even a 10 per cent market share, 2.5 per cent better than anything achieved so far, would still demand a disciplined approach to TA selection and concentration. Better for the customer as well if there are six rather than sixteen companies concentrating on CNS. Focus makes strategic sense. It is also common sense, but is easily postponed, pending the search for an ideal merger partner.

WHAT ARE THE IDEAL SIZE AND FOCUS FOR LONG-TERM SUCCESS?

It is said that it is in development that 75 per cent of major investment costs are incurred, rather than in discovery, manufacturing or marketing. That being so, a more disciplined choice of businesses (therapeutic areas and indications within areas) should be made and regularly reviewed. Similarly, organizational competence in both discovery and market understanding should be integrated more by intent than by default or serendipity. Scale is important in basic research and in clinical development.

> Sandwiched between the two is drug development, where clever chemistry – and cunning experimentation – can turn an unassuming compound into a

promising new medicine. Here, creativity counts for something. (*Economist*, 2000b, commenting on the GlaxoSmithKline merger)

The organizational challenge, therefore, is to build independence and innovation into the disciplined processes of discovery and development. GlaxoSmithKline aspires to giving its free thinkers room to manoeuvre through the formation of six stronghold discovery centres. Roche Bioscience consists of two autonomous business units: inflammatory diseases and neurobiology. Each unit includes basic, pre-clinical and early clinical research staff, as well as strategic marketing and business development. Pfizer goes one stage further in harmonizing discovery and marketing understanding, putting all candidate drugs through the 'CRAM' programme (Central Research Assists Marketing). Although scientists account for 90 per cent of the development team, it is 'captained' by people from marketing.

There are always occasional 'off-strategy' opportunities, such as Viagra. In such events, the more focused the business, the easier the task of managing the exception and maximizing its value. There must be a consistent logic used that connects resource/competence building across the typical business functions within a pharma business. Such logic, the most persuasive argument for merger candidate selection, cannot be deduced easily from recent public statements of strategic intent.

WHAT MATTERS IN THE ORGANIZATION DEVELOPMENT OF A GLOBAL COMPANY?

If you are a main board director of a life sciences or healthcare company, your influence on the growth and direction of the business has to penetrate through the many layers of the organization. Frustration can therefore be relieved easily by the decision to pursue a merger. The major corporate task is setting the context. For a life sciences company there are two or three corporate HQs – life sciences and/or healthcare and/or pharma – each capable of embarking on a quest for a merger. The feel-good factor of being busy and justifying your existence, combined with any personal motives to be seen to succeed at something, drives the process forward. When the business really needs focus and a radical organizational overhaul in the face of external change, merger mania can be hypnotic. The attitude taken can be: do nothing; we are about to merge.

The ideal sequence of events would be as follows:

1 To leave corporate strategy to the pharma company.
2 To organize development into autonomous therapeutic area businesses.
3 To encourage the senior management team in each TA to put forward a brief statement of strategic intent, indicating which enabling technologies, which substances, which lead markets etc. are going to drive future growth.
4 To obtain commentaries on those statements from the major functions.
5 To allocate priorities and existing resources.
6 To produce a shopping list for additional resources.
7 To decide on any major initiatives arising from the shopping list, choosing, if appropriate, the ideal merger candidate(s).
8 To select and set up the negotiating team. The strategic driver is the TA, hopefully the point of confluence for the critical knowledge streams.

The AstraZeneca merger appears to come close to this ideal and, with good strategic discipline, should hold or secure dominant positions in anaesthesia/pain control and gastro-intestinal, with strong positions in respiratory and oncology. Success for the company in cardiovascular could well depend on a disciplined choice of activities, within particular indication/therapy combinations. These are now relevant issues for the corporate parent to address, once the reorganization and rationalization of its non-pharmaceutical activities is complete.

The real risks with a merger are introspection for a time and debilitating after-effects. It is wrong to condone the political realities of life, but the primaeval source of acute discomfort is usually personality clash, followed by the equally primitive school playground process of appointments, equity demanding that equal numbers from both sides should occupy the key positions in the new organization. Parents should set a good example, but rarely do so. Then there is the risk of indigestion, with denial of some of the difficulties arising from integration. Paranoia over early loss of market share encourages myopic thinking. Experience dictates that an initial share loss is the inevitable side effect of the post-merger organizational disruption and the pursuit of cost savings. No one should be at all surprised by this or simplistically assume it to be a symptom of merger failure. Such outcomes need strategies for prevention or amelioration. Much can be learned from the misfortunes of others. Pharmacia and Upjohn span the cultural Atlantic divide and have struggled to uncover the Holy Grail of synergy. Pfizer and Warner-Lambert, Glaxo and SKB have their interests and intentions more simply focused on the US market. Perhaps single-mindedness rather than ambiguity is the essence of parental involvement in the building of a substantial global pharmaceutical company.

IS THERE A THINK GLOBAL, ACT LOCAL DILEMMA?

The tension exists in all the top pharma companies between the scientists and the marketers, the intrinsically curious and the extrinsically pragmatic. As the medical need to address, treat and eliminate disease is largely global, discovery and development are centralized. Contact with the patient, physician and healthcare provider is, in contrast, local and selling (detailing) is decentralized. Knowledge of the product and contact with the market come together through the extensive and expensive process of clinical trials. No other industry is faced to the same extent with this necessary but delaying product-proving process. Generally speaking, it is centrally driven and locally administered in the pursuit of regulatory approval. The seamless two-way flow of knowledge, product and market is still a distant dream, even for the best. Serendipity remains more likely to produce a successful drug than the smooth-running, process-based organization. Multidisciplined, multinational project teams are evident everywhere. Essential supporting technologies are the subject of serious review. The opportunities for improvement are infinite, but so are the formidable obstacles. Both are addressed in the context of product development below.

WHERE ARE FUTURE INVESTMENT AND EFFORT BEST APPLIED?

As the compelling struggle to launch blockbuster drugs intensifies, contradictions are emerging. Attention may well prove to be misapplied to mergers, given too much to licensing and even, it might be argued, be more than is really needed on scientific discovery. The 'Cinderella' perhaps is, rather, the simpler, more essential task of improving the selection and development processes. There was a time when one successful drug every five years or so satisfied the appetite. It is now very different. Three new active substances each year is Astra-Zeneca's target. This equates to one for every $750 million R&D spend or necessary to sustain $4–5 billion annual sales. As for retaining market leadership in a chosen therapeutic area, a constant flow of breakthrough products is now essential. AstraZeneca or Glaxo in respiratory, Merck or Aventis in cardiovascular, are compelled to protect their competitive advantage and build their specialist capabilities in these markets.

Convention has it that 'R' and 'D' fit together, and in most industries that makes good sense. Pure research invariably attracts the biggest slice of investment. For pharmaceutical companies, scientific discovery offers the prospect of a gargantuan feast. High throughput screening, pharmacogenomics, computer-based molecular design and biological advances provide a rainbow of bewildering choices. But quantity never ever means quality. Current behaviour conveys low self-esteem on the part of top management in assessing their ability to combine science and serendipity. Mergers, acquisitions and high-price licensing deals are the strategic answer to the impoverished pipeline. Such universal initiatives are expensive and also accompanied by significant hidden costs.

A *McKinsey Quarterly* article (Aitkin *et al.*, 2000) suggests a growing propensity to license in promising compounds, rather than to nurture more discovery initiatives closer to home. Sadly, each successive post-merger rationalization seeks to take out costs equivalent to the savings forecasts. Far-flung discovery outposts are easier prey than those development and marketing bastions defended by entrenched barons on either side of the merger. The McKinsey article draws particular attention to the failure to track the relative profitability of both internally and externally developed drugs.

The consequences of this externally focused growth addiction are a middle-heavy organization, fed on a diet of 'takeaways', not inclined to lose weight through a sensible, sustained lifestyle. There are exceptions, Merck certainly and Pfizer until the Warner-Lambert Lipitor connection forced its hand. The healthy lifestyle motto could well be a different external focus, none better than the Accenture website line, 'find out what your customer values most and deliver only what you do best'. This simply means an organization that is equally market and competence focused.

The bigger issues are thus not with research. The central problem lies in the narrow, inordinately expensive and time-consuming development pipeline, from pre-clinical to launch. Only 32 new products successfully emerged in 1999. To be more specific, in respiratory, a market worth $20 billion and with significant unmet needs, only one new product was launched. Yet there are 2000 respiratory patent registrations, 650 pipeline products and 120 products in late stage development. The top seven companies have 55 of the latter. Total development expenditure in respiratory over the next ten years is likely to exceed $60 billion. The arithmetic appears far from attractive. There are just too many candidates gathered at the pre-clinical door queuing up for capacity in a development process that is very likely over-organized, over-staffed, over-complicated and, through no fault of the pharma company, over-regulated.

IF CORPORATE OBESITY IS THE CONDITION, WHAT IS THE IDEAL TREATMENT?

The challenge is to choose and adopt the most effective change capabilities and to improve radically the new product selection and development processes. The first issue applies particularly to the impact of science and technology on discovery, in as much as independence needs to be respected and preserved. Pure research requires global devolution, autonomy, discretion and a set of underpinning values that encourage serendipity and stubbornness, free flowing imagination and intuition. For example, interferon-based treatment for multiple sclerosis was pioneered within a programme of AIDS research, not by a rational process but by following a hunch. Viagra came out of the Pfizer laboratories in Kent, UK and research targeted on heart failure. Variety and diversity need champions. Pharmaceutical companies also need strategists who can cope with apparent contradiction, convergence and divergence, centralization and devolution, global and local, focus and freedom, insourcing and outsourcing, ownership and alliances, networks and hierarchies, science driven and market driven and so on. The loose/tight capability championed years ago by McKinsey is often the accidental 'collateral' casualty of the post-merger cost-cutting programme. When Glaxo-SmithKline finally emerges as a corporate giant, for instance, in which part of its anatomy will the Wellcome values reside?

The second issue is growth. Once again, contradiction is healthy. A comprehensive network of discovery alliances, in-house initiatives and selective 'licensing in' agreements ideally feeds organic growth. The selection process should not reside within the research function or with specialists in legal negotiation. Development business units with the necessary competences and global perspective must determine the appropriate candidates for entry into the time-critical, inordinately expensive clinical trial process. Choice of indication is an essential early stage and requires a development unit-based understanding of markets. This is easier said than done, given the dominance of the US, the fragmentation of Europe and the introspection of Japan. The respiratory portfolio, for example, in asthma, in rhinitis and in chronic obstructive pulmonary disease (COPD) in particular, needs a dynamic understanding of the market, less data and more shared knowledge. Such a competence is easily assumed, but requires the right initiatives in explicit and tacit knowledge access and awareness – a process that is often unrecognized, resides only in specialist pockets or is inadvertently destroyed by such interventions as mergers or major management consultancy initiatives.

The contradictory aspect of a merger is also sadly that talent inevitably leaves early, knowledge networks atrophy and a battle of will and personality places politics before products. Corporate consultancy assignments, both pre-merger and post-merger, offer alternative routes to either a better organization or more effective integration. Inevitably, they also promise a seductive additional technique or process, for example claiming more efficient product life cycle management or fast-track status for super brands. There are no prescribed diets that ease the process of weight loss and the fight for fitness, however. Corporate lifestyle management, a stable structure and self-discipline are the essentials. Add cross-cultural complexity, and continuity becomes even more essential. Organizations have a complex metabolic structure that is easily disturbed. Cost reductions add weight in the longer term.

The third issue is the strategic development process itself. Patients, physicians, prescribers and payers are all customers whose needs are best articulated as early as possible in the target market profile. There are inevitable tensions in the confinement phase from pre-clinical through to launch. Research is concerned to hand over a perfect embryo. Development is anxious to begin the efficacy and safety-proving processes with a minimum of delay. Marketing wants to know the product characteristics in advance of approvals, to name (brand) the child and to begin to position it for life. This particular issue is dealt with in more detail later in this chapter. All are essential roles, but they create a complicated set of relationships around ownership and responsibility. Development must be a multidisciplinary function, competent in product selection, fully conversant in market understanding and nurturing value proposition-supported products from pre-clinical trials to pre-launch. Strategic responsibility should begin and end here.

Parallel responsibilities are dangerous tensions potentially leading to conflict, confusion, uncertainty, neglect and delay. Add merger or consultancy fad to the mixture and the mess becomes a maelstrom. Matrix organizations and cross-functional teams have proved difficult to manage and are over-complicated answers to the simple formula: competence plus authority equals accountability. Sequential responsibility is easier to operate and therefore more effective, providing that development in particular is well informed, well led and skilled in multinational team working and communications. It is easy to criticize from outside looking in. Experience and observation of other industries do, however, signal an urgent need to sort out the development process now and to protect best practice through the trauma of major merger.

Perhaps good global sense will prevail. If so, those with respiratory problems could look forward to a fivefold increase in new product launches, to more cost-effective targeted treatments and to something closer to a normal lifestyle. Most other therapeutic areas offer even greater potential for radical improvement. The global pharmaceutical industry is not the automotive industry at an earlier stage of maturity. It is different and has a unique set of challenges that cannot be addressed by a generic formula such as merger and consolidation. Capturing the essence of discovery, never losing sight of value for the customer and being smarter and cleverer in development are the best foundations. Marketing then has an essential role to play, but with 'e' now before everything there lie other issues and other lessons to unlearn in the pursuit of the lean mean, fit and fertile organization.

The daunting prospect of having to spend almost $1 billion in R&D for every new successful drug launched is the one major issue eclipsing all the rest in the pharmaceutical industry. No other industry faces such a formidable regenerative task. The pressure on people, procedures and processes will progressively build as one blockbuster drug after another ends its short patented life. Replacements will be few and far between, even though the number of patented prospects has never been higher. The cause and the effect are the same. Life expectancy has increased faster than affordability. We live longer and healthier, therefore we need lengthier and bigger clinical trials to show improved efficacy.

IS THERE A SIMPLER SOLUTION?

> With a laser you can drill a hole in a diamond – when you focus a company you create the same effect. (Ries, 1997)

Partnerships in all their forms, both global and local, should ideally be a consequence of focus rather than focus being the outcome. Partnership is therefore a seductive but illusory distraction from the real issue.

There are the familiar strategic options available, further global mergers, acquisitions, alliances and licensing agreements. Mega-mergers take time and energy, rarely deliver the promised benefits of real synergy and are often a late knee-jerk parental response to the call to do something. The escalating trend of rising development costs has to be reversed. There is only one serious strategic option available: focus. Tough decisions and choices over where to concentrate effort and resources are inevitable and unavoidable, if the billion-dollar hurdle is to be lowered in real terms. The key questions are:

- In which broad areas should discovery resources be concentrated and with whom should a network of alliances be built?
- In which therapeutic areas should development and marketing expertise be applied?
- Should the aim be to lead in a therapeutic area (TA), be a drug category or be an indication niche player?
- Should marketed product portfolios be built essentially from within or by alliance or both?

Integrated development and marketing are the essence of a profitable and growing pharmaceutical company. Their deployment and enhancement are the real source of added value. So far, there is little evidence of effective integration. There are many reasons why progress towards it has been slow. The pressing issues have tended to be elsewhere. Pfizer and GlaxoSmithKline are attending to post-merger rationalization, Aventis and Novartis are trying hard to manage their bigger life sciences portfolios or divesting parts of them. Others such as American Home Products are desperately seeking partners in order to achieve critical mass. None of these external initiatives directly addresses the issue of escalating development costs. It might even be argued that they add fuel to the fire. Decisions over best practice have to be revisited each time a corporate entity is disturbed. Best practice embraces both organization form and processes and the old adage 'if it ain't broke don't fix it' has a great deal of relevance in the easily done dismantling of existing networks and their associated tacit knowledge centres of competence. Strategic focus first is the more secure route to sustained profitable growth.

WHAT CAN BE DONE AS A BETTER ALTERNATIVE TO IMPROVE THE RATIO OF DEVELOPMENT COSTS AND SALES REVENUES?

There are three overlapping components to manage, both independently and sequentially:

- Pre-clinical development from patent to target product profile (TPP) selection.
- Pre-regulatory approval from choice of first indication to new drug application.
- Pre-marketing activity from target market profile (TMP) to launch.

Who should do this is the more debatable question, given the traditional functional structures within the industry, the silo conventions of discovery, development and commercialization and the more recently based emphasis on processes, matrix organizations and multidisciplinary project teams. This issue is not new. The Japanese automotive industry built its global success on a number of *shusas* or heavyweight product managers responsible for leading a team of functional experts from product concept to patent expiry, cradle to grave and maybe beyond.

Toyota and Honda, both highly focused organizations, have benefited in particular from the single-minded concerns of the designer/engineer champion. Each product portfolio needs a director. Each chosen market sector by indication deserves a champion, who steers a series of products through from pre-clinical to launch. An effective champion has the personal skills, team competences and explicit/implicit authority to attract the necessary development and marketing resources towards products with prospects. It is the clarity of the role that can have more of an impact than anything else on future development expenditure and its effectiveness. A champion's responsibilities include early termination where insoluble problems arise and continued investment decisions where both the clinical trial and market signals are positive. Essentially, the idea of having a champion to oversee a product through its gestation and to prompt much earlier decisions on its welfare fundamentally changes the whole way in which, in this industry at least, a global product is developed.

WHAT MIGHT THIS PIVOTAL LEADERSHIP ROLE FOR THE CHAMPION INVOLVE?

There are three components:

- reception (selection or rejection);
- construction (design and development);
- promotion (position and perception).

Reception skills include a capacity to manage the discovery interface, the construction and application of a current and predictive market 'map' of the therapeutic area and the finite number of target market profiles (TMPs) derived from it. In respiratory, for example, one TMP might be for COPD and another for the ultimate and ideal relief plus control asthma combination therapy, and a third for severe asthma and avoidance of high hospitalization costs. The reconciliation of a target product profile and a target market profile is the essential disciplinary gateway. This process has been applied to some extent already, described by such phrases as 'market aligned planning' (GlaxoSmithKline). However, there needs to be an even better and deeper understanding of unfulfilled market needs than has ever been developed before.

The different content and scope of each profile are illustrated in Figure 9.2. The development process in the absence of a TMP requires the provision of a market context for each product through new market research initiatives or a reliance on later market assessments of potential. Either option is more expensive when measured in terms of delay (less time in patent) or in proceeding with unhelpful clinical trial programmes.

Construction skills are heavily weighted towards regulatory approval. Product concept design and development protocols will dictate the choice of discipline, but flexibility is essential here, the acceptance

PRODUCT	MARKET
■ Vision	■ Statement of portfolio strategic intent
■ Competitive environment	■ The therapeutic context – prediction to
■ Main customer groups and their	stability (trends)
unmet needs	■ Patent needs/experience zones
■ Pricing strategy	■ Patent and pipeline activities
■ Key claims for launch	■ The opinion leader argument
■ Route of administration	■ Issues concerning treatment and
■ Dosing regimen	compliance (physiological + psychological)
■ Label indication	■ Global numbers – treated/untreated,
	growth/treatment trends
	■ Disease progression parameters (reality)
	■ Information sources, Internet/action groups
	+ emergent influencers

Figure 9.2   Target profiles.

by the development team of a set of specific goals, communicated through an e-commerce-based networked organization. Manufacturing processes, often an afterthought, are now adding greater complexity to this process and contribute to the potential for setbacks and delays. The inherent uncertainty of clinical trials can be managed more effectively with the essential competences and the decision processes simplified through the overall direction and control of better-informed global project teams. Their enemies are over-elaborate procedures, big committees and an organizational separation of competence and judgement. Such constraints exist in every organization. Management consultancy thrives on their proliferation. The relevant issue is the extent to which they lengthen the development time frame, once again eroding the 'in patent' window of opportunity. Development is not a three-stage relay race following a good discovery start. It is much more a three-lap race for the champion and his or her team. Construction anticipates reception. Design and development are geared to the selection of appropriate candidate drugs. There should be no surprises.

Similarly, promotion anticipates both reception and construction. There are critical strategic marketing protocols to be met before pre-marketing can begin. These protocols are particularly the preparation of a value proposition and its essential derivative, a comprehensive and demanding positioning statement. Neither discipline is common practice within the industry and, when applied, both often lack the necessary rigour in choice of word and phrase. If they are prepared in advance of any pre-marketing or marketing initiatives, they can speed up the translation process, taking clinical trial outcomes into positive end result benefits and experiences for the intended patients and prescribers. There are some marketing issues that need to be addressed as early as five years before launch, in particular those concerning pricing, branding and opinion leader development. Such needs can be met by drafting an outline value proposition early and amending the phrasing in the light of clinical trial and market research outcomes.

The value of pre-marketing lies in its use in building perceptions. There are, however, ethical considerations. Pre-marketing can imply pre-selling, a dangerous game of promise before delivery. The challenge is to build awareness and interest in the product to create an earlier desire to use it and therefore encourage a faster growth in both sales and acceptance. Pure marketing skills can and do make a big difference. Perceptions do matter. This process has to be managed sensitively both globally and locally. The disciplines of the value proposition are the guarantee of the right balance being struck between promise and delivery.

The new disciplines in product development are interwoven and interdependent. The people, processes and procedures must reflect this mutuality if the escalating trend of development expenditure is to be reversed. Key questions asked and unequivocal answers generated will assist the task of resource focus. But above all, it is the context that must change. While discovery can be allowed some generosity in range, development and marketing must be laser like in their concentration.

GlaxoSmithKline will continue to dominate the respiratory market for years to come. Its current market share (30 per cent) is matched by a formidable pipeline of patented, pre-clinical and pre-regulatory products. Its marketing muscle and reputation are similarly specialized and dedicated. This is the benchmark for Glaxo to apply to other therapeutic areas and for its competitors to emulate in their own chosen centres of excellence. The consequences will be a leaner and healthier industry for all.

WHAT ARE THE LIKELY FUTURE TRENDS AND THEIR PROBABLE IMPACT ON INDUSTRY STRUCTURE AND GROWTH?

Threats and opportunities are both global and local. The top competition will continue to be concentrated around the US lead market in terms of product development, regulatory approval and marketing. To compete on equal terms, non-American companies will set up HQs and other major interests inside the US pharmaceutical and biotechnology regional clusters. Europe will continue to play a secondary role until regulatory harmonization is achieved and the market pricing and preference listings show greater consistency across boundaries. It is unlikely that those macroeconomic factors described elsewhere will have a major impact on the future development of the industry. Good health is high on most personal, family and social agendas within the advanced industrialized/information economies. One significant change will be the lower-cost availability of off-patented drugs, however. This predictable and inevitable development will lower the drugs bill in the developed world, creating budgetary space for the new expensive drugs sought in particular for genetic and geriatric-based diseases. The only contentious issue is who pays for such treatment and for a prolonged active life.

In the rest of the world, cheaper generic drugs will be much more readily available to those economies that can afford it. A soft-landing recession in the US and continued economic under-performing in Europe and Japan will favour the US-based pharmaceutical giants. This may lead towards more selective acquisitions than mega-mergers, building global development capabilities across chosen therapeutic areas. In discovery and in marketing, collaborative partnerships, licensing in and out should grow exponentially. The global development 'queen bees' may command a hive of innovative worker bee scientists, accessing a wide discovery field of new active substances. Access to global marketing muscle will suit the local producers of potential blockbuster drugs. Portfolio management will be more disciplined and focused.

Those are the ideal trends. They should happen sooner rather than later, particularly if healthcare cost becomes an even more serious issue for both providers and payers. While a continued but slower pace of horizontal consolidation is likely, convergence with biotechnology and genetics should stay out of fashion for a few more years. Vertical integration, as seen in Merck and AstraZeneca, will remain a corporate parental whim, unless real therapeutic breakthroughs depend on it. A fully integrated disease management programme will be inhibited by continued global differences and an imperfect market. There may nevertheless be exceptions, such as specialized cancer treatment and combined therapies for such serious lifestyle diseases as obesity.

Perhaps the most significant future change will be in product harmonization and global marketing. Branding, packaging and point-of-prescription promotion can only improve. Standards have been low, creativity misapplied and last-minute strategic decisions taken outside the context of an integrated marketing plan. Psychology plays a significant part in the healing process, if only in resolving many of the difficulties arising from non-compliance – failing to take the medicine. The expertise exists within the industry. Novartis, Johnson & Johnson, GlaxoSmithKline, Procter and Gamble and others have strong 'FMCG' or 'OTC' pedigrees.

Parental influence is already having an impact here. The driving force is the opportunity through global branding of extending the product franchise long after patents have expired.

The twenty-first century offers challenging opportunities for the pharmaceutical company, big or small or even stuck in the middle. Further consolidation among the giants should hold the combined market share of the top 20 above 65 per cent to 2010 and the market should double to $680 billion (Bastianelli *et al.*, 2001: 118). There will be a few significant breakthroughs from the new technologies giving the emerging pharma company entry into global markets. The temptation of access to development/marketing resources and a deal with a big player, has recently forged this kind of alliance: Protherics to Eli Lilly, Interneuron to Pfizer/Warner-Lambert, Vertex to Novartis, Millenium to Aventis and Oxford GlycoSciences to Glaxo.

The greatest pressure will fall on those companies ranked 21st to 100th, not big enough to attract or search for the new blockbuster drugs. A middle-market squeeze is a familiar and present characteristic in other mature markets such as automotive, computing or banking. Niche strategies are a way forward, since smaller target markets lower entry costs and strengthen portfolios through handpicked licensing deals. Thinking small before the giants lessen their fixation on blockbuster drugs is the narrow growth corridor for 50 or so medium-size companies in Europe alone. In Germany, the largest European market, Merck, Byk Gulden and Schering could press Bayer and Boehringer Ingelheim for a place in the top twenty. To support such rapid growth they need, in particular, long-term access to the $100 billion US market, only achievable through equal partnerships with others of a similar size.

WILL THERE BE ANY MAJOR BREAKTHROUGHS IN TREATMENT AND DISEASE CONTAINMENT?

The completion of the human genome programme marks a beginning rather than an end. It offers a real opportunity for breakthrough in treating some of the rarer diseases where genetic defects have always been seen as the cause. It offers the opportunity for better diagnosis and access to new treatment pathways. It offers the potential for personalized drug therapies that recognize differences in reaction and metabolism. It offers hope of an eventual cure to the killer diseases where in reality only palliative care is at present available. It offers the prospect of a better quality of life for those suffering from such life-limiting diseases as chronic asthma or multiple sclerosis.

Insight into genes widens the scope of discovery. Rapid screening provides more drug candidates for development. The bottleneck remains, however. Clinical trials and regulatory approval procedures have to be radically overhauled and their escalating costs contained. Electronic monitoring and submission may be part of the solution. Many more new technologies are on offer. Progress in a mature market is more likely, however, through further consolidation and business focus. Even in areas with high growth potential, such as cancer treatment, expensive effective new treatments will be balanced by a shift into low-cost generics for standard therapies. The net result will be modest growth and continued unfulfilled needs.

In such circumstances, top managers need to be smart and long-sighted, leaving the thrust of business development to the new technology generation. Those that do will last the century. Those that follow twentieth-century conventions will be easily overhauled within the decade. The pharmaceutical industry began as an offshoot of the chemical industry. It enters a new phase as a major global industry, a significant employer and provider of essential healthcare services. It will need to respond to the challenges of continuous change by adapting successfully itself. It can and, for the good of humanity, it must.

References

Aitkin, M., Baskam, Lamarre, Silber and Waters (2000) 'A licence to cure', *The McKinsey Quarterly*, 1, 80–89.

AstraZeneca (1999) *Annual Review*, statement by Chairman Percy Barnevik, 1.

Bastianelli, E., Eckhardt and Teirlynck (2001) 'Pharma: Can the middle hold?', *The McKinsey Quarterly*, 1, 117–25.

Economist (1998) 'A survey of the pharmaceutical industry', *The Economist*, 21 February, 1–16.

Economist (2000a) 'A farewell to "life sciences" ', *The Economist*, 18 November, 125.

Economist (2000b) 'Business Britain: Glaxo's expanding galaxy', 25 November, 40.

Naisbitt, J. and Aburdene, P. (1988) *Megatrends 2000*, Sidgwick and Jackson, London.

Ohmae, K. (1990) *The Borderless World*, HarperCollins, New York.

Pursche, W.R. (1996) 'Pharmaceuticals – the consolidation isn't over', *The McKinsey Quarterly*, 2, 110–19.

Ries, A. (1997) *Focus: The future of your company depends on it*, HarperCollins, New York.

Woolley, S. (1999) 'Science and Savvy', *Forbes*, 11 January.

FACES OF
GLOBALIZATION

**Sarah Burns, Piero Dell'Anno,
Samreen Khan and Alex Poppleton**

CHAPTER 10

FACES OF GLOBALIZATION

*O*ur perspective on globalization and our interest in contributing to this book came out of our own experiences as inhabitants, consumers and citizens of an increasingly globally interconnected world. We are relatively well placed to benefit and profit personally and professionally in a new 'global' reality. Between us we have parents of British, Irish, Indian, Venezuelan, French and Italian origin. Aside from these birth connections, we have lived, studied and worked in other countries, including El Salvador, the US, Belgium, Austria and Sweden, and we have travelled to many more. We work in an international team of business consultants in which our colleagues and clients value our 'global' experiences. We are each very different as individuals and yet we share many attributes deemed desirable in this new world. At the start of the twenty-first century there is little unusual in such a group of colleagues.

However, what brought us together was our sense of unease about the phenomenon of globalization. We wanted to put forward some of the thoughts and issues we have discussed in trying to understand the globalization phenomenon and our discomfort with it. We put these forward not as answers or as the only issues to be discussed, but merely as prompts for thinking and discussion on globalization. We do not pretend to be proposing a theory or a point of view, but to be beginning a debate that seems pertinent to us – and we hope to you.

Our initial conversations left us puzzling over some compelling and yet unanswered questions. We wondered why globalization is perceived and portrayed as so glamorous and seductive to corporations and individuals alike. We were struck by how many assumptions about globalization remain unspoken and unchallenged. We speculated about globalization's seemingly inexorable shifting of power from the nation state to the corporation and argued about what space remained for ethics in a globalizing world, indeed whether the concept of ethics has much relevance. And we wondered most of all where that leaves us as 'global' individuals: what sense can we make of our experiences, what are the implications of globalization for how we are to live in the future and what sort of future can we expect?

In this chapter we seek to discuss some of these unanswered and perhaps unanswerable questions. We are well aware that our own perspectives, despite being international, are far from global. We offer our thoughts not as the answer, or even a possible answer, to some imagined globalization problem, but rather to stimulate thought and provoke debate about the present and the future.

THE GLAMORIZING OF GLOBALIZATION

Globalization is clearly an interesting topic, otherwise there would be no audience for books such as this. But why does 'globalization' currently seem not only a business imperative, but also so glamorous and seductive? If one reads the national and international press and the business journals, 'global' is used to denote importance, desirability and sexiness. Companies that are merely 'local' seem to be viewed as unsophisticated, provincial, ignorant and even inadequate. It seems that a global corporation is, or at least feels, more powerful and unassailable –

immune from the vagaries of national or regional economic up- and down-turns, not accountable to a specific country or region and with a booming market somewhere in the world. Global corporations span great territories, have their own empires and, significantly, their staff are always on the move.

In the global economy, knowledge has become critical. Knowing about something is a way to 'own' its value and to have power over it and over other people. Knowledge has become a way of 'owning' resources, carrying as much importance as the ownership of primary resources like oil, coal and steel did during the Industrial Revolution. The ownership that counts in the global world is increasingly knowledge and control of information through patents, licences and technology.

Perhaps some of the glamour comes from a rather Western view that novelty is desirable and tradition is less interesting. New things are inherently more attractive and to be sought after – it is cool to be the first, to be a pioneer. Going into new markets, doing things that have not been done before is more glamorous than being a late follower; although research shows that often being second, learning the lessons and avoiding the pitfalls are more profitable (Bartlett and Ghoshal, 2000). Acquiring the artefacts or even philosophies of other cultures can offer novelty, at least as long as they are in fashion.

We would laugh at someone who claimed to 'know' Japan without ever having been there – it seems we have to travel for the glamour of owning pieces of the world. Even then, how well do we really understand our newly acquired property? Experience suggests that many corporations are tourists rather than travellers, picking up scraps of information and then failing. Famous examples include companies losing money in China by trying to sell things like toilet cleaner, which a few weeks living outside those international hotels would have shown would be unlikely to succeed.

Money is, of course, one of the most glamorous factors associated with globalization. Globalization makes money – for some. And money offers power, a theme that we return to later in the chapter. First, however, we propose to explore in more depth some of the taken-for-granted ideas about globalization.

WHAT UNDERPINS THE TREND TO GLOBALIZATION?

There are numerous possible definitions of globalization. For example, the Organisation for Economic Co-operation and Development (OECD) defines globalization as the process through which markets and production in various countries become increasingly interdependent as a consequence of the dynamic of exchanging goods and services, and through the movement of capital and technology. Others use it to describe the increasingly worldwide movement of information, of money and of people. In Anthony Giddens' view (Hutton and Giddens, 2000), globalization began with the launch of the first communication satellites in the 1960s, allowing instant information transmission world-wide. But goods and people had been moving around the world for considerably longer. Take for example the two world wars of the twentieth century, when for the first time soldiers might find themselves fighting anywhere in the world. There is little doubt, however, that globalization was given impetus by the relaxing of the restrictions on global capital movement in the late 1970s and early 1980s.

Perhaps the biggest kick given to the globalizing process was the collapse of the Soviet Union in 1989. Some would argue that this fall was inevitable because of the globalizing of information and money. But it is also possible to take the view that globalization did not merely contribute to the collapse but also gained significant momentum from it. Once the Berlin Wall had fallen peacefully, it was clear that capitalism had won the Cold War. Throughout the Cold War, communism seemed such a powerful and evil enemy that anything that could defeat it must be even more powerful and an indisputable force for good. So in the early 1990s the fetters that still bound global corporations were released and governments accepted that as capitalism had proved itself to be the only way, its consequences must be both unavoidable and acceptable, any disadvantages a small price worth paying. With the transition from planned to market economy of the central and eastern European nations and China's cautious relaxing of control came further proof that capitalism is good. Globalization is a way of spreading capitalism that assumes that it is inherently superior and enlightened.

A further strong assumption underpinning the virtues of globalization seems to be that investment is good and the investor should be privileged. This seems to ignore the distortions of the local economy that globalization can create. The original idea was that investment would stay, at least for the medium term if not the longer term. But since the introduction of the free movement of capital this is no longer the case. Investors can withdraw at short notice. Market-driven economics assumes that allowing markets free reign ensures the best outcome for everyone in the long run – but the existence of regulation and social structure acknowledges that this is not always the case. Regulation around social matters particularly shows that we do not like the idea of people being treated as commodities, in the West at least we set limits to the flexibility of the labour market.

Within market-driven economies there is an assumption that there is a ladder of economic and social development that nation states seek to climb that follows a basic model of underdeveloped to developed. There is still an inherent assumption that the globalizing nations of the G7/G8 will remain at the top of this pecking order and that others will eventually benefit from the increasing wealth in both social and economic terms. It is worth noting, however, that for many developing countries this is not the case.

Box 10.1 Human Development Indicators (HDI) from 1975 to 1997

Of the 31 countries classified as having a low level of human development and for which statistics were available, 18 had a negative or zero annual average change to their HDI.

Of those 42 countries with a high human development index, 37 had a positive average annual change in their HDI.

Source: UN Human Development Report (1999) UNDP Human Development Report Office (HDRO).

Globalization assumes that economic growth is good, even for the poor. A 1999 World Bank report (Dollar and Kraay, 2000) concludes that 'growth generally does benefit the poor and that anyone who cares about the poor should favour the growth-enhancing policies of good rule of law, fiscal discipline and openness to international trade'. But what globalization is really doing is changing the shape of our economies and the relationship between them away from the old hierarchical national development models. Mark Weisbrot (Weisbrot *et al.*, 2000) found that the relationship between economic growth and the incomes of the poor is less close than had been assumed. In many instances, not only the poor but the majority of the labour force has failed to share in the gains from economic growth. For example, per capita income in the US has risen by 70 per cent since 1973. However, the median real wage in the US today is the same as it was 27 years ago: and for the bottom quintile of the labour force real wages actually dropped by about 9 per cent between 1973 and 1997.

Research from the Institute of Development Studies (Tang and Wood, 2000) indicates that globalization increases the earnings of highly skilled workers in developed countries by widening the market for their services, but lowers the wages of other workers in developed countries by eroding their privileged access to jobs in production. Initially this lowering happens mostly for unskilled workers, but it then spreads to medium-skilled workers. There are two important mechanisms required for these changes to take place – the falling costs of moving people and their services around the world, and falling trade barriers – both of which widen the gap between medium-skilled and unskilled workers in developed countries and narrow it in developing countries.

Despite increasing talk about triple bottom line accounting (financial, social and environmental), there is little challenge to the idea that organizations' pursuit of shareholder value is entirely appropriate, or that shareholders can and do affect the behaviour of the corporations in which they invest. The idea of shareholders grew out of personal investment in people's business ventures – sea voyages, for example. But is this still an appropriate model when shareholders are increasingly corporate institutions investing funds on behalf of individuals and other corporations? Does it remain appropriate when there is no longer a personal connection to the investment or the people who run the companies in which they invest? In the UK, the National Association of Pension Funds represents the owners of about 80 per cent of British shares, who have no say in how their money is invested (*Economist,*

1998). In the US, 95 per cent of people think that US corporations should have more than one purpose, that they also owe something to their workers and the communities in which they operate, and that they should sometimes sacrifice some profit for the sake of making things better for their workers and communities. Given the un-challenged focus on shareholder value for corporations listed across the world's stock exchanges, there is little likelihood of these other purposes being supported by financially driven organizations.

However, the primacy of shareholders is upheld by an individualistic culture that pervades the West. One of the most popular responses to a BBC radio poll seeking to find the word of the twentieth century was 'individual'. This emphasis on the rights and privileges of the (privileged) individual appears to be an important component of globalization. More than at any time, the rights of the individual (to life, self-actualization, health, enjoyment, wealth, bearing arms, free speech, democracy) have been privileged over those of the broader community. Those privileged individuals are largely residents of the northern hemisphere/developed world, and there seems to be a shared view that these western or northern lives are more valuable than others. For example, in recent conflicts the US body count has seemed to be more important than the overall number of deaths. The idea that an individual's rights are paramount is not shared by many non-western societies, who regard individual rights or human rights as a luxury for rich people: the good of the community comes first.

The export of capitalism also often assumes that Western cultural values, such as the primacy of the individual, are the right ones. We tend to believe in rationality, favouring it over intuition, and we see our own cultural values as rationally to be preferred to those of non-western cultures. We see our own cultures as more successful (at least economically) and therefore better. If local things disappear in our own culture or in others', it does not matter because global things are inherently superior — whether that means food, traditions, clothes, way of life, values or language. But often we don't even know or understand what exists before we start replacing it, nor how important it is to its local context, nor do we even consider what we could learn from it. We assume that if other people are not like us and do not value what we value, it is only because they are not yet enlightened and have yet to see our 'right' way of doing things. And this cultural flow is in one direction: from the richer countries to the poorer.

A huge part of this 'enlightenment' is the exporting of English as the language of globalization. There are currently around a billion speakers of English, but in 10 years' time there will be more people speaking English as their second language than as their mother tongue. How might this change the globalization agenda? We also tend to assume that where the US leads, Europe will follow, the UK in the vanguard and other European partners later. We see this as inevitable – is it really? *The Economist* (2000) certainly thinks that globalization can be reversed, but warns of the dire consequences of this reversal.

Building on the assumption that western–style capitalism is the right system, it is generally taken for granted by western nations that capitalism must be exported to other countries rather than importing people into it. The anxieties over immigration highlight this assumption – migrants who show themselves to be enterprising by raising funds to leave their home countries and finding routes to the West are refused entry or vilified as bogus asylum seekers. So, despite the economic rationale at the heart of global capitalism, 'economic' is an adjective with negative connotations when placed in front of the word 'migrant'. The US no longer wants the 'huddled masses' who were offered refuge at its founding, and while there is free movement of capital, labour is held captive.

Paid employment is one of the cornerstones of globalization. Paid work creates the ability to be a consumer in global consumer markets. A good job in a multinational should be the aspiration for the worth-while global citizen. Large companies need markets; Henry Ford was quick to realize that if he paid his workers well they would be able to buy his cars. So global companies create jobs for people who literally earn the right and the capability to become consumers, part of the market for the products of global companies. This assumption has helped devalue important caring roles such as looking after the elderly, the sick or children, work that is largely unpaid. But what does this do to our social structures? And to self-esteem when economic models are based on the idea that there will never be full employment? How can the unemployed feel valued by their families and communities in such a society? And what will be the effects on western societies and their markets of a growing population of the socially and economically excluded?

We assume too that the upsides of globalization will last well into the future, and that any disadvantages do not represent serious long-term problems. However, the profits of globalization can often be taken quite quickly, while the costs in terms of environmental, social, health and other effects may take much longer to appear. We return to this theme later in our thoughts on ethics.

THE SHIFT IN POWER

In an increasingly corporate world, it is difficult to see what meaning democracy (one person, one vote) has if power is shifting into the hands of corporations and if shareholders do not exercise their votes. For example, in the UK only 20 per cent of British shares are voted (*Economist*, 1998). However, is this perceived shift in power real?

Perhaps the most obvious manifestation of power is money. A striking statistic is that of the 100 largest economies in the world, 51 are now global corporations and only 49 are countries. The combined sales of the world's top 200 corporations are far greater than a quarter of the world's economic activity. The accusation (Anderson and Cavanagh, 2000) is that far from creating an integrated global village, these firms are weaving webs of production, consumption and finance that bring economic benefits to at most a third of the world's people – the rest of the population is at best left out, at worst marginalized or hurt. Nevertheless, it is how this money is being used that makes the difference, particularly in the fields of global investment and the global communications media.

In the 1970s, many western governments stopped being able to afford to create jobs, investment was required from outside, and the free flow of capital made it possible to invest freely across borders. But what corporations put in they also take away – money can easily be moved out again. For example, the Siemens factory in north Tyneside was mothballed in 1998 after only 15 months' operation and with the loss of over 1000 jobs. This pattern of investment and rapid disinvestment is repeated elsewhere. The International Monetary Fund (IMF) is accused of contributing to the Asian financial crisis (Weisbrot et al., 2000) by encouraging the opening up of financial markets to large inflows of portfolio investment, which subsequently flowed out even more rapidly, contributing to the financial panic and currency crisis.

The power to invest and disinvest does not have to be exercised to be real – just the threat of it is enough. Governments are forced to accede to corporate demands to secure investment and create jobs.

> Globalisation, moreover, has enabled companies to hold a gun to governments' heads: if it [governments] refuses to meet their demands, they threaten to disinvest, move their plant to Thailand, and damage its credibility by making thousands of workers redundant. The sheer size of the new trans-national corporations also enables them to swing an unprecedented weight. (Monbiot, 2000)

In southern Italy, Fiat secured taxation concessions and exemptions from employment rights in return for its investment. It was harder to disinvest in the days of heavy industry – and it is still difficult to move a coal mine or an oil field. But for much of the twenty-first century's industry production can be shifted much more easily to seek the lowest labour costs or most manageable labour force. Some e-business start-ups, dissatisfied with their web designers in the UK, have transferred the work to India at a couple of days notice.

Even in more traditional industry things have changed. The British government had little influence over what BMW decided to do with Rover – so little that the company didn't feel the need to inform ministers in advance of its plans to close the Longbridge plant in 2000. This power is power to create or remove employment and a single big investment creates much better news than the painstaking work required to support the growth of SMEs. There is power over the workforce too – with workers spread between different countries, freedom of association loses its meaning. Far from their being alongside you, you may not even know who your fellow workers are. In belated recognition of this loss of power, there is talk of creating pan-European unions, global worker associations seem a distant prospect.

POLITICS AND LEGISLATION

As well as wielding the power to create and destroy jobs, corporations can influence governments by injecting money into the political process and into universities. This can be rather different in Europe than the US. In the UK there are limits on what political parties can spend on electioneering and what individual candidates can spend; accounts have to be produced and donations are visible. This doesn't hold for many other countries, keeping power there in the hands of the wealthy and the corporate.

Box 10.2

- 72 per cent of Americans say that business has too much power over many aspects of American life.
- 74 per cent of Americans feel that big companies have too much power over government policy, politicians and policy makers in Washington.

Money gives control over intellectual property rights and information, and over its distribution. Over 90 per cent of all product and technology patents are owned by transnational corporations (Corporate Watch, 2000). The top five firms in the world have over 30 per cent of global sales in airlines, aerospace, steel, oil, personal computers, chemicals and the media (Anderson and Cavanagh, 2000). Control over the media allows you to influence what information people possess. Despite many channels of US broadcasting, effective control over the media is in the hands of a few large corporations, with heavy reliance on their corporate advertisers and vested interests. For example, Rupert Murdoch's News International in China has been accused of failing to report negative news about China for fear of failing to secure lucrative access to the Chinese population. The information base for many in developing countries can be very small – the TV programmes *Dallas* and *Dynasty* can be the main source of information about what it is like to live in the US, or CNN the only 'real' news of what is going on in the outside world, despite being perceived widely in Europe as superficial and US oriented.

Control of information and media gives you the power to write or rewrite history, including business school case studies and even wars.

Box 10.3   Western domination

- Ruper Murdoch, Australian by birth, is an American citizen and makes use of the world's most powerful persuaders – information and entertainment – to access 75 per cent of the world population.
- Cumulatively in the past 20 years, the most watched television programme in the world is *Baywatch*, an American series containing sand, surf, lifeguards in action and beauties.
- The US's single largest export is entertainment. Hollywood films grossed more than $30 billion worldwide in 1997 (UNDP Human Development Report, 1999).
- The average American consumer is hit with 3000 marketing messages a day. What percentage of this sample is actually coming from non-western cultures or emerging economies?

For example, consider the case of the US-based Southwest Airlines. It was not the first to adopt the low-cost, no-frills business model, but it has claimed it. And look at the furore over the American-made film U571, rewritten to claim for the Americans a British Second World War battle success. In 1941 British divers took huge risks to retrieve code material from a crippled German submarine: in the film the heroes are American. The justification for the rewriting was that it made the film more appealing to the US market. The change attracted huge criticism in the UK, but was little noticed elsewhere and the US version is now accepted as a 'true' account of history because people cannot challenge what they do not know about.

The Internet is often cited as a possible solution to a lack of information, which it may be for the privileged with access. But it may also contribute to the problem by overwhelming people with information. Eventually, giving people too much information can be as powerful as withholding it.

SOCIAL ASPECTS OF GLOBALIZATION

It would be easy to examine the shifts in power associated with globalization and see a simple choice between being a supporter of a free-trade-based system of integration, or a passionate opponent of its homogenizing tendencies. Might there be other, somewhat broader perspectives? The OECD's definition of globalization, based on the exchange of goods and services and the movement of capital and technology, has seemed rather limiting to many commentators such as Rosabeth Moss Kanter. She rightly points out that viewing the phenomenon from this perspective results in our seeing the world merely as a supermarket of global proportions. But globalization is clearly more than a merely financial or economic phenomenon, and a globally connected world is more than a hypermarket. Globalization is not new, in fact Marx and Engels talked about it more than 150 years ago in the Communist Manifesto. What is new is the growing criticism of its impact on both environmental and social long-term sustainability.

Previously poor countries have increased their GDP as corporate globalization has increased. What does this mean in social terms for the distribution of benefits? What is happening on a global scale? How are economic hierarchies behaving in terms of global growth? The IMF says that during the second half of the current decade, the combined GDP of the emerging economies will be 50 per cent of the global total. But is it helpful to measure development only in terms of GDP? It seems clear who has benefited in financial terms from this growth, but what is happening to those who have fallen behind? Are there suitable mechanisms in place for ensuring that the benefits of globalization are shared, for example that taxes are collected and that tax income is distributed?

Box 10.4

> In the last 30 years the income gap between the world's richest fifth and the poorest fifth has doubled. It is now 74 to 1.

Source: UN Human Development Report 1999, UNDP HD Report Office.

It is too simple to see the process as one by which large, faceless corporations from the North inflict globalization on a passive and impotent southern hemisphere. Although there have been significant shifts in power from governments to corporations, questions should still be asked about appropriate roles for government in this new world.

Governments may be limited in some of the measures that they can take, but they still find ways to intervene. For example, they can create barriers to the free movement of labour forces characterized by low education, but permit almost unlimited freedom for the well educated and highly skilled. The Asian tiger countries became successful in the global economy following a very strong programme of protectionism. The only real example of a free capitalist economy in the last years has probably been Russia, but here *laissez faire* has produced disastrous results, both for corporations and for individuals. Globalization is not necessarily a problem in itself, but its effects may be if governments, society, corporations and institutions cannot find a way to work with it.

Box 10.5

In 1980, the average company CEO was paid 42 times the earnings of the average factory worker. Today it is 475 times.

Source: Corporate Watch, 2000.

In the same way, technology development cannot be said to be the main cause of high rates of unemployment in those countries that have embraced it, otherwise the US and Japan would not have been able to reduce unemployment respectively to 4.1 and 4.4 per cent versus the current 9.1 in the EU (*Economist*, 1999). But globalization has created feelings of uncertainty and instability both for those who work in transnational corporations and for those who live with the consequences of global corporate actions without having a part in making the decisions. In extreme examples this might include people whose environment and means of subsistence are destroyed by the actions of a multinational corporation acting together with government, such as the U'wa people of Colombia or the Amungme in West Papua. Do those of us who work in governments, in international or transnational corporations, and who do have some influence over those actions need to assume some responsibility for what occurs?

Europeans often criticize the American social and welfare system for not having a strong moral or ethical basis. And yet in 1998 Ralph Dahrendorf (1998) wrote that during the past 20 years EU countries increased their wealth by between 50 and 70 per cent. And yet they have 20 million unemployed, 50 million poor and 5 million homeless. Where has the wealth gone? Europe still has a welfare system, but how attractive is it? What quality of service does it still provide? What does increasing wealth mean if this is not coupled with an intelligent and useful investment in welfare? How is it possible that governments haven't promoted decisions that could have guaranteed a certain stability and acceptable standard of living for the less advantaged within wealthy economies? Is this the sign that wealth is increasingly in the hands of an elite that has the power to exert considerable influence on the decision-making process at government level? Does globalization require us to think about new forms of governance, both social and corporate?

Dahrendorf went on to say that globalization today means that competition is written in capital letters and solidarity in lower case. It seems we will need to decide how we want to see these words written in the future. Do we want to extend the notion of Darwinian competition to encompass social Darwinism? Are individuals who cannot meet and overcome the challenges of global competition destined for a global scrap heap? If we imagine what this might mean in social terms, we may see the privileged protecting what they have with ever greater security, in effect living in gilded cages, while the disadvantaged look on without a stake in the future.

This may mean we need to think about ethics – not blaming corporations or governments for where we find ourselves, but examining what part we play as individuals and whether we can find a coherent role. Too often we can find ourselves acting differently in our roles as managers, consultants, investors, consumers or parents: sometimes working with or inside a global company, sometimes profiting from their successes, using their products, often deploring the effect they have on our own quality of life or on our children's development. In these circumstances it is easy to lay blame, ignoring the fact that we *are* the corporations. We cannot expect Greenpeace or Amnesty International to draw attention to the next potential social or ecological problem and take responsibility for its resolution: we must take our share of responsibility for what occurs.

WHERE DOES THAT LEAVE THE INDIVIDUAL?

So far this chapter has discussed what we believe are the key assumptions underpinning globalization, the shifts of power and how ethics relate to anthropology and further developments in the globalizing world. What it does not fully capture is the 'So what?'. What does this mean for us, as managers, consultants and inhabitants of this world? Although globalization may or may not aim to have effects on an individual scale, our experience suggests that it does. We share below some of our thoughts about what globalization means for the individual, for family life and for social identity: how does it feel to be global?

This book in itself is emblematic of the surge in interest in globalization. There is no doubt that the topic is hot, or that tremendous hype surrounds it. The desire for organizations to globalize is continuously accelerating. We illustrated ways in which it has been glamorized earlier in this chapter. A 'global' lifestyle or culture has become the desirable life to lead. Global workers today aspire to travel, to relocate and to live the expatriate life. Around the world, young graduates fresh out of university look for jobs with international opportunities. At the same time, however, many older executives tell how tedious it is to live out of a suitcase, moving from one anonymous international hotel to another. They speak freely of how little time they spend at home, how rarely they see their partner or spouse, of the monotony of airline food and lounges, of the missed birthdays and forgotten anniversaries.

This missing out at home is a little-discussed aspect of globalization. Those of us who have lived abroad do not always find it glamorous to uproot our families, lose touch with our friends and miss out on whole chunks of our children's lives and our contemporaries' cultural experience. Perhaps the idea that moving abroad should be glamorous has its origins in the American immigrant philosophy: what matters is not where you have come from, but what you make of yourself in the new land of opportunity. Travelling and living abroad offer the chance to escape from humble origins and transcend nationality, class and background. Worrying out loud about what we are losing or leaving behind casts us in a distinctly unglamorous, unadventurous light. Globalization tells us that to be rootless, to be a global citizen, is to be free, and yet the experiences of one such 'global citizen' (see Box 10.6) suggest that this can make us uncertain rather than confident and miserable as well as marketable. Can we feel comfortable belonging everywhere, or does that mean that we belong nowhere? And if we belong nowhere, do we feel moved to vote, to pay our taxes, to invest time in schools and communities?

Box 10.6

> My nationality was always a puzzle to me. My father once told me that when asked where I was from, I should not answer, 'I was born in Venezuela, my father is from India, I study in an American School and live in England.' He said it was too complicated, and suggested that I said to people, 'I'm a global citizen', a lot simpler and far more sophisticated. 'It will give you an edge above others, remember that.' At the time it was quite confusing as most of my classmates, friends, teachers were from the US, Venezuela or a particular nationality. I tried saying it once and it did not fly high – I think the teacher thought I was trying to be a smart-ass.

And what does this mean for our relationship with our employers, the globalizing companies? When individuals have no single coherent set of values from their family life and upbringing, how do they cope with corporate life? Do we automatically take on the implicit values of the corporation and then find ourselves unable to question them or influence them? It is often seen as high status to work for a global organization, a reflection of your global personal worth. However, US commerce department statistics imply that about one million US workers lose their jobs every year as a result of imports or job shifts abroad (*Business Week*, 2000). So, in the face of this increasing uncertainty, there may be no secure identity in corporate life either. What happens when you lose your job?

Rootlessness and its associated flexibility may pay off for global companies now, but will this really be a long-term source of competitive advantage? Some might argue that in order to work in a global setting without coming across as culturally naïve, globally inept or internationally unsophisticated, one has to have been born in an exotic country, lived or worked a diverse portfolio of places or done something quite outlandish like move to a developing country and marry a tribal chief or princess. Another view might be that long and deep experience in one culture provides a more grounded basis from which to work with other cultures. For example, knowing several languages is usually seen as desirable, but some multilingual people end up without a native language and feel limited in their ability to express themselves in comparison with individuals who have excellent command of only one language. How can a global company make good decisions about what experience and knowledge to value, and how can it develop the individuals who form part of its community?

CONCLUSION

The globalization debate is gathering force and weight. As we write, protesters against globalization are seeking to disrupt the meeting of the World Bank and the IMF in Prague, and the mainstream press is becoming ever more interested in the phenomenon. In the words of *Business Week* (2000), people are wondering how a term that once connoted so much good for the world has fallen into such disrepute and are looking for a more intelligent approach to globalization. Economists, social historians, ecologists and managers are all seeking a better understanding of what is happening and its implications for our future. A debate that has been dominated by extremists at the end of the spectrum, the free marketeers versus the radical anti-capitalists, is turning into a serious discussion that merits everyone's attention.

We can now choose to see globalization not as an irresistible force to which we must either submit or resist, but rather as a process that can be influenced and shaped. As global managers and workers, we are more than mere recipients of the changes that accompany the process. Rather we are active participants, capable of noticing what is happening, of thinking hard about our actions and of influencing it through our work in large international and global corporations. Our scope of influence extends well beyond the confines of our own company's success and includes the social, economic and environmental fabric of our society. We hope this chapter has illuminated just how far.

References

Anderson, S. and Cavanagh, J. (2000) 'Top 200: The rise of global corporate power', *Corporate Watch*, http://www.globalpolicy.org/socecon/tncs/top200.hhtm.

Bartlett, C.A. and Ghoshal, S. (2000) 'Going global: Lessons from late movers', *Harvard Business Review*, March, 78, 2.

Business Week (2000) 'Global capitalism', *Business Week*, Nov 6, 3706, 40.

Corporate Watch (2000)' Facts from the corporate planet: Ecology and politics in the age of globalisation', http://www/corpwatch.org/trac/feature/planet/fact_1.html.

Dahrendorf, R. (1998) 'Towards the authoritarian century', *Die Zeit*, 2 January.

Dollar, D. and Kraay, A. (2000) *Growth Is Good for the Poor*, World Bank, March.

Economist (1998) October 31, 74.

Economist (1999) *The World in Numbers*, Economist Books, London.

Economist (2000) 'Labour pains', September 23, 29.

Hutton, W. and Giddens, A. (eds) (2000) *On the Edge: Living with global capitalism*, Jonathan Cape, London.

Monbiot, G. (2000) *Captive State*, Macmillan, London.

Tang, P.J.G. and Wood, A. (2000) 'Globalisation, co-operation costs and wage inequalities', unpublished paper, http://www.ids.acc.uk/ids/global/ttint.html.

Weisbrot, M., Baker, D., Naiman, R. and Neta, G. (2000) 'Growth may be good for the poor – but are IMF and world bank policies good for growth? A closer look at the world bank's most recent defense of its policies', draft paper released August 7 2000, http://www.cepr.net/response_to_dollar_kraay.htm.

AUTHOR BIOGRAPHIES

THE EDITOR

Paul Kirkbride BA, MSc, PhD, FIPD, FHKIPM

Paul Kirkbride rejoined Ashridge in 2000 as Research Fellow reporting directly to the Chief Executive, having previously been from 1991–94 a Faculty Team Leader responsible for Change, Leadership and HRM programmes. Paul is also a Visiting Professor at the University of Hertfordshire and Managing Director of The Change House Ltd. and Full Range Leadership Ltd.

Paul has been, over the years, an HR professional, a researcher, a 'proper' academic, a trainer, a consultant, a businessman and a life-long Carlisle United supporter. From 1989–91 he was British Aerospace Professor of Organizational Change and Development at British Aerospace (Commercial Aircraft) and the University of Hertfordshire. He has taught in universities in Oxford and Hong Kong and has been a visiting professor at the Australian Graduate School of Management (AGSM), the Fuqua School of Business at Duke University, North Carolina, and the University of Maryland.

In his consulting work Paul specializes in advising top management on change processes; developing strategic leaders; building new cultures in mergers and alliances; and developing and delivering project-based management development programmes. He has lived, taught or consulted in many countries including Argentina, Australia, China, most of the countries in the European Union, Hong Kong, Macau, Malaysia, Mexico, Philippines, Singapore, South Africa, Taiwan and the United States.

His current research interests include the post-modernist organizational change and structural inertia theory as well as the more pragmatic areas of leadership, strategic human resource management, international/cross-cultural management and organizational culture. He has published over 60 journal articles, 15 book chapters and four books. His research work has been published internationally in journals such as *Asia Pacific Human Resource Management, Industrial and Labor Relations Review, International Journal of Human Resource Management, Journal of Industrial Relations* and *Organisation Studies.*

Paul gained a degree in Business Studies and a Master's in Personnel and Industrial Relations before completing his PhD at the Centre for Organisational Change and Development, University of Bath.

CONTRIBUTORS

Marcus Alexander MA, MBA

Marcus Alexander is a director of the Ashridge Strategic Management Centre. His work combines consulting, research and teaching with leading international organizations. The main focus of this work concerns the corporate strategy process, the relationship between strategy and organization in a broad sense, and the use of strategic alliances and strategic outsourcing. His publications include *Corporate-Level Strategy: Creating value in the multibusiness company*, and articles in *Harvard Business Review, California Management Review, Planning Review* and *Long Range Planning*.

Prior to joining the Centre, Marcus worked at the Boston Consulting Group in London, Australia, continental Europe and Boston. Subsequently, he founded a consulting firm with colleagues from Boston Consulting Group and McKinsey & Company. His work there was particularly focused on development of strategic thinking in senior management teams and on building strategic capabilities within client organizations. He has also worked in merchant banking on mergers and acquisitions and project finance, served as a non-executive director of several start-ups, and been a tutor in Business Economics at Harvard University.

Marcus holds an MA with Congratulatory First Class Honours from Christ Church, Oxford, and an MBA with high distinction from Harvard Business School, where he graduated first in his year, and was a Harkness Fellow, Ford Scholar, Loeb Rhoades Fellow and winner of the Wolfe award.

Sarah Burns MBA

Before joining Ashridge as a consultant, Sarah was a diplomat in the British Foreign and Commonwealth Office. In a variety of assignments in the UK and overseas, her focus was on creating and developing long-term relationships in multicultural contexts, particularly within Europe and the Middle East. She has worked extensively leading strategy in fast-changing and unpredictable environments.

Sarah developed her interests further during an MBA at the University of Bath, taking a particular interest in the emotional aspects of leadership, in team working and in unconventional approaches to change. While at Bath, she conducted research with a blue-chip engineering company into ways of facilitating strategic business-to-business relationships.

She prefers to take a whole-organization approach, working collaboratively to uncover assumptions and develop fresh insights to stimulate and support both personal and organizational change. Sarah has been using these ideas to consult to clients in the pharmaceutical and IT industries, in professional services firms and to entrepreneurs, working both in her native English and in German.

Piero Dell'Anno BA, MA

Piero studied government law and economics at University of Rome La Sapienza. He also completed a series of post-graduate diplomas in project management, organization development and learning (London School of Economics, New York University, Columbia University and Boston University) focused on how learning can enhance and sustain organizational development and change.

Piero has worked for a number of consulting companies in Italy, United States, the Sultanate of Oman, Ukraine, Armenia, Russia, Uzbekistan and Northern Africa identifying, designing, managing and implementing projects aimed at promoting management and organizational learning in the periods of radical change.

Piero has also worked for the European Commission helping the Directorate General XXII (Training and Education) to manage and assess the impact and the results of the European Open and Distance Learning programme and for the European Training Foundation.

Piero's current interests are innovative learning and creativity as a means to foster organizational development, team building and incidental learning.

Jim Durcan BA, MSc, MA(Oxon), MIPM

Jim Durcan has been Principal of Ruskin College, Oxford since 1998. As Principal, Jim combines the roles of academic leader and chief executive to enable the college to respond to the rapidly changing world of adult education. Ruskin is a small specialist adult education college with close links with many UK and international trade union organizations and community groups.

His employment record includes three years as Leverhulme Research Fellow in Industrial Relations at Nuffield College, Oxford, and spells at Oxford Brookes Business School and at Ashridge Management College. As a client director at Ashridge his clients included BAA, Deutsche Bank, Fisons and Glaxo Group Research. His teaching and consultancy contributions were heavily focused on issues of organizational change, strategic implementation, leadership and coaching, organizational and national cultures, strategic human resource management and the personal development of individual managers. He has worked in Asia, the USA and widely across Europe. As a second-generation member of the Irish Diaspora his work on global labour markets reflects personal as well as professional and academic interests.

Jim has published a number of articles, three books and presented papers at national and international conferences. His 1994 book *The Manager as Coach* – a study of the impact of delayering and empowerment on the role of managers – has also been published in Spanish and Italian. His 1996 book *Career Paths for the 21st Century* (Random House Publishing, co-author David Oates) received a great deal of attention for its treatment of individual responses to career opportunities. His articles have covered such diverse topics as change, leadership, bargaining power and cross-cultural issues in management. His other research interests include mergers, partnerships and alliances, cross-cultural issues and adult learning.

David Hennessey BS, BA, MBA, PhD

 David is an Associate Professor of Marketing at Babson College in Wellesley, Massachusetts, USA. He is also an associate of Ashridge Management College, where he was the Director of the Advanced Marketing Programme, Bausch & Lomb European Marketing Programme and the Thorn Senior Management Programme, a joint venture between Babson and Ashridge. He also contributes to the Electrolux International Business Leaders Programme and the Philips Mastering the Semiconductor Industry Programme. At Babson he has contributed to executive programmes for DSM, Ares Serono, SAP and the Swedish Management Institute.

After gaining his first degree in Economics and Business Administration at Norwich University and an MBA from Clark University, Worcester, MA, David worked first as a senior marketing analyst for the American Can Company. He then became Marketing Director for a division of the Interpace Corporation based in New Jersey.

In 1979, he moved into the educational sector to teach business studies and marketing. He completed his PhD at New York University and joined Babson College in 1982. He has taught on courses on global marketing, marketing strategy and sales management, and written numerous articles and case studies. He has co-authored two books: *Global Marketing Management: Strategy and cases*, 1988, 1992, 1995, 1998 and 2001 (with Jean-Pierre Jeannet) and *How to Write a Marketing Plan*, 1986, 1990 and 1998 (with Robert Kopp).

Alongside his teaching commitments, David has continued his varied business interests including running his own consultancy company that specializes in strategy and marketing. His clients have included ATT, Jardine Matheson, BBC, Maersk Sealand, ICI, Compaq Computers and others.

David has had executive teaching experience on a wide variety of programmes at Babson College, Ashridge and IMD, as well as in Costa Rica, Finland, Germany, Switzerland, France and Japan. Participants are from many companies, for example Electrolux, Unilever, IBM, ICI, Novartis, Procter and Gamble, Cable and Wireless, BT, Zeneca, Unisys, Philips, Shell and Nokia.

David is a founder and owner of Winthrop Hill Properties, with his wife Elizabeth, which renovates luxury properties in Boston. He holds both US and Irish passports.

John Heptonstall BA(Hons), MSc, MBA (Harvard), DBA (Harvard)

John Heptonstall is a Programme Director at Ashridge, Professor at the International University in Geneva and visiting professor at the American Graduate School of International Management (Thunderbird) and at the European Institute of Purchasing Management. He was for ten years a visiting faculty member at IMD, and previously Chairman of faculty at the International Management Institute in Geneva. He holds a BA from the University of Durham, MSc from Cranfield and MBA and DBA degrees from Harvard. He lives in Switzerland and in France.

Samreen Khan BA, MSc

Samreen joined Ashridge Consulting in 1998. Her consulting is informed by her particular interest in creating space in organizations where individuals are encouraged to reflect on, explore and share personal value sets, culture and experience in order to conceive learning communities that can build tacitly rich organizations. She is also fascinated by the e-world and the implications its rapid development and maturity will have for the 'organization' as an organic and human system.

Samreen's previous experience was in research in overseas government, editorial and marketing within the publishing industry and international portfolio management. Since joining Ashridge, she has worked with the National Health Service focusing on waiting list reduction initiatives, conflict and change and programme/project management using Theory of Constraints Methodology. Medical bodies she has worked with include Norfolk & Norwich Healthcare Trust, Radcliffe Infirmary, Wiltshire Health Authority and Southampton University Hospital. She has worked with Novartis Animal Health, Pharmaceuticals and Corporate divisions on the development and organizational ownership of a coaching culture. Samreen has dedicated significant time, however, to helping clients unleash hidden learning potential within their organizations. Clients within this context include Prudential Portfolio Managers, Infinium and Novartis.

Samreen did an MSc at City University in London. This degree introduced her to techniques such as Soft Systems Methodology and Object-Oriented Analysis and Design, as well as Project Management and IS Strategy. Her undergraduate degree was in Political Science and was gained at Colgate University in Hamilton, New York. Samreen is half Venezuelan, half Indian, and has lived in Europe and America in recent years. She is bilingual in Spanish and English and has a basic conversational background in French.

Mike Malmgren MSc, MBA

Mike is Programme Director for e-Business programmes at Ashridge. His main interest is strategy and organizational development, with a particular focus on the emergence of the Internet and its implications for business transformation. He works with a range of international clients such as Volvo, Electrolux, Volkswagen, Groupe Bull, as well as Internet start-ups and new ventures.

Born in Sweden, Mike gained an MSc in Thermodynamics from the Royal Institute of Technology in Stockholm in 1983. After graduation Mike joined BTG, a Swedish international high-tech company, before embarking on an international management career spanning the USA, Australia and the UK.

Mike gained an Executive MBA from London Business School in 1998 where he specialized in strategy and issues relating to high-tech start-up companies, including raising of finance and development capital.

He has extensive experience as managing director for several high-tech companies, including an executive board position with Spectris GmbH, a German international technology company. His roles have involved managing organizational change through acquisitions and integration of companies, as well as growth through international marketing and sales to a wide range of industry sectors, including the automotive, chemical, power and the pulp and paper industry.

Paul Pinnington MA (Oxon)

Paul is a member of the Ashridge board and leads the strategic management and director development activity stream, a group of tutors concentrating on senior-level strategic and international management programmes. His current clients include Electrolux, PricewaterhouseCoopers, Royal and Sun Alliance and ICL, for whom he designs and runs highly tailored global programmes.

He is particularly interested in marketing and business strategy and is currently researching, developing and implementing strategy in a global context.

Prior to Ashridge, Paul worked for Stauffer Chemical Company (now part of Zeneca) in sales and marketing management positions, first covering the UK and Eire operations. Then based in Geneva as marketing manager for Europe and Africa, he held a short-term 'troubleshooting' assignment for the Johannesburg-based operation and managed several pan-European product launches.

His earlier career after Oxford University was spent with Massey Ferguson and Fisons in both sales and marketing management positions and with Marketing Improvements Ltd as a senior consultant responsible for training and consultancy assignments in Europe and South-East Asia.

Paul has experience in many industries including chemicals – especially petrochemicals, pesticides and pharmaceuticals – white goods, retail and technology. He has worked for Ashridge throughout Europe and Japan, and is a visiting professor at Babson College, Boston, USA, teaching business strategy on tailored programmes.

Alex Poppleton BA (Hons)

Alex works for Ashridge Consulting and is currently completing a Master's degree in organizational change at Surrey University. Prior to working at Ashridge she worked as an organizational change consultant, both independently and for KPMG after beginning her career in financial services.

Alex has particular interest and expertise in working with groups on personal development and training, as well as operating more effectively together. She has conducted extensive developmental work with clients, including acting as an internal training and development consultant within KPMG. Over the last few years she has developed supporting and coaching roles to consulting or project teams, as well as working as a consultant directly with clients.

Previous career history includes some design, media and retail experience before moving to Midland Bank/HSBC and eventually leading the Strategic Management Information team. The team delivered critical management information to all sectors of the wholesale banking business and required close collaboration with the business, finance and IT teams within the bank on an on-going basis.

Alex's consulting career has been a mix of financial and service sector, with experience in technical banking work, business processes and project management. In recent years her focus has been developing her experience in organizational change roles, including working with top teams on leadership; developing communication, facilitation and consultancy skills; working with team assessment and performance; mentoring programmes; and large-scale organizational change programmes. She has trained in a number of facilitation, assessment and change techniques, including psychodynamic, Transactional Analysis and Gestalt approaches.

Roger Pudney MA, DipEcon

Roger teaches and consults in international strategic management, strategic alliances/partnerships and acquisitions, key account management and innovation.

After leaving Oxford University with a degree and post-graduate diploma in Economics, he worked for the Ford Motor Company in marketing and sales roles, in the food industry with Spillers, including marketing management and general management responsibility for major business developments in Europe, USA and West Africa. This included leading acquisition and joint venture teams.

After a senior role in an international publishing company (part of the Thomson Organisation), he joined the consultancy MIL and worked on major business developments in European and South-East Asian markets.

Recent consultancy and development work in Europe, North America, Asia-Pacific, Latin America and Africa has included assignments for automotive, retail, publishing, drink, chemicals, petrochemicals, tourism/hotel, defence, electronics and public-sector organizations.

He leads a major Ashridge international research study identifying best current practice in strategic partnerships between major companies. He teaches and consults extensively in the area of creating competitive advantage from strategic alliances (including joint ventures, supplier–customer partnerships and the integration of acquisitions).

His clients include ITT Industries, Volkswagen, Inchcape, GKN, Anglo American, BP, Electrolux, BHP, The Post Office and Aga Khan Network.

Malcolm Schofield BSc(Econ)

Malcolm joined Ashridge in 1983 to teach marketing, and after retiring in 1995 became a retained associate. Previously he was responsible for the Strategic Management Programme and in 1987 was appointed Director of Studies for the Management Development Group. From April 1991–94 he led a new team specializing in building market-focused organizations. He now concentrates on tailored programme development.

Malcolm read Business Administration at the London School of Economics. He worked in marketing and general management with AEI and GEC, and then joined Urwick Orr in 1970 as a consultant concentrating on business appraisal and organization development assignments. His activities extended into Europe in 1974 and into international consultancy in 1977 when he was appointed a senior partner of the Urwick Group. In 1978 he joined Thomas Cook as Sales and Marketing Director of the banking division. He subsequently became International Director, establishing new operations in 12 overseas markets.

Malcolm is involved in programme design and related assignments, specializing in strategic market planning. He has a particular interest in the development needs of businesses within the automotive, pharmaceutical, computer and professional services industries. More recently he has worked on issues concerning strategy implementation and the critical role of leadership in market-driven organizations.

Karen Ward BSc (Hons), Msc, MCIM

Since January 2000, Karen has been working in an associate capacity with Ashridge after being a full time member of faculty for three years. Prior to Ashridge, Karen had a range of management and organization development roles within organizations in the pharmaceutical and financial services sectors. She began her career with PA Consulting Group, where she worked across both the private and public sectors.

Karen teaches and consults with a range of global organizations on issues related to the effective implementation of strategic choices. Her work focuses on organizations trying to work across boundaries, whether national, functional or organizational. In particular Karen has extensive experience of the integration issues of mergers and acquisitions. She worked in the integration office during the merger of GlaxoWellcome and has subsequently consulted to a number of organizations on integration issues.

Her book, *Leading International Teams* (McGraw-Hill), draws together her academic and consulting experience of enabling organizations to develop global capability through the successful creation and maintenance of complex teams.

She is joint client director for the Strategic HR Management and the Leading Complex Teams programmes at Ashridge. Her current and recent clients include Volkswagen, Aventis, SAP, Bull, Bank of Scotland, ICON and GlaxoSmithKline.

INDEX

Heartland

How to Build Companies as Strong as Countries

Mark C Scott

In *Reinspiring the Corporation* Mark Scott explored the lessons corporations could learn from the world's great religions on harnessing the committed energy of its members. In *Heartland* he takes this thinking further and tackles the issues of the Global Firm – an organisation whose constituent parts transverse many communities.

Few companies have yet acknowledged that competitive advantage is fundamentally dependent on understanding and managing the dynamics of their own internal 'societies'. Scott suggests that the key to creating the commitment required for truly sustainable success is to move away from accepted structural perspectives and think of the firm as a society of national communities – The Corporate State.

- Shows how, by learning the lessons in longevity from the Nation State, today's large but short-lived firms can become enduring global societies.

- Shifts the focus of business competitiveness from the structural orientation of corporate strategy to the social dimensions of the firm – social strategy.

0471 49936 6   224pp   June 2001   £17.99   Hardback

WILEY
Independent Thinkers